Travel Writing 2.0

EARNING MONEY FROM YOUR TRAVELS IN THE NEW MEDIA LANDSCAPE

Second Edition

Tim Leffel

Published by Al Centro Media

Printed on acid-free paper.

© Al Centro Media
2016

Second Edition

DISCLAIMER

This book details the author's personal experiences with and opinions about travel writing, web publishing, and blogging. The author is not a licensed financial consultant.

The author and publisher are providing this book and its contents on an "as is" basis and make no representations or warranties of any kind with respect to this book or its contents. The author and publisher disclaim all such representations and warranties, including for example warranties of merchantability and financial advice for a particular purpose. In addition, the author and publisher do not represent or warrant that the information accessible via this book is accurate, complete or current.

The statements made about products and services have not been evaluated by the U.S. government. Please consult with your own Certified Public Accountant or financial services professional regarding the suggestions and recommendations made in this book.

Except as specifically stated in this book, neither the author or publisher, nor any authors, contributors, or other representatives will be liable for damages arising out of or in connection with the use of this book. This is a comprehensive limitation of liability that applies to all damages of any kind, including (without limitation) compensatory; direct, indirect or consequential damages; loss of data, income or profit; loss of or damage to property and claims of third parties.

You understand that this book is not intended as a substitute for consultation with a licensed financial professional. Before you begin any financial program, or change your lifestyle in any way, you will consult a licensed financial professional to ensure that you are doing what's best for your financial condition.

This book provides content related to topics finances and economic living. As such, use of this book implies your acceptance of this disclaimer.

Dedication

To the next batch of brilliant travel writers, creative bloggers, and inventive entrepreneurs with something original to say.

Contents

Introduction

When I pulled up my bank balance online I started to feel a bit uneasy. It showed a lower amount than I was comfortable with and I knew I had a bunch of bills to pay when I got back home from the trip I was on. I'd been traveling a lot, generating a ton of material for current and future stories, but for now none of that was bringing in income. I was moving to a new city soon and that meant a load of one-time expenses that would be hefty, plus I'd just put three plane tickets on a credit card for me and my family.

I was flying home from a six-day hosted trip, working a few hours in the early morning in my room, touring around all day gathering notes and photos, then answering e-mails late at night. I'd usually get to bed after midnight and be up at 7:00 or earlier. There's no getting ahead on a trip like that: the best I could do was address what was urgent and keep the gears spinning.

I had payments coming that I was waiting for, but one advertiser was already three weeks late in paying and two publications that owed me money for past articles were ignoring my e-mails.

I had two more freelance things due from other publications though and I could invoice $550 for those once I turned them in. I knew from experience that they paid their bills quickly. It was 1:00 in the morning but I was stuck all night in the airport anyway after a weather delay resulted in a missed connection.

So I opened my laptop and got to work.

I finished one article about Oaxaca and one about USA bed and breakfasts with brewpubs attached. Never mind that I was doing this after a week of trying to absorb everything I could about a third destination--Guatemala. At 3:30 I sent the two articles off and caught a few hours of sleep curled in an airport chair.

When I dragged my suitcase up the 32 steps to my house on a hillside the next day, my wife greeted me with a kiss and asked, "Did you have fun on your trip?"

"Fun" wasn't the first word that came to mind.

A couple of weeks later the late payments came in and on top of my passive income streams, it was enough to pay the bills. A few more opportunities came through too, for small ad deals and other article commissions.

The month after that I felt downright rich. A client renewed for a big six-month campaign. A website I had put up for sale through a broker a few months before finally got a firm offer. One week later we had a deal hammered out and a week after that the money was wired into my account. My checking account went from three figures to mid-five-figures at once. In the space of eight weeks between mid-May and mid-July I went from stressed about money to feeling loaded.

I'd love to pretend this was an odd turn of events that will never occur again, but after doing this for more than 20 years, I know better.

The life of a freelance travel writer or blogger is far from predictable. No matter how much swagger we display in our drool-worthy social media streams full of photos from exotic locations, we continually grapple with an uncertain road ahead of us. What if Google changes its algorithm and my blog traffic drops in half? What if Amazon switches things up and stops recommending my books next to others? Will I stop getting freelance gigs related to my niche because there's more competition? Will advertisers decide the package I'm pitching is too expensive or that budget cuts have taken it out of their mix? What if the destination I'm covering has a terrorist attack or a disease outbreak?

Amidst the fun and the glamor and the freedom, there can be a lot of uncertainty and upheaval. The phrase "roller coaster" comes up a lot when you ask bloggers or freelance writers about their income. If you do it right you can get close to being "antifragile," able to ride the waves of change and profit from them. If you're not flexible and persistent though, you can get smashed up and broken like a fishing boat stuck in a hurricane.

Getting paid to do what you love—a dream job, right? I could make you salivate from the start with all kinds of dreamy weeks I have experienced while getting paid to explore exciting locations around the world. I'd promise you lots of wonderful perks and a life of leisure. I'd open with all the ways I'm going to give you the keys to the kingdom. I'd promise that in 90 days you'd be staying in an overwater bungalow in Tahiti with a nice magazine feature assignment that will earn you a few thousand dollars.

But that's not fair. It's not fair because there's a long journey involved before any of that happens. We do this because it's what we love and sometimes we can't believe how lucky we feel. There's no denying that the perks can be great. Only after you reach a point where you are influential enough to deserve them, however. Despite appearances of frolicking fun, this requires real work.

> *I am a one person shop who does everything from managing my own SEO to editing all my own photos. Just downloading the 200+photos I take each day, naming them, cataloging them, uploading to the cloud, and backing them up on an external hard drive takes a lot of time, and that's before I've done the first bit of research for my stories.*
> ~ Barbara Weibel of HoleInTheDonut.com

Many travel writing seminars and classes focus on the glamorous side of the business because that's what brings in the students and the bucks. Heck, it's even what most books about travel writing do. They lay it all out like a display of pastries at a French bakery, with lots of exclamation points in their come-on copy. Get paid to travel! Free trips! Luxury suites at beach resorts! Fine dining just for writing a quick review!

You can find similar ads for seminars on how to break into modeling, how to break into acting, or how to make it as a songwriter. It's all about the payoff, with very little about the tough odds you face to get there—or the vast majority of aspirants who never make it at all.

You deserve to hear the real story instead.

Beginning writers struggle with how to turn this passion for travel into real income and many experienced writers struggle with the problem too. You probably picked up this book because you want to start off on the right track or you're not earning what you think you should be earning from your efforts. If you read this book you'll have a much better chance of being a success story rather than a broke and frustrated writer.

The chapters to follow will outline the ways to make money as a travel writer and blogger in the new environment, with the pros and cons of each. It's clearer every year that the old highway is cracking in the heat behind us, so most of what was written in earlier travel writing books is becoming more fossilized all the time. Following the traditional road of endless query letters, slowly breaking into print magazines, and making good money writing guidebooks doesn't cut it anymore for the new writers arriving on the scene—or even some that have been doing it for ages. Just starting a blog and hoping for the best is not the answer either. Here you'll get advice for succeeding in a media landscape that favors the creative and the bold, the self-starters and the platform makers.

Most travel writing books you pick up spend most of their pages on the craft itself and the earnings part is treated as an afterthought.

I think that's backward.

There are already a thousand other books out there on how to be a good writer. They'll instruct you on how to be observant, avoid clichés, construct a narrative, define characters through action, and write tight sentences. These skills are 90 percent the same whether you are writing about sports, business, food, politics, or travel. Go to your local library and you'll probably see shelves and shelves filled with these books. Check out a few and heed their advice. Read four or five of them to recognize the common threads. I have yet to meet a writer who thinks she is so skilled and talented that nothing she has written can be improved. We spend our whole lives learning and improving.

Since that "how to write well" job has already been done in fine fashion by others over the course of decades, I'm not going to dwell on it all that much. Writing travel articles, even good ones, is not as demanding as being a great novelist. I assume if you are holding this book, you are already a decent enough writer to get published or you are in the process of getting there soon on your own. If not, why enter this hyper-competitive, crowded, low-paying field with the deck stacked against you? Go get educated and read this later when you're prepared. Or choose a path of less resistance.

Travel Writing 2.0 will cover some of the 10% of writing well that is unique to travel (and is unique to appealing to search engines, which is not covered in most writing books). Otherwise this is a handbook for the business and marketing side of things, where most of your effort will be concentrated. The resource section lists other good travel writing books that take the opposite approach and I suggest you pick up at least one of those as well at some point.

Good writing matters, don't get me wrong, but although I've won my fair share of awards, I want you to actually get paid for that writing. This book will tell you how to succeed, get noticed, and make money. Perhaps more important than the reality check, this is a book about the here and now, not about what used to be. The elements of the book itself are meant to illustrate that point. The title (*Travel Writing 2.0*) refers directly to the new age of self-directed writing we have already entered. The means of production I am using (e-books and print-on-demand) reflect the reality that the publishing system of the last century is not serving us well in the new one. The methods of gathering data and advice for this book are also appropriate to the participatory climate the Internet has created, rather than the top-down declaration-making that has existed since the dawn of the printing press.

As many writers will tell you in these pages, the best way to learn is to constantly practice, stretch, refine, and improve. Thanks to the digital media world, all that is far easier than it used to be. You no longer need to get past a gatekeeper to tell your story.

Why me?

I have learned how to do a lot of things from "how to" books. I've learned to invest well, buy real estate overseas, grow vegetables, brew beer, write creative non-fiction, start a business, code HTML, market my own book, teach English overseas, and relocate my family to another country. And yes, more than 20 years ago I read a book on how to be a travel writer and decided I was going to find a way to make it work.

My two main questions when deciding whether to plunk my money down on one of these how to books are always, "Why should I trust this person?" and "Does the author know what he/she is talking about?"

So here's why you should trust me.

I've been at this for more than two decades, from part-time to full-time, doing almost every kind of job available to writers—travel and otherwise. This includes writing five travel books, ghostwriting business books and articles, editing two travel webzines, editing one business webzine, working as an RFP writer, publishing articles in dozens of magazines and newspapers, publishing even more on other people's websites, running multiple travel blogs, writing copy for multiple corporations, and writing for the trades. I am quoted in the major media regularly as a travel expert. If you put "travel writing blog" in a search engine mine is usually at the top.

I've won a whole lot of nice awards for articles I've written and get invited to speak at conferences. I'm an author who actually makes five figures annually just from from book sales and my travel website company is profitable enough to pay all the bills for a family of three and put some money away for later. (See my portfolio site at www.TimLeffel.com for the full shebang.) So I think at this point it's safe to say I'm a successful travel writer.

Just in case my litany of published work is not enough—which it probably isn't since I'm still just one guy with one set of opinions—I have crowdsourced much of the content for this book. In the first edition I turned to 52 working travel writers I knew and respected to answer some burning questions I had. This time I got input from more than 100 working writers, editors, and bloggers. So if you don't trust my opinions, you've got plenty more to pick from in the following pages. Some of these people are pros who have been full-time travel writers for most of their working lives, some have been at it just a couple of years, and others are permanent part-time travel writers who have another source of income.

In different ways, they'll show you how to get to where you might want to go, though the paths might be more meandering than they used to be.

I know what most travel writers and bloggers struggle with. I ask them on a regular basis. If you're just starting out in this field, *Travel Writing 2.0* will help you avoid years of trial and error and enable you to start earning money for your efforts more quickly than those just winging it.

If you're an experienced writer looking to consistently increase your income, this book will be even more helpful as you learn from me and lots of other success stories who have found various paths to real earnings. You'll learn how to make actual money and enjoy yourself, with eyes wide open on what to expect along the way.

If you want to dive in deeper afterward, sign up for my monthly newsletter (TravelWriting2.com/newsletter) or see the intensive course options at RealMoneyWriters.com.

Let's start the journey!

Travel Writing in the Digital Age

It is commonplace among artists and children at play that they're not aware of time or solitude while they're chasing their vision. The hours fly. The sculptress and the tree-climbing tyke both look up blinking when Mom calls, "Suppertime!"

~ Steven Pressfield in *The War of Art*

There's one ad for a certain travel writing seminar that says, "Live your life like a permanent vacation!" I don't think any of the writers included in this book would classify their work as anything close to being a "permanent vacation." For a guidebook writer, it's more like "permanently working my butt off while everyone around me is on vacation."

I love my job and it's a blast. Even in the home office, sometimes I'll forget to eat lunch because I'm so involved in what I'm doing and am enjoying it so much. The travel part can be a lot of fun—at least after the flight is finished. But it's unfair to tout the positives without detailing the corresponding trade-offs—especially the financial ones.

Thomas Kohnstamm laid it out well in the intro of his controversial book *Do Travel Writers Go to Hell?* He said, "I imagine that the difference between traveling and professional travel writing is the difference between having sex and working in pornography. While both are still probably fun, being a professional brings many levels of complication to your original interest and will eventually consume your personal life."

There are some writers/bloggers/solo publishers making a good living, and I'm encouraged by how many more there seem to be even since I published the first edition in 2010. Most worked hard to get there and didn't get permission from some editor in an office to make it happen. Roger Wade runs three websites, including the popular PriceOfTravel.com. He says, "This will be my third year earning more than six figures. I thought to myself if I could ever ever get to $100K by doing this stuff, this would be the dream career for the rest of my life. It took four years to get to that point, but now it's wonderful."

When Shelly Rivoli, author and family travel blogger at HaveBabyWillTravel.com, was asked about how she broke in to travel writing she said, "I got there early, I worked hard, and I held on for dear life."

This is one of the most interesting and fulfilling jobs on the planet, but at times it can be one of the most frustrating. It can pay off handsomely for a few, both in real earnings and great fringe benefits. It can also batter and break many who dive into travel writing without a clear sense of the challenges ahead and the necessary persistence to break through a lot of adversity.

The Fun Stuff

Everyone I meet thinks I have a job that's barely one step removed from a wish granted by a genie. "Wow, how did you pull that off?" they'll ask, incredulous, like I just told them I'd hit four 21s in a row in Vegas after doubling down each time. When my daughter tells classmates what I do for a living, they say things like, "That's the coolest job *ever*!" So I get how fortunate I am to be working for myself doing something fun I am passionate about, traveling the world without having to pay for it all.

This vocation sure beats harvesting lettuce, cleaning toilets, or pouring asphalt. It's not fair to talk about all the hardships and ignore the perks, so yes, there are some great perks. *After* you achieve some level of success, you get invited on free trips or have editors paying your expenses. You get paid to go places most people you know will never visit. You get VIP access, get wined and dined, and you may get to travel in a style you would never be able to afford on your own. If you act like a journalist instead of a lazy hack, you will also see more of a place and its culture than you ever would as a casual tourist.

I could spend pages on the great trips I've gone on and if we have a beer together sometime, I'll regale you with all the tales of excess and excitement. Right now though, that's like taking a 16 year-old boy to a strip club. All in good time, but first you need to reach a level of maturity—in this case career maturity.

Most fun jobs invite lots of competition and this fun job is as competitive as any out there. With success comes a whole range of wonderful byproducts, but you need the success first before you get the goodies. I hope the information I present here will help you get to that point. Yes, it can be a blast eventually, no doubt about it. But you have to want it bad enough to put in the real time and effort required to get to the payoff. Then, even with those perks in place, you've still got to get the income part right. Otherwise you'll just be a broke person who travels instead of a broke person who watches TV all day.

Nearly all of us travel writers are in this because of a love of exploring new places. I backpacked around the world for years before I ever started making real money as a writer. The travel came first, then the writing, which is how it is for most. Krista Luisa's start is typical: "After almost ten years of international travel, I decided to combine my passion for world exploration with my love for writing. I started a blog, read as many books and articles as I could on travel writing, and set off on my career path."

If you don't already use every vacation and holiday day you have available and take off traveling every chance you get, then you may not have the stomach for this ride. If there's not a thrill from the travel that drives you, there are certainly far more lucrative pursuits available to you instead.

The Murky Future

The rules were changing fast at the beginning of the '10s and if anything the changes have sped up. The way many successful travel writers earn money is morphing so fast that what worked really well two years ago may be completely off the table now. The people really doing the best are the ones ignoring the traditional paths of depending on others for a check and are charting their own course. They're constantly experimenting, adapting, and forming partnerships that will endure through platform changes and new flavors of the month. I believe 100% that this is the best path to success for those who have nailed down a specific subject niche and have both a good work ethic and a good head for business.

At the same time, I'm a big believer in multiple income streams, so it makes sense to keep writing for others too in order to keep income flowing from more than one place. Run your own show, but don't be afraid to go get more cash where you can.

While this book is big on practical advice, it's not so big on most of the specifics you historically find in travel writing books. The main reason is, the real money is going to the most creative thinkers. They are making their own rules.

> *Too much of the community is concerned with how everyone else makes money. Those truly doing well put their nose down, work hard and don't worry about what others are doing.*
> ~ Ayngelina Brogan of BaconIsMagic.ca

If you want easy answers, checklists, and the Yellow Brick Road to success, that period has passed. The writers profiled here have found 100 different routes to happiness as travel writers. Another batch of writers would present even more routes in the new digital age. We're all finding our way into a future that nobody can see clearly and the clouds are not going to part anytime soon.

Just as a great language teacher is a facilitator rather than a lecturer, my goal is to show you what to do so you can go develop your talent and skill as a writer and maybe even as an entrepreneur. I and the other writers profiled here are going to give you great tips on how to succeed and make money, but despite what any seminar may promise, there are no shortcuts in this vocation. The only thing that's reliably short is the number of digits on the paychecks during your first year or two.

So if you want lots of blueprints to copy for breaking into print media, get a library card and start checking out other tomes on the subject of freelance writing. Or go load up your Kindle or Kobo. There are plenty of good freelance success books out there. Instead, I'm going to tell you to go find great writing yourself, take lessons from it, and learn what the marketplace wants to hear from you. Then I'm going to tell you to work your butt off on marketing so that people actually read what you've typed.

Hacks wait for shortcuts they never seem to find. Like true explorers, successful travel writers pull out a machete and a compass and start moving. I'm just handing you the map.

Travel Writing 2.0 will, I hope, inspire you and get you jazzed up, but also prepare you for the real life of a freelance travel writer or better yet, an independent content creator. It will give you a kick in the seat of the pants sometimes, and be the wise advisor telling you to get your answers for your specific situation the way most journalists do: by going and finding them.

But first of all, can you *really* make money while having fun traveling around the world? Let's go find out.

How Do Travel Writers Make Money?

One hundred percent of my income comes from my blog. Most of the income now is affiliate sales and ebooks.

~ Matt Kepnes

One hundred percent of my income is print magazines. I may be the last person working that way. And I'll continue that way until they pry my fingers loose from the magazine stand.

~ Edward Readicker-Henderson

My income sources are diverse, and are lots of little sources as opposed to one big one. They've changed by adding more strings to my bow.

~ Michael Huxley

As you can see from the quotes above, there's no single path to success. The real question should be, "Is there a way for me to make real money in this vocation? Yes, there definitely can be. Freelance travel writers and bloggers—those not employed by a corporation—make money in one of three ways.

1) They write for someone else and get paid by that organization, with a set fee for a specified amount of work.

2) They run their own publication(s) and earn money the same way organizations do: by selling advertising, selling products, earning a commission on others' products featured in their publication, or earning money for services such as consulting or leading tours.

3) They depend on some combination of numbers 1 and 2.

For most freelance writers and bloggers, this endeavor is like the setup of a mom and pop business. Count the revenue, subtract the expenses, and there's your profit. Divide what's left by the hours you worked to figure out the earnings from your efforts. If you worked 50 hours a week and have $1,400 in earnings at the end of the month, then you've *almost* made minimum wage. Will that pay your living expenses?

So let's start out with reality: Unless you are a staff travel writer/editor at a magazine or major newspaper—and there are fewer of those full-time jobs left in the whole English speaking world each year—then you will be a freelancer or you will run your own enterprise.

If you can score one of those staff jobs, then more power to you. The normal path to that is to intern for nothing while in college, work for really cheap for many years as a junior editor or copywriter, then move up to an actual living when someone else leaves or gets fired. Or you are already the food or lifestyle editor at one publication and you end up making a leap to travel editor at another publication down the street. But in an annoying irony that can be a real bummer, travel editors don't actually travel that much. They have too much to do in the office. As Leslie Terew Magraw, Intelligent Travel editor at National Geographic online said, "I do get to travel once in a while, but I'm mostly chained to my computer. The good thing is that I can do my job from just about anywhere, assuming there's good Wi-Fi, so that gives me a lot of flexibility."

Every other travel writer—which probably means 99 out of 100—is self-employed.

So first let that idea sink in and decide if it's for you. Are you comfortable forging your own path and being responsible for your own income? Having all the responsibility on your own shoulders? Not being able to make an accurate household budget because you can't forecast your income?

If you move from freelancer to business owner as a blogger or web publisher, even more falls upon your shoulders. Here's what Robert Safian, editor of *Fast Company*, said in one issue of that magazine: "Entrepreneurship is hard work that requires both high-intensity risk taking and a steel stomach capacity for absorbing disappointment. Some people are psychologically suited for the roller coaster. Many of us are not."

If you're a "punch the clock and pick up a paycheck" type, you may want to stop reading now and pass this book on to someone else who's just the opposite. Travel writing may look glamorous, but it involves a lot of very real work over a very long period. This "job" is closer to that of a business owner than it is to a person sitting in a cubicle.

Many writers who have been at this for a decade or more are just now getting to the point where this is their "real job." Brad Olsen runs CCC Publishing, with a whole range of books under the imprint, but says, "Do it for the love of writing, don't expect much, work hard and hopefully in a decade you'll be able to support yourself! As in don't give up your day job too soon."

You *can* get paid handsomely now and then if you land the right assignment. There are plenty of big feature stories assigned by magazines each month that pay 50 cents to $2 a word. So for 2,000 words the writer is getting between $1,000 and $4,000. Those are the elite assignments, the ones that generally go to writers with plenty of experience. Expecting that to happen quickly is like a news anchor in Greenville, South Carolina looking at what a Los Angeles anchor makes and expecting the same salary.

A more common fee that a freelancer will get for a story of that length is 5 to 25 cents a word, or $100 to $500. Get into the online world and it can be lower still, to the point where you don't want to even think about what you're earning per word because it's a fraction of a cent. Most freelancers who make good money put together a *lot* of assignments on a regular basis and have regular columns or blog appearances on top of those.

The bad news is, it's not getting any better when it comes to pay scales. Writer Mariellen Ward expressed a sentiment shared by many when she said, "My biggest frustration by far is the downward spiral of pitches and opportunities to work for free."

The flip side of the negativity though is a clear improvement in lifestyle factors. As Mark Johanson says, "I made a lot more money when I was a travel editor than I do now as a freelancer. That said, I have so much more freedom now to travel and write the kind of stories I always wanted to write when I was a desk-bound editor".

The Freelancer's World

It is not childish to live with uncertainty, to devote oneself to a craft rather than a career, to an idea rather than an institution. It's courageous and requires a courage of the order that the institutionally co-opted are ill equipped to perceive. They are so unequipped to perceive it that they can only call it childish, and so excuse their exploitation of you.

~ David Mamet

Playwright and director David Mamet was speaking to actors in that quote, but it applies to any creative field where people are scrambling for the next gig and piecing together streams of income instead of settling for life in a cubicle. Being a writer is not for the faint-hearted or the easily scared. Showing up each day and getting a paycheck is easy. To pursue the independent path takes real courage and fortitude.

Most travel writers are freelance. They wield a lance—or pen, laptop, or netbook—that is for hire. They sell their output to someone for an agreed-upon price or they run their own business and make money from what appears next to or in their writing. Or more often in the digital age, it's a mix of both.

The travel freelancer's life involves lots of yin-yang trade-offs. I've lived through every one of the ups and downs and have the gray hairs to prove it.

- You have freedom, but not much certainty.
- You report to nobody, but there's no mentor in the next room either.
- Your hours are your own, but you end up working more of them than most office drones.
- You can go on vacation when you want, but you often end up working while you're away.
- You can work at home, but you buy all your own supplies and equipment.
- You can pick and choose what you work on, but sometimes that means having no work.
- You don't have to follow someone else's workplace rules, but you have to arrange your own health insurance and fund your own retirement account.

I worked for more than a decade in the corporate world, but I left it for good in the mid-'00s and can't imagine ever going back to the constraints of a routine job in a structured environment. I love having control over my life, my career, and what I spend my days working on. That doesn't mean it's always easy. Every freelancer I know talks about the "financial roller coaster" that comes with the territory: one month of everything going right followed by a two months of not being able to make the checkbook balance. Even the people I know who are making six figures complain about this. Over the course of a year their earnings are great, but some months are just plain tough. It takes serious financial discipline and the ability to be what most people would call "a hustler." (In a good way of course …)

> *I've become very comfortable with rejection, in a way that friends in other fields don't understand. It takes a lot of time and dedication to be a successful travel writer and blogger, and you can never really 'take a break.' But if you love it, you don't mind the full-on work.*
>
> ~ Kenza Moller, freelance writer

I don't think it's fair to talk about "the job" without talking about what that means for "the life." As writer Alison Stein says, "There are better ways to make a buck than being a writer, period, and second, there are other subjects to write about that are more lucrative than travel."

If you get one point of reality from this book, let it be this: travel writing is not something to go into because of the potential earnings. When I asked Gary Arndt, one of the most successful bloggers around, what advice he had for aspiring travel writers, he had this to say: "Be prepared to do this for many years before making any real money."

As blogger Nora Dunn said, "Give it time. It took me two years of almost full-time work to develop a writing career that paid the bills."

I have no way of knowing what would work for your life situation, but here are a few alternate income sources to consider in the early years to make life easier:

- Any full-time day job
- A second (steadier) source of part-time income

- A spouse with good earnings and benefits
- Social Security and retirement income
- Savings that will support you for a year or more while you get ramped upUnemployment payments/the dole
- Parents who don't mind you living at home and eating their groceries
- Teaching English overseas by day, writing by night
- Being a teacher or professor who has the whole summer off to travel
- Being a seasonal worker with long stretches of time off to travel.
- Working abroad or moving to a country with a much lower cost of living
- Investment or rental property income

It may seem crazy that I am talking about alternate income sources at the very beginning of this book, but for 95% of the travel writers out there, this is reality. Unless you are charmed and remarkable, or already wealthy, you need to think about where the money will come from that pays the bills for a good while.

The only viable way to skip this part would be by investing some capital. "Buy a website that's already successful," says GoNomad.com publisher Max Hartshorne. "Find someone who wants out, make a deal, and build from an already successful website."

If I were starting out today, this is the path I would take for at least one site or blog to hit the ground running.

The rise of new media has not changed the growing process. If anything it's worse because pay scales are flat or declining if you write for established organizations. There are more ways to make money now, including ones totally in your own hands, but all of them take time to build. Travel writing and overnight success do not go hand in hand unless you're a famous actor who can get a meeting with any editor in her office.

There's nothing novel about going through these backup scenarios and figuring out how you'll pay the mortgage or the rent. The same is necessary for wannabe actors, sculptors, musicians, songwriters, and other creative types.

As we'll talk about later, you can't expect that anyone owes you an income just because you've declared yourself to be a writer. Electricians and plumbers need a license. Architects need five years of schooling plus an apprenticeship. Cops need to graduate from the academy and prove they can shoot straight. All a travel writer needs to do to claim the title is order business cards from VistaPrint. Some don't even do that—they just sign up with Examiner.com and say they're a writer.

This doesn't mean you are thinking of "something to fall back on" because then you are setting yourself up to "fall back." A better outlook is that you are going to have multiple streams of income and that you will keep building to a point where you are making what you need to be comfortable from just your writing-related activities.

For a retired person, that may just mean a few hundred dollars a month on top of Social Security. For a stay-at-home mom or dad, maybe enough to cover the grocery bill. For a full-timer, enough to drop all the other stuff that is not fulfilling. Only you know what the magic number is, but once you know it, work toward that and look at any "falling back" as temporary.

For some people, this is just something to do on the side, apart from their day job, and that's fine.

I have a corporate day job, so success for me is landing enough trips that I'm happy, and enough coverage that my host partners are happy. I don't write for free, but I don't make a living on writing (never have, never intend to) so I'm meeting my own goal for success.

~ Sarah Deveau, part-time freelance writer

Some writers find the balance by mixing in speaking or consulting jobs. These generally are not pursuits you'll be thinking about in your first few years of travel writing, but it is a part worth considering after you have paid your dues and built up a solid portfolio.

Some travel book authors have discovered that speeches at colleges and conferences pay a whole lot better than the book did. They show up, engage the audience with some fun stories and good

PowerPoint slides, sign some autographs, and get a check. What a gig!

It's a great job if you can get it, but that assumes you're reasonably famous, are seen as an expert, and are a good speaker. That doesn't happen overnight. If you're writing a book, however, it's worth keeping this goal in mind as a possibility. Will this translate to the stage? Will people want to hear more about it in person?

Others spend part of their time writing and part of their time leading tours. Amanda Mouttak of the MarocMama blog started a Marrakech food tour company that has become a major business. I started a street food tour company in my sometime home of Guanajuato, Mexico, that carries on without me when I'm not there, thanks to three local guides I have in place. Other bloggers lead city walking tours or getaway excursions their readers (and others) can book online.

Beth Whitman, who runs WanderlustAndLipstick.com, leads tours to destinations such as Papua New Guinea, Bali, and Bhutan, gaining much of her business through her books and the website.

How Much Do Travel Writers Make—Really?

Some people make very little writing about their travels. Some make a very comfortable living.

Take the following chart as an unscientific snapshot of the full-time writers/bloggers I surveyed for this book plus me, but I think if you tracked down 50 or 100 working travel writers yourself, you'd probably find a pretty similar income breakdown.

Here are the collective annual earnings of the full-time writers quoted in this book.

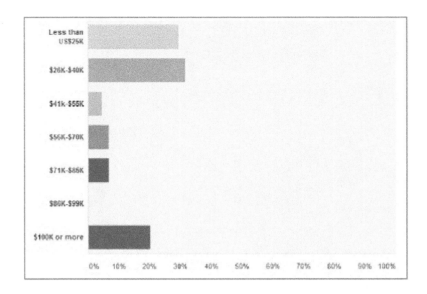

This is only a little different than the results I got five years ago. The main difference is an accentuation of the reverse bell curve. The two largest responses are for $40,000 a year or less annually. That's lower than the median household income level in the US, UK, or Canada, so it's not encouraging. Then there is a big drop-off after that point.

The most interesting, however, is that if you get past that dip, the rewards can be great. A full 20% of respondents have passed the proverbial six-figures level and another 5% are earning between $71K and $85K. These people are making as much or more as cubicle jockey VPs stressed out in a job they hate, but are reporting to nobody but themselves. That's encouraging.

On the next page, there's a chart for people who are part-time earners. They are usually part-time because they want to be. There's nothing wrong with that, and it's a nice place to be if you have another source of income (or a spouse) paying the big bills. Then you can relax and have fun with it. Earning $10,000 won't cut it for a full-time job, but it can be a nice side hustle income for a parent or retiree.

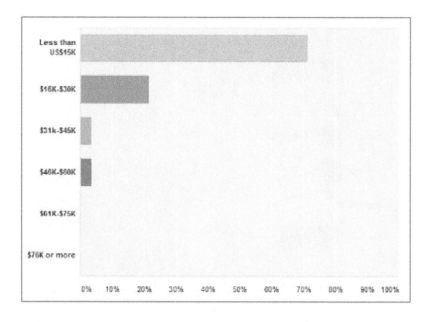

What makes you special?

To make it as a freelance writer covering any subject, it has always helped to have "a beat," something you can write about better than others. In travel this can mean a subject area, a place, a style of travel, or many other differentiating factors. Being without this—a beat, a niche, a specialty—means you are just another face in the crowd.

My beat, for instance, has traditionally been cheap places to travel, with the natural sub-niche of how to travel well on a budget. Later I branched into travel gear that is a good value—on a completely different blog—and I can fairly be considered an expert on both. I am friends with the go-to guys and gals on destinations like Turkey, Mexico City, Brazil, Cambodia, Thailand, Portugal, and Chile—and I could tell you who to call for 20 other places. If I ever invited all the travel food specialists I know into one place we could have the dinner party of a lifetime. Another acquaintance is an amazing resource on wine and cocktails, another on responsible travel/eco-tourism, and another on traveling with disabilities. These people have a leg up on anyone trying to do it all.

> *You need to find a niche. It is no longer enough to just write about travel - there is too much competition for a little guy to rank for the search term "travel." Find something about travel that you love (scuba diving, mountain hiking, volunteering, etc.) and focus on that theme.*
>
> ~ Barbara Weibel

Writers with a clear focus don't have to try very hard to get assignments or to get quoted as an expert. Anyone who puts the appropriate terms into Google is going to see these people at the top of the rankings. They are therefore recognized as authorities. If they have a book out, that adds even more credibility and they're beyond question.

So what makes you special? What can you cover better than anyone? For a lot of people that's their own region, but they don't take advantage of it. Here's what Sheila Scarborough, a contributor to my Perceptive Travel blog said: "My best advice? Quit thinking about *going* someplace and pitching stories from there; look around your very own town but see it as a travel writer would, and pitch that. Write what you know. Paris, France has been done. Someone needs to totally rock Paris, Texas."

As Nikki Pepper says, "Start with local content. You don't have to travel to exotic and undiscovered destinations. Bring your favorite experiences to life through your writing to show your mastery."

South Pacific travel expert David Stanley says if he had it to do all over again, he'd also pay more attention to his own back yard. "I would focus on my local area more and become 'the' expert on it."

Writing about what you know, and where you already live, may go against your idea of "travel writing," but traveling locally has a lot of advantages. You can pitch to regional magazines that aren't inundated with queries. You don't have to get on a plane. You can make local phone calls to reach people and meet them at their office or for coffee. You can change your schedule easily for interviews. You don't need a hotel room. You already know the lay of the land. And this may be the most important factor: people trust you. You are not an outsider who has parachuted in for the weekend; you are a local.

This doesn't mean you have to stay where you are for life and just be a specialist on Fargo, North Dakota. There's still a serious lack of good English language resource sites and blogs once you get beyond the most popular destinations. It wouldn't take long to establish yourself as the travel expert on Mendoza, Zihuatanejo, Moravia, or Sapa. Granted, there's not as much potential in those as being the expert on London, but it's certainly a path of far less resistance. Stake your claim and own it.

Jack of All Trades, Master of One

Eggs in one basket or multiple baskets?

As Seth Godin says, "Putting all your eggs in one basket and watching the basket really carefully isn't nearly as effective as the other alternatives. Not when the world gets crazy."

The world *has* gotten crazy. In a good way for us.

Today it pays to be nimble, adaptive, and opportunistic. Anyone who depends on a single stream of income from a specific company or even one type of media is going to get a nasty surprise sooner or later. As Nassim Taleb so effectively laid out in the book *Antifragile*, a freelance worker or solopreneur is, over the long run, in a much better position than a stockbroker. The latter may have a "safe" salary, but that salary can go to zero at any time. A taxi driver may have a bad day now and then, but his income won't drop to nothing.

Here's some advice from Beth Whitman, who wears hats as a blogger, publisher, author, and tour company leader. "Travel writers must have a multi-pronged approach in order to succeed. It's a small percentage who can actually make a living strictly from their writing. The trick is to be able channel it all into the travel world so you're not working as a barista during the day (not that there's anything wrong with that) and then blogging and writing at night."

While it's very important to find a niche you can dominate, that doesn't mean a laser focus is going to fatten your bank account, especially in the short term. Even the most specialized writers still have something else they do "on the side," and often that "side" pays their mortgage every month.

I believe strongly that you cannot make it as a freelance writer year after year if you do not have some knowledge or expertise to set you apart. But if there's one thing I can say with certainty about the future of travel writing, it is this: you need to diversify your income streams.

This may sound contradictory, but specialization in a subject area does not mean narrowing your sources of revenue. Be the master of your niche, but find lots of ways to make money from that expertise.

You can pitch articles to local publications and you can pitch to national or international ones as the go-to person for that area or subject. You can blog on that subject or area, attracting readers on your own. You can connect with sponsors or advertisers who are naturally interested in reaching that tribe. You can sell products that answer the questions or fix the problems your readers have.

There was a time when one publication you were tight with could keep your bills paid. There was a time when a relationship with a single editor was enough to enable you to sleep well at night.If you're starting off now, however, my advice would be to follow the "multiple streams of income" path instead—the more streams the better. It's just plain reckless to depend on one outlet, one type of media, or one source of advertising income. You want to be antifragile, thriving on disorder and taking advantage of new opportunities. Once you become an authority, some of those new opportunities will come to you naturally.

Many travel writers also ghostwrite books, do corporate writing, or make a significant portion of their income from advertising that runs on their own site or blog. Before I went full-time, I had a day job as a proposal writer for a tech company, blogging and writing books in the evenings. After that, I worked for a while for a national media placement firm where I had complete control over my hours. Both paid better than being a barista, thankfully, since I had a wife and a new daughter to support. The key was, both allowed me the flexibility to pursue what I really wanted to do with my time and eventually turn it into my real job.

Holding down a conventional day job while trying to be a travel writer is tough, especially if you're American and get a pitiful amount of vacation time for travel. After all, it's hard to be a travel writer if you only get two weeks off per year, unless you can just cover your local region on weekends. Or if you can just be a reporter doing research remotely around a specific subject. Many writers have better luck juggling writing with less structured positions. Seasonal workers, teachers, and professors have it a little easier:

> *I strongly recommend to bloggers to not give up the main job (for example, being a teacher) if they love it, as the symbiosis between blogging and teaching has done a lot for me.*
>
> ~ Lillie Marshall, freelance writer and blogger

Diversity of income is incredibly important, whether you are making $200 a week from your writing or $2,000. If you take the attitude that any source of income could go away at any time, you will be much better prepared for reality than the person who takes joy in a fat paycheck without considering the future clouds on the horizon. Getting an assignment is great, but that's just the first step: you still need to get paid.

At this point I've done writing work for more startups than I can count. Usually these companies are funded by venture or angel capital and have a sizable budget out of the box. They post an ad or call with a great assignment at a good pay rate and life is good. Eventually, however, reality sets in and those fat paychecks start dwindling. Sometimes the companies go under for good—so watch how much you do up front without getting paid.

Other times I've done work for a reputable magazine, only to see my story die on the vine because the invincible-looking publication got into financial trouble. With all the magazines that have gone away or gone digital-only all of a sudden in the past decade, you can't rely on a big brand name as a sign that your check's in the mail, on time. Blogger and freelancer Amy Whitley says her biggest frustration of all is "getting paid by magazines in a timely manner." It should be a simple transaction, but it seldom seems to turn out that way.

There are two ways to fight this inevitable buzzkill: 1) Run your own show completely or 2) Have multiple streams of income.

I would argue that even #1 requires a bit of #2 because even if you run your own website or blog, your income could be from Google, direct ads, networks, affiliate ads, e-book sales, or all of the above. If one of those is half your income, raise the big red flag because what if it goes away?

My income is only partly from my own site, but a lot of it comes from ghost blogging for other sites and for travel brands.

I also make a piece of my income doing marketing and SEO consulting, so I am entirely outside of the travel writing space for about 40% of my income. I don't see a lot of long-term income in travel writing, so I have been successfully transitioning into other areas.

I also do a lot more ghost writing now, which is something I did not do before, but I am happy to continue doing in the future as it's a bit easier to write to others' specification than to pitch work or write stories for my own site. I find it's more like a job when I ghost write, and for now, I like it.

~ Shannon O'Donnell of AlittleAdrift.com

Out with the Old:
Buggy Whips, Carbon Paper,
and Fortress Journalism

> *The punchline is this: the gatekeepers are dying. You, sitting in your apartment, can communicate with anyone on Earth more effectively than any media company 20 years ago.*
>
> ~ Taylor Pearson in *The End of Jobs*

A t this part of the book, you're probably itching for practical how-to advice. "Where do I start? What do I do right now? Just show me how to turn this career on!" In the past, the advice was fairly consistent and tried-and-true. You study the publications that are a good match for ideas you have. Then you send a targeted query to the right editor and wait to hear back. If you get an assignment in all the rejections, you then turn in a well-written piece on time and try to parlay that into more assignments. You start small and build your collection of clippings, thereby getting better and larger assignments as time goes on. Maybe you even get signed up as a guidebook writer, spending months gathering info about a particular destination and turning it into chapters or the whole book.

For more than 50 years, this was how things worked. There were variations on this theme, with trade magazines, staff editorial positions, and narrative books offering other paths, but in the end they all depended on you getting a yes from a powerful gatekeeper—an editor, agent, or publisher.

Some have called this fortress journalism. Everything we readers were fed in the pre-Internet age was controlled by gatekeepers and publishers in their mighty towers. You either played by their rules or you didn't play at all. It didn't matter how much talent you had or what kind of great ideas you had if you didn't get to the right people and get them to listen. If you sucked at writing short and cutesy "front of the book" articles but were brilliant at writing feature stories, well too bad. You weren't allowed to skip to C without going through A and B. If you had so much info to share that people would line up to hear your advice, it didn't matter if the gatekeepers didn't want to give you a forum. Nobody would see what you wrote.

Those days are not completely gone and if you want to break into the elite magazines or the *New York Times*, it still might as well be 1950. With print media, the only things that have changed are that you use e-mail instead of the postal service and in inflation-adjusted dollars they are paying you far less than they used to pay. Oh, and you don't have to make duplicate Ektachrome slides and mail them with fingers crossed. Otherwise it's all about working your way up a ladder slowly, building relationships (while praying the editor who hired you doesn't get fired), building up a portfolio, and trying to snag better assignments over time.

Financially, it can be a tough slog. As you can imagine, this is no way to make a living from the get-go. I'd say 8 out of every 10 freelance travel writers I know spent at least a year getting established before they made more than a good night's bar tab from an article. Most spent many years, working another job at the same time, doing this on the side, or using severance/savings/a spouse to support them while they built up a body of work. Most of the exceptions are people who got a staff job: the intern who became a junior editor with a salary; the junior copy editor who worked her way into the travel section; the guidebook company minion who moved out from behind a desk to go research a guidebook on a place nobody else wanted to go.

I studied journalism in college, worked at a slew of newspapers and magazines in my teens and 20s, then landed a research job at Newsweek in 2005. I served a brief stint in the New York office before moving to Europe and becoming a stringer for the international editions. Somehow, I then found myself contributing restaurant and hotel openings monthly for the next five years or so; during that same year abroad, I landed my first guidebook gig for Frommer's and went on to pen more than a dozen.

cont'd ...

> *At the time, I didn't even realize at the time that travel writing was a legit career; I wanted to be a sports reporter and somehow fell into travel writing instead.*
>
> ~ Kristin Luna, freelance writer

There's hope though. In the Internet Age, a new route has opened up, one that is self-directed and has nothing to do with getting buy-in from an editor or publisher. It's an entrepreneurial path, a marketing path, and a path requiring greater discipline. It's one that depends on pleasing an audience of readers, not pleasing one busy person in a cramped Manhattan office. Some people in this book are still 100% on the old path, some are 100% on one of the branches of the new path. The majority are somewhere in between, trying to figure out how to optimize the mix. You'll meet a lot of them in this book and hear their stories.

Before we look at the future though, where are we right now? What's wrong with all those books on travel writing 1.0?

For starters, the media in place since World War II is fading fast. We are in the midst of a major transformation, one not seen since the mass adoption of television. That was 50 years ago. Many magazines are hanging on by a fraying thread and most of the editors have no idea if they'll still have a job in 2020, much less the job they have right now.

Print will probably never really go away. Video didn't really kill the radio star after all—at least for the radio star who could adapt. We've come full circle with podcasting actually and many podcasters are bigger than the radio stars of old.

Any medium that has thrived for so long is not disappearing in the space of a few years. The *New York Times* added its millionth digital subscriber in 2015 and makes a very respectable level of revenue from those subscribers. But they're one of the few that has gotten people to pay for an online subscription and unless you're on staff, writing for newspapers and magazines is looking less dependable every month. It's not the bloodbath we saw during the Great Recession, but it's steadily getting uglier.

- As has been the case this whole decade, Yahoo's market value is higher than the sum of all U.S. print media companies added together. Just as an example, Yahoo is worth six times more than Scripps Interactive, producer of The Travel Channel, HGTV, the Food Network, the DIY Network, and more. And Yahoo is considered an also-ran, worth a fraction of Google or Facebook.

- A slew of magazines went under at the beginning of this decade. Today there's more of a general decline than a dive over a cliff, but 82 shut down in the USA and Canada in 2012, 56, shut down in 2013, and 99 closed in 2014. Most of the new launches now are confined to very narrow interests, for example *Construction Las Vegas* and *Mantra Yoga & Health*.

- Several other magazines went digital-only this decade including *AdWeek*, *Golf World*, the *Hollywood Reporter*, *Budget Travel*, and just about every magazine having something to do with tech (except glorious *Wired*, thankfully).

- In the UK, 432 magazines folded in just a two-year period and a media trade publication said, "Even though small and major magazine houses have added new titles to the newsstands, the industry is shutting them faster than it can launch them."

- More than 100 newspapers folded this decade and others, such as the *New Orleans Times-Picayune*, cut its staff by 50% or more in one year. *USA Today* bought out or laid off its whole veteran travel editorial staff, some of the most respected names in our industry, and closed their weekend magazine. You can now count the full-time newspaper travel editors in North America on one hand.

- Britain's *The Independent* newspaper sold for £1 plus assumption of debts at the beginning of this decade and *Newsweek* sold for $1 plus assumption of debts. More recently, the *Boston Globe* sold for $70 million and Amazon's Jeff Bezos paid $250 million for the *Washington Post*. The latter sounds pretty rich until you consider that a German publisher bought a controlling stake in online-only *Business Insider* for $343 million.

- Speaking of the *Washington Post*, here's how they reported on *National Geographic* selling 74% of its media operations to one of Rupert Murdoch's companies: "The magazine's domestic circulation peaked at about 12 million copies in the late 1980s; today, the publication reaches about 3.5 million subscribers in the United States and an additional 3 million subscribers abroad through non-English-language editions. Advertising has been in steady decline."

- A 2001 *Travel & Leisure* magazine issue I found in my mother-in-law's garage had 308 pages. A new one that landed in my mailbox recently had 148 pages. The same month, *National Geographic Traveler* was only 94 pages. Less and less print advertising means less and less editorial as well.

- Some once-respected publications with big brand names are now teetering so close to insolvency that their whole output is top-10 posts and listicles surrounded by desperate-looking paid brand advertorial. Even venerable Smithsonian.com has links under its articles to stories like "20 Child Stars Who Have Grown Up Hot" and "15 Horrible Crimes Committed by Famous Celebrities."

Some of this could be chalked up to a bad economy when I put out the first edition of this book and ad sales have predictably picked up as the economy has improved dramatically in the US. But will print media ever recover from the blow? It feels like we've collectively moved on, already seeing print publications as yesterday's news.

My 15-year-old might open a teen magazine because it comes with free posters, but last time I was perusing my city's alternative weekly she said, "Who reads a *newspaper* anymore?" About the only time I see American and Canadian 20-somethings reading a magazine is when they're waiting for a battery to recharge. They see magazines as a retro novelty, the same way they look at vinyl records, Polaroid cameras, and fountain pens. Newspapers aren't even that—they're something grandpa reads.

Statistics Canada's Survey of Household Spending found that average annual spending on periodicals and newspapers was less than $45 per household. In the US it's slightly less. Think about it:

that annual expenditure is less than the average voice and data plan *monthly* bill for someone with a smart phone. So how important is non-book print media in the average person's life?

There is a sea change happening that does not bode well for the future of newspapers and magazines. Most readers have moved to the web and the advertisers are following them. Without readers or advertisers, what does a publication have left?

> *Almost all of my income still comes from writing for newspaper travel sections (those that are still hanging in there). This can't, and won't last. I feel like a deckhand on the Titanic, but don't see any way I can stop the thing from going down.*
> ~ Peter Mandel, freelance writer and author

In a survey conducted at the beginning of this decade, 48% of the editors who participated said that "without a significant new income stream, their organizations could not remain solvent for more than 10 years; 31% gave them five years or less." We're at that five-year mark and for many of them, their prediction has come true. An increasing number of freelance writers see the writing on the wall in their pocketbooks. "The top tier print publications are drastically reducing rates, making freelancing financially challenging," said Beth Blair, author of *Break Into Travel Writing*.

They can move the whole operation online, as some have done already, but without the scarcity that fortress journalism created, they can't earn nearly as much money there. Instead of competing with their peers, they are competing with everyone—and usually "everyone" includes a few good one-person websites with similar traffic levels but 1/100th of the overhead.

In the print world, England has a handful of newspapers that still publish robust travel sections and a there are a few travel magazines that matter. Go online though and there are probably a thousand travel blogs and websites just based in England—with free content. Cross the ocean to the United States and the difference expands exponentially: maybe 25 travel magazines that still have a sizable readership (counting regional ones and airline magazines), but probably at least 4,000 travel content websites and blogs with decent enough traffic to earn some advertising revenue—and growing every month.

When faced with those numbers, how can *Travel & Leisure* charge advertisers a premium for their web traffic like they do for their magazine spreads? Sure, they're a recognized brand, but some travel websites that weren't even around five years ago get more traffic and their readers stick around longer. It's a different media world now, and the big publishing brands just don't have the power or influence they once did. So usually what they do instead is cram as many ads on a web page as they can and do so in the most obnoxious way possible so they can charge a higher rate. The resulting user experience is then far from ideal of course, which drives readers to less intrusive one-person blogs that feel more authentic.

Travel media is still incredibly important. By some estimates travel itself is the biggest industry in the world by revenue. It generates some $65 billion a year. People are reading more about travel than they ever did. Exotic places that nobody used to visit are now hot destinations. That's all very positive. But now there are more places to get information and that information is sliced and diced into smaller subsets that better fit varying needs. The pie has expanded, but it has thousands more pieces.

We can fight this trend or we can embrace it. Embracing it means recognizing all the sliced-up micromarkets and anticipating where the new ones are headed. It means capitalizing on the new hunger for more specific information. Twenty years ago, how many publications talked about eco-tourism, voluntourism, gay tourism, or medical tourism? Who was taking a vacation in Albania, Nicaragua, or Cambodia? Ten years ago, who needed information on the best flight tracking apps for the iPhone or stories on how to get around airline baggage fees and fuel surcharges?

Nobody. There wasn't a big enough market to support these niches when all info was in print, or the niches didn't even exist. On the web, writers can meet those specific information needs and make money from being a trusted resource. The people answering the new questions are getting lots of readers as a result.

> *My biggest key to success was stumbling on a niche that I could work in three different ways: I parlayed my expertise from my former career as a Certified Financial Planner into the realm of travel by writing for travel publications about finance. Conversely, I wrote for finance publications about travel. And on my own site, I combined the two to write about how to travel full-time in a financially sustainable way.*
>
> ~ Nora Dunn of TheProfessionalHobo.com

What About Books?

In the book publishing world the news is much more positive in most respects. Every author has one man to thank for allowing books to weather the digital revolution: Jeff Bezos. Thanks to the Kindle, most authors are making more money now than they did in the fortress publishing days. No matter what developed country you look at, print book readership is down somewhat, and from a base that was already pretty low to start with. Couple that with a ridiculously inefficient distribution system and you've got a situation where as few as 20% of all print books released turn a profit—including travel guidebooks. All the ones that don't sell get recycled at best or go into a landfill at worst, after being shipped back and forth to several warehouses and stores before that point, burning more fossil fuel. The vast majority of authors are lucky if they end up making more for their time spent on a book than a teenager stocking shelves in a supermarket.

Fortunately, there is more hope here than with other traditional media. Electronic books have now become accepted the way digital music has been accepted—without the piracy part. Also, there are more reasons to own a physical book than a physical CD, so it's more likely that print books will just plateau or slowly decline over decades rather than dropping through the floor. Plus the new book landscape is much more tilted in the author's favor than the old one.

> *Sales of my self-published books on Amazon now represent at least one-half of my total writing/publishing income. Work for regular publishers such as Fodor's varies from year to year, depending on their guidebook publishing schedules.*
>
> ~ Lan Sluder, freelance writer and author

Nothing is assured, however, and travel publishers that did well in print are having trouble matching that revenue from electronic media. While self-published authors love the new landscape, traditional publishers are less than thrilled. Their main reason for being—access to distribution—has disappeared as a competitive advantage, since anyone now can put out a print book directly through Amazon or via a general print-on-demand publisher. Since Amazon is (for now) a benevolent dictator that controls more than half the book market, getting into bookstores is now "nice" rather than essential unless you're putting out something very illustration-heavy like a coffee table book, children's book, or cookbook.

Many of the publishers don't pay large advances anymore and some don't pay an advance at all, which eliminates one of the only other reasons authors had for getting a publisher in the first place: money up front.

In this setup with no advance, you are signing away your rights to a book, getting only 10-15% of the income, yet taking the bulk of the risk yourself. Sure, the publisher has costs related to formatting and printing, but you're the one who slaved away months of your time to create the product. From a business standpoint, this doesn't make any sense, especially since the author does the bulk of the promotion as well. Why not just arrange your own cover and proofing?

More and more, smaller publishers are blurring the lines between traditional and print-on-demand, passing all of the risk onto the authors, with no payment up front. Will they go the way of music labels as a result, relegated only to the superstar acts and those needing full-blown retail distribution? We'll see, but just as many rock bands now fill 2,000-seat venues without being attached to a major label, authors are finding they can do better on their own than by signing a lopsided contract with a book publisher and getting very little in return.

If you have a good platform, now is a brighter time to be a non-fiction book author than any time in the past. It's a terrible time to be a music label executive, but a great time to be a band with a following. It's probably soon going to be a terrible time to be a book publishing executive, but a great time to be an author—*if* you're good at marketing. As we'll explore in more depth later, being good at marketing is more important now than it has ever been for writers. Nora Dunn of The Professional Hobo said, "The release of my latest book (*Working on the Road*) in February 2015 was very lucrative, and despite working less, I'm lined up for my biggest year yet in terms of income."

There's also a golden opportunity for someone, maybe a few someones, to take the available publishing tools and produce their own great guidebook by being a person who is truly on the ground researching. Stuart McDonald of TravelFish says his main frustration is the growth in "remote updating" of traditional guidebooks "and nobody calling them on it."

Could you do better? One of my contributors, Jim Johnston, did just that with his Mexico City guide and it is frequently No. 1 for that city on Amazon, beating titles from the likes of Lonely Planet and Fodor's. Another resident there who I know is doing one just on the Roma neighborhood, niching down even more. For a traditional publisher, that makes no sense, but for someone who can make a profit with 500 copies sold, hell yeah!

The Changing Definition of "Writing"

Futurist and professor Marshall McLuhan coined the saying, "The medium is the message" and the Internet Age has magnified his point. People consume information very differently on a computer monitor than they do in a magazine or newspaper. They consume it differently still on a small portable smartphone. When communicating on Twitter and Facebook, they have the attention span of a fruit fly.

From a writer's standpoint, it is hard to see any of this as a positive development. When reading electronic articles, attention spans are shorter, people do more skimming, and they are searching for answers more than reading for enjoyment or enrichment.

Some publications defy this trend—and profit by being different—but in general writing for the web requires adjustments. The engaging lede (often referred to as "the lead") meant to draw readers in, often gives way to a paragraph stuffed with keywords for the search engines. An article that would go on interrupted for two pages now requires subheads to break it up. There's no easy way to insert the kind of information-packed sidebar you see in newspapers and magazines. There's a limit to how large and how detailed photos can be. Conversely, the web has lots of advantages. It's searchable. There are hyperlinks. You can insert video. You can match ads to the content. There's an infinite supply of pages to hold the content. Stories live on forever instead of being tossed in the recycling bin when the next issue arrives.

So what does it mean to be a good writer in this environment? It depends on the medium. In a later chapter we'll break it down by outlet type.

Survive or Thrive

In the first edition of this book I said, "Maybe for another three to five years the old guard of print writers can keep doing what they've always been doing. There will still be some writers who get enough big feature assignments from surviving magazines (especially trade magazines) to still do well. The really great ones can probably keep going strong for a decade or more if they get a steady stream of book royalties and speaking gigs."

Five years later as I'm doing this update, I can count on one hand the number of travel writers I know personally who make a real living doing primarily print articles. When 2020 arrives, I won't be surprised if there are just one or two left standing.

This is the path of most resistance for a new writer, like studying to be a buggy whip maker just as Henry Ford was revving up his factories. Somebody still makes buggy whips of course—there's the Amish/Mennonite market if nothing else—but it's a *very* niche business. It's going to be mostly a winner-take-all game, with just the best hustlers and writers getting the bulk of the spoils.

People like Jill Robinson, a freelancer who frequently writes for the likes of *Afar, San Francisco Chronicle, Robb Report, Islands, and Delta Sky*:

> *My migration to print came as a result of online outlets paying poorly. For me, that will only change if my better-paying sources end.*
>
> ~ Jill Robinson, freelance writer

For those who want to excel in the new digital world, a whole different mindset is required. The old way of building up clips, establishing a track record, and getting cozy with a few key editors is going to be less and less effective. Some will still manage it as a print-only freelancer, others will get staff positions, but most will need to either give up or find another way.

The old model will eventually go the way of the pay phone and the fax machine. Like it or not, it's time for Travel Writing 2.0.

In with the New: Unleashing the Writing Entrepreneurs, the Solopreneurs, and the Gig Creators

If you want to write the fortunes for the cookies that don't exist anymore, you may need to make your own organization, lead your own tribe and hire yourself.

~ *Seth Godin*

So if old media outlets—and their nice paychecks—are fading fast, what is replacing them? As far as money goes, that's still an open question on the freelance side. Most websites don't pay anything close to what comparable print publications pay, primarily because what they are earning in revenue isn't close to what a healthy print magazine pulls in on a monthly basis. Plenty of people I know are making great money as a new type of travel writer, but most of them are content owners, not just writers.

Fair or not, the era of "user-generated content" has also devalued the worth of the written word. We're all drowning in words and can only consume a fraction of even what interests us the most. TripAdvisor has more pages posted than most other travel sites added together—and they haven't paid for hardly any of the content. Yelp's review numbers grew from 8 million to 83 million in just the first five years of the '10s. All but the fakes were posted by volunteers who wanted to rant or rave—typos and bad grammar be damned.

Then consider all the "content marketing" going on by people who only see the words as a means to an end: to get e-mail signups, get people into a marketing funnel, or enhance their authority in order to get paid speaking engagements. It wouldn't cross their minds that this is a paid service done by professionals.

Getting mad at all these people who "write for free" and devalue the work of those who want to get paid for it is a fruitless exercise. The genie is already out of the bottle and it likes the fresh air.

To survive in the new media landscape, you'd be wise to go back and study Charles Darwin. "It is not the strongest of the species that survives, nor the most intelligent that survives. It is the one that is the most adaptable to change."

Those who are really "making it" as travel writers and feel confident about their futures are those who are adapting best to the new reality. They are finding ways to meld their skills to new demands and markets. They are antifragile, profiting from change rather than complaining about it.

That's not easy, no matter what anyone's *Make a Fortune Blogging in Your Underwear* e-book may tell you. If you're going down this road, expect plenty of detours, breakdowns, and potholes along the way. In other words, a good road trip—if you have the right attitude.

I've seen a lot of change, and watched many old school travel writers end up sidelined because they refused to write for online publications and develop a social media presence. I've always watched popular bloggers with big numbers try to make the move into travel writing, and fail miserably because they can't write compelling travel stories, which are very different from most blog content. Hone your craft and stay on top of new trends. Attend professional development sessions, network and make yourself memorable in a good way.

~ Sarah Deveau, freelance writer

In my survey for the first edition of this book, nearly two-thirds were still making the majority of their income from work they did for others. Fast forward five years and it's the reverse. Now two-thirds are making the majority of their income from travel content and among those who consider themselves full-time writers, 46% are making 100% of their revenue from their own content or platform. No matter where the money comes from, the equation is the same: make enough revenue to be left with a profit.

Economics and Accounting for Freelance Writers

Making money as a writer entails understanding the same basic formula that guides all types of freelance or self-employed work:

$r - e = p$

That's revenue minus expenses equals profit. In the real world that formula can get much more complicated in a hurry, for example:

$(r1 + r2 + r3) - (e + o + t) = p$

That would be revenue from three stories minus travel expenses, office costs, and taxes. What's left is what you actually earned. Take it further as a full-time freelancer and you also have to factor in real living expenses, pesky costs like housing, health insurance, and food.

"Hey egghead, I'm a writer, not a math whiz," you're probably thinking. Well too bad. You had better get good at understanding your finances to be a freelancer or you won't have anything that equals "p" in that equation. (Of course if you are completely supported by a spouse or retirement income—more on that later—then you can stay blissfully unconcerned about how much you actually earn.)

In simple terms, the goal is to make more money than you spend. If you finance your trips and write for tiny publications—or are a beginning blogger—it's tough to make that formula look positive. It's noble, but in a starving artist kind of way. If you're paying for your own travels and writing, it's usually more sane to look at those earnings as gravy, a byproduct, not as your main source of income. Otherwise you'll find you are permanently in the red unless you reach a level of true success.

Here are a few things travel writers do to make the formula work out so that p=real **profits**.

1.   Write for publications that pay expenses. In these situations you agree on what it will cost, you submit expenses to an editor, and you get reimbursed.

2.   Go on press trips or accept hosting from tourism bureaus and hotels.

3. Cover the local region so expenses are far lower.
4. Make sure the article or guidebook project fee is at least double what will be spent.
5. Write for a self-owned publication where advertising and/or product income is higher than expenses

We collectively have to get better at understanding basic economics. If TravelKingpin.com makes $2 a page per month on the article you wrote for them from advertising, they're not about to pay you big bucks for your article, even if it's great and even if you turn in another 99 great ones. They'll probably pay you a fraction of what they are bringing in—which in this case is only $200 a month from your 100 articles. If you run your own site though and average $2 a month from each of 100 pages, your revenue actually *is* $200. That's still not much, but it's yours and it'll keep being yours every month, increasing as your traffic goes up. TravelKingpin.com is not evil. It's a business. In general terms, the site is not going to pay you more money than the revenue you generate. Their risk, their reward. If you work for yourself, you take all the risk and reap a higher reward.

If you understand this basic tradeoff, you can evaluate opportunities in a better light. JoeNobodyBlog.com may only pay you a few dollars a post. One that's more established may do a revenue share or pay you $6 to $15 a post. An established blog network funded by venture capitalists may pay you $25 for 400-500 words. Keep moving up the ladder and you get $100 to $400 for a real article or corporate blog post. Get into the rarified air where major sites pull in millions of visitors and you start getting closer to the print world, like $200 to $1,000 for a quality piece that hundreds of thousands of visitors will read.

That range goes from peanuts to the monthly rent, but all of these options can make sense for the right person at the right time and I'll admit that I've done work for all of the above. Sure, I'd rather have $1,000 than $6, but compensation takes many forms and the dollar amount is just one of them.

In my case I took the low-paying blog posting jobs because I wanted an outlet for something specific, I wanted a valuable link back to my sites (more on that later), I knew it would sell books, or it helped me help someone who helped me. Any gig can be a good gig if it serves a purpose for you, especially when you are just starting out as a writer.

I am also firmly in the camp that believes what Malcolm Gladwell proposed in *Outliers*: most people who are great at something have spent at least 10,000 hours practicing.

Think about that number. It equates to about three years and five months of writing eight hours a day, seven days a week. Or about five years if you work at it 40 hours a week and don't take many vacations. (And don't spend half your day sending glorified text messages on Facebook and Twitter.)

> *My biggest frustration is trying to balance freelance writing for magazines with building my own blogger brand. It's an issue because monetizing the blog is a full time business, but the freelance writing market is getting more difficult because a lot of "free" sites have pulled down the pricing on many freelancing gigs.*
>
> ~ Susan Lanier-Graham, freelancer and blogger

Still, compared to some activities, 10,000 hours is not all that daunting. Clay Shirkey, author of *Cognitive Surplus*, estimates that a person born in 1960 has spent five times that amount sitting passively in front of a television. That's more than five and a half solid *years* of a 50-year-old's life. The obvious lesson: turning off the TV is a great first step in becoming a better writer.

Ask any writer who has been at it for a decade or two and most will tell you, "I'm still improving." Most years I can say the best story I ever wrote came out last year. But I'll probably write something better this year. Then I'll improve again the year after that.

Write often, write a lot, and write about different things in different styles—that's how you become great. So those who evaluate every potential job by whether it's going to cover the car payment or not are going to lose out on a lot of valuable practice, practice that comes with immediate (and sometimes brutal) feedback.

> *I was a full-time corporate accountant and technical writer, and wanted to get out of the rat race. I transitioned to freelance technical writing and sent out a bunch of travel pitches.*
>
> *I landed regular gigs with meetings & event magazines and online at TravelGolf.com when online wasn't cool. Over time I've expanded on those to write for dozens of print and online publications and run two of my own blogs.*
>
> ~ Diana Rowe, freelance writer and blogger

Diana's meandering path is actually more typical than any straight one in today's media world. In an environment where it's increasingly hard to make a living from just one or two outlets—or even one or two kinds of media—hustling for multiple income sources is key.

Part of being a financially savvy freelancer is also making sure the organization you are writing for can actually pay you. Before, freelance writers didn't think much about the financial health of the publications they were writing for; you got the assignment and were happy to have the work.

Most of us have gotten burned at least once by a magazine that crashed and burned, taking the IOUs with it to the graveyard. In the new climate we have to be more vigilant about dying print publications—even century-old newspapers that once seemed invincible—and also web startups that could disappear as fast as they began.

A friend of mine wrote for a New Jersey magazine called HudsonMOD that is still in business, but partly because the publisher keeps stiffing her freelance writers and photographers. When some of them took to social media to shame the publication, at least one of the writers received a nasty cease and desist letter from a lawyer. (We're assuming the lawyer got paid just fine.)

Unfortunately this happens more often than you hear about: a condition of getting paid 50% of the back pay for my friend would have been to sign a non-disclosure agreement. In other words, "Shut up and we'll pay you half what we promised for all your hard work."

Why Becoming a Business is Better Than Working for a Business

We're in a golden age of entrepreneurship, in which the earliest phases of bootstrapping have never been so inexpensive. A fledgling entrepreneur who is committed and passionate has no appreciable barriers to testing her hypothesis, interviewing potential customers, and building a minimum viable product.

~ Dave Lerner, serial entrepreneur, angel investor, and Columbia University professor

There are multiple ways to make a buck at this writing endeavor and other ways to profit that don't involve a direct exchange in cash. I want to be clear, however, that nearly all the big money success stories I know are people who have complete control over their destiny. The path of running your own real business may not be the easiest or the quickest, but it's certainly the one where you're leaving the least amount of control in other peoples' hands.

As that quote at the beginning says so well, the other reason to start your own business now is that it's so cheap. Never in history have so many great tools and so many great people been available so conveniently and inexpensively. I can point to 20 things I do in my business that would have been prohibitively expensive when I started that are now very much in anyone's reach. I'm talking about hiring WordPress experts to fix something for $10 or having ones at your beck and call for $69 a month. We have social media scheduling apps like Hootsuite, Buffer, MeetEdgar, and ITTT (If This Then That). Although it may be hard to believe now, when I launched my first blog there was no Dropbox, GoogleDocs, Facebook, Asana, Slack, or YouTube. Skype was just getting started. There was no service that matched people who wanted to hire remote employees with those willing to do the work. As I write this, massive time savers like Fiverr and Canva are only a couple years old.

Many people look at stories of how entrepreneurs got started and assume they had investors, but that's seldom the case. In a survey of the Inc. 500—the fastest-growing small companies in the US—nearly half of them were started with less than $5,000. For a web-based business like ours, you can do it for a tiny fraction of that.

It is so incredibly easy now to launch something as a test and have it look totally professional that it's almost crazy not to try. There are people launching new ventures every day from a laptop that are making more than their previous salaries ever did just by solving a problem or meeting a market need. Much of the time this is done with an information product comprised mostly of...content. Which mostly requires...writing.

See the resources section at the end for the things I've listed above and plenty more, but don't get hung up on the tools. The ways to launch and execute will keep evolving. The market needs will change, requiring regular adaptation. What won't change is the need to buckle down and get it done. Ideas are everywhere. The hard part is showing up and making them happen, day after day.

I started this chapter with a quote from Seth Godin and I'm going to end with another one. If you're running your own show as a solopreneur or business owner, you probably ought to have his blog at the top of your weekly reading list and be looking at every post. He also offers a free podcast series on iTunes called The Startup School that will be 10 of the best-spent hours of your life if you want to launch a real business. He gets his ideas across a few paragraphs at a time, without a lot of wasted words. That's a good model for any writer.

Just because you're good at something doesn't mean the market cares any longer.

The Marx Brothers were great at vaudeville. Live comedy in a theatre. And then the market for vaudeville was killed by the movies. Groucho didn't complain about this or argue that people should respect the hard work he and his brothers had put in. No, they went into the movies.

Then the market for movies like the Marx Brothers were making dried up. Groucho didn't start trying to fix the market. Instead, he saw a new medium [television] and went there.

~ SethGodin.typepad.com

The 104 Faces of a Travel Writer

"My husband and I are developing cookbooks at the moment, and we're doing far fewer guidebooks than we used to. I'm also writing for the weekend edition of the Phnom Penh Post, Cambodia's national newspaper.

I've also been offering bespoke travel itineraries for the last couple of years, mainly for high-end clients, including some of the world's best chefs and restaurateurs. That happened organically. I did it for friends and then they started recommending my services, so I started creating them for a fee.

I do a bit of fixing work as well, and have started—along with my husband—hosting culinary travel writing and photography tours and will also be hosting some creative/writing retreats.

So I guess you could say we're diversifying more, but then we've always had our fingers in many pies since we started working in the mid-80s. I've never in my life ever done one thing at any one time."

~ Lara Dunston, writer and blogger

Lara and her husband make a comfortable living and have for many years. As you can see from that "what we're doing now" description though, they're still hustling for it. They're also smart enough to know that income diversification is a key element of continued success.

What does it mean to be a "travel writer" in the second decade of the new millennium? Articles writer or editor? Book author or webmaster? Blogger or corporate writer? There's no one answer that is going to work for everyone. And for some people it's all of the above.

Here are examples of a few people who are making a full-time living at this to show you how diverse the paths and outcomes can be.

Stuart McDonald started by self-publishing a couple of guidebooks in the 1990s. "I made my money back plus I got to travel. That was enough to give me a taste for it. I've only ever very rarely done freelance, so I 'broke into it' I guess by starting my website." His TravelFish.org has been the best online resource for Southeast Asia for more than a decade.

Nora Dunn's writing career started very organically in 2007. Like many before and since, she started a blog to chronicle her travels. "Shortly thereafter I connected the dots and realized that my lifelong penchant for the written word, plus my laptop and an Internet connection, could lead to an income to sustain my travels. Thus, I started seeking out freelance travel writing gigs, and over the next few years, built up a portfolio of bylines and columns that eventually started generating a full-time income. Most of my travel writing is online, however I've had a few print columns as well. Over the years as my own travel blog gained notoriety, it too, started generating income through advertising, affiliate income, and digital products."

Mark Johanson used his blog to prove (and improve) his writing skills before parlaying that into a full-time gig about a year and a half later. "I was hired on as a travel editor at a young digital publication. I got in with the publication in its early days, and by the time I left three years later, it was a major player in the digital landscape, helping me to raise my portfolio. Along the way, I took every opportunity I could to write the kind of stories I knew would build my career and be useful clips when I left to become a freelancer."

Beth Whitman broke into travel writing with a multi-pronged approach. "I wrote a book, *Wanderlust & Lipstick*, to establish myself as an authority in the world of women's travel and then launched a website and blog to help promote the books." Beth has parlayed that expert status into a line of other books she publishes herself and a business running tours to places like Papua New Guinea, India, and Bhutan. She has turned WanderlustandLipstick.com into a full platform, hiring other bloggers to write different sections of the site. Writing has become just a piece of the whole, as much a marketing tool as an income source. "As other parts of my business grow, I think that my writing will continue to be less of a revenue generator and more of a means to help promote and sell the Wanderlust and Lipstick tours."

Brian Spencer says his big, life-altering break came when he was hired as an editorial assistant at an ahead-of-its-time travel site called IgoUgo. "I was sorely underpaid, at least at first, but this came after working in a Brooklyn grocery store for 1.5 years to help make ends meet while interning at *Paper Magazine*, so I jumped on it, thankfully. The best job perk was a free extra vacation day and $500 in travel money once a quarter, in exchange for publishing a 'travel journal' about the trip on IgoUgo. That money took me to places that until then I'd never dreamed of seeing—Rio de Janeiro, Berlin, Buenos Aires, Hong Kong, many others—and got me started on a travel writing (and editing) career that I'd not previously thought possible."

Gary Arndt started his now-successful Everything-Everywhere.com blog when he began traveling around the world a decade ago. It's something many people do when they take off, but Gary kept at it and turned his blog into a full-time job, now making more than enough to pay his bills, support his globetrotting, and put some money away. "The keys to my success have been Internet marketing and constant attention to the site," he says. "I don't view myself as a travel writer. I view myself as a travel blogger."

John DiScala (a.k.a. Johnny Jet) was one of the travel website pioneers but says he just got lucky. "I used to be afraid to fly. I started learning all kinds of tips and began helping others' travels." He put up one of the original travel resource websites and it took off. He now flies around 150,000 miles and visits more than 20 countries each year. He and his website JohnnyJet.com have been featured over 1,800 times in major publications, including most of the major U.S. media outlets. He makes serious money as a travel writer, but not because of the articles he writes for others—that part is gravy. He makes his living from advertisers who want to be a part of his site or tap into his influence.

The strategy employed by Gary and Johnny—the last two on that list—is the common thread among most of the financially successful travel writers I know: they write for themselves and own their content instead of giving it away to others for one-shot article fees. They earn money as publishers do: from selling advertising and sponsorships that tap into their readership and influence. But as the examples above illustrate, "travel writers" have many different faces. You'll hear stories and advice from many other writers throughout this book.

For some, it's not really about the money, and that's fine. I once got invited on a blogger summit sponsored by Gore-Tex. They flew a bunch of us to their headquarters, wined and dined us a couple nights, and taught us about their product lines. Yes, I got some cool gear to try out—which of course I reviewed later. Outdoor apparel companies have been way ahead of travel destinations in understanding the power of the web and this summit was a great example. Only three of the 16 people invited were full-time writers. One was a geologist, one worked for a TV network, one had a communications job with a big software company, and one worked at a gear retail shop.

The thing is, they all ran influential blogs or websites that landed on Gore's radar. These people ran some of the most respected sites around on mountain biking, snowboarding, skiing, hunting, rock climbing, and backcountry hiking. (And in my case, a blog about useful travel gear.) Some of these writers were making serious money from their sites, while others were barely making enough to buy a season pass to a ski resort. The common denominator was that they were passionate about their particular niches and had become known influencers—industry experts. For many people, that's enough.

I met Jennifer Miner and Kara Williams at a conference called Travel Media Showcase many years ago and have kept in touch with them ever since, even hiring Kara to write for me at two publications. They are two of the founders/writers at TheVacationGals.com, a family travel blog. Neither of them is getting rich from their efforts and they both contribute to a long list of different publications, but the writing from that site and others provides both a good income stream while letting them get some nice perks and write about what they enjoy. Jennifer says, "The web has been, and continues to be, a great source for novice travel writers. There are many sites that accept "newbies," where we can learn the ropes as freelancers—despite the low wages therein."

Kara broke into travel writing by "covering her own backyard," writing $25 articles for GoColorado.com. She also wrote for free for BellaOnline.com covering honeymoon travel. "I took my travel writing career up a notch by taking an online course from Amanda Castleman. Soon after I landed more lucrative web and print assignments."

I started this section with a crazy quilt of income from one writer and here's another that shows how the ability to hustle and adapt is what leads to long-term success.

The bulk of my income used to come from advertising directly on my blog, in the days when companies were buying text links to artificially inflate their Google ranking. When Google clamped down on this practice, I lost every bit of that income within a year and had to completely change my focus. These days, aside from a pittance I earn in affiliate advertising fees, I use my blog to create authority within the industry and as a platform where potential publishers can see the quality of my work. As such, most of my income now comes from sources outside the blog, such as freelance writing jobs. I am also developing alternative sources of income that also use my blog as a launching pad (redirecting traffic to purchase a product).

I'm also starting to make a little money with Plansify, which allows people to hire me to answer travel questions via e-mail or Skype. My next project is a couple of eBooks, assuming I can carve out some time to get them done. Basically, I earn a little here and a little there, doing whatever it takes to stay on the road.

~ Barbara Weibel

Does Location Matter?

For a freelance writer, location used to matter a lot. There's a good reason half the working magazine writers seem to live in New York City: it's the biggest publishing center in the world. Apart from a few outlier magazines like *Outside, Afar,* and *Southern Living,* most editors of national magazines work in Manhattan. So do most book publishers and literary agents. So do a whole slew of organisms that depend on these industries, like PR agencies, ad agencies, and tourism boards. The same goes for London if you're a British writer or Sydney if you're Australian.

Whenever I return to New York, I understand the allure of living there. It's a blur of parties, of event invitations, of rubbing elbows with people that matter. One time when I visited the city for a conference, author David Farley talked me into going to a party that a liquor PR company was sponsoring. In a city I hadn't been to for two years, a place I hadn't lived in for more than a decade, I ran into four people I knew within a half hour of arriving. The Six Degrees of Separation principle is in overdrive in Manhattan.

The problem is, it's really ridiculously expensive to live in New York City. Your normal American spends less on a mortgage for a three-bedroom house with a yard than most New Yorkers spend on rent for a cramped studio apartment. You get invited to parties, but good thing because you don't have money to buy booze on your own. You have a better chance of meeting editors, but you need lots and lots of assignments from them just to cover your expenses.

As print media becomes less and less important, it follows that living in New York (or London) will matter less and less. As digital media has become more and more influential, we're seeing writers live where they can afford to live instead of living where they feel like they have to live. When nearly every communication is by e-mail, why do you need to even be in a city? Rolf Potts seems to do fine on a farm in Kansas. For that matter, why do you even need to be in your home country? I have freelancers working for me who are living in Argentina, Chile, Mexico, Hungary, Singapore, and Australia.

I'm one of those people who thinks the fragmentation of media is a healthy development. As someone who lived and worked in the New York City area for many years, I know first-hand how myopic a place it is. There's a tremendous amount of groupthink going on and most New Yorkers will freely admit they have no grasp of how people in the rest of the country live or what motivates them. So it will probably help us all if the media decision-making gets spread out to a wider base.

The beautiful thing about the environment we are entering now is that location doesn't matter much. Why do you need a New York or London publisher if most of your books will sell through Amazon and Kobo anyway? Why does your website need to be in a major city if you are posting from the road or a home office, not even knowing where your server is located? Why do you need to be rubbing shoulders with editors in their hometown if most of your income is derived from content you own yourself?

For three of the past five years I've run my business from Guanajuato, Mexico. I'm now back in the United States so my daughter can finish high school here, but it doesn't really matter where. In the digital age, with all the communication and file sharing tools we have, who cares where you plug in your laptop? You can adjust your expenses to enable the pursuit of your dream. (For my book on that subject, see CheapLivingAbroad.com.)

The one caveat is that the solitary life of a writer becomes more solitary—in a physical sense anyway—if there's no community of writers around you. I never ran into another travel writer when I lived in Nashville. Susan Barnes and I have put a group of them together in Tampa, but we're only up to a dozen members. If you live in Seattle or San Francisco, however, you can't toss a hacky sack in a coffee shop without hitting one.

If having a community of people to meet with and bounce ideas off of is important, move to a place where your type already lives. With a little effort you'll have a built-in support group.

Otherwise, live wherever you want and get on a plane to attend conferences and go on group press trips. Join online groups. Then stay in touch with the people you have met in person: often those bonds are much stronger and longer lasting than those established with an online avatar.

The Key Qualities of a Travel Writer

You never know where or when your big break is going to come from. But you definitely won't get it by doing nothing.
~ Peter Moore, author of multiple travel narrative books

You cannot spot a travel writer in an airport like you can a pilot, a pro basketball player, or a priest. There's no uniform, no typical physique, and no telltale sign of a specific profession. Except for times when you'll see one taking notes in a notebook, there are few clues projected through appearance or action.

There are some common characteristics the good ones have in common though, qualities that separate the winners from the losers across all kinds of travel writers. If you don't have a good number of the following in your personal arsenal, start working on them now. Otherwise you are going to struggle.

Self-motivated. I think it's safe to say that all writers covering any subject have their moments of self-doubt and it's hard to not feel you have some faults when editors repeatedly reject your ideas. We get over it though because we have to. Like a great salesperson who measures success by the number of times he hears "no" in a day, a freelance writer needs to have the motivation to keep plugging away to score the next assignment or pull in that next batch of subscribers.

It's very easy to get discouraged, which is why the self-motivated writers are the ones still working ten years after they started, while others give up and move on to another vocation that's less of a struggle. It's easy to give up on this tough gig if you don't have the fire in your belly to push on when the going gets tough.

> *How does a travel writer go on vacation? It's constant, and even though I love the work I do and would never trade it for anything, it is overwhelming and takes a great deal of time, energy, and brain space. I'm hoping I'll get more used to this and be able to find a good rhythm as time goes on.*
> ~ Jackie Laulainen, of The Budget Minded Traveler podcast and blog

Persevering. Motivation can't be fleeting and temporary. The writer who perseveres and keeps at it is the one who will succeed after the others have dropped out. This is true in traditional media, where you are pitching to editors, and in the blogging world, where most writers make little to no money in their first six months or a year of work. "Instant success" is so rare as to be statistically impossible in the travel-writing world. It takes a long view and perseverance to survive and eventually thrive.

Flexible and Adaptable. If you've ever been a backpacker for months or years on end, you've got this one down already. Travel is, by nature, unpredictable. Things go wrong on a regular basis. There are a lot of moving parts on any journey: airlines, ground transportation, a parade of hotels, attractions, restaurants, people to interview, and places where you can log on to the Internet—for a start. You roll with the punches when things fall through and learn to adapt. Quoting Darwin again, "In the long history of humankind (and animal kind, too) those who learned to collaborate and improvise most effectively have prevailed."

This need for flexibility also applies to the actual writing. Different publications require a different style and voice. An editor may make changes to your article that you don't agree with, but she is the boss so you learn to live with it. That angle you had so carefully researched before leaving may turn out to be a crappy angle once you've arrived and you need to change course. Roll with it.

Confident. If you don't believe in yourself and your abilities, there are hundreds of people out there ready to supply negative feedback. There are also hundreds of more confident writers ready to leapfrog over you at any given time.

This doesn't mean your story is great when every editor has told you it's awful, but if you've got a reason to believe you're a good writer—from classes, writing groups, awards, publication credits, blog traffic—then exude that confidence and use it to energize your efforts. There is no shortage of people who will write nasty blog comments, ignore your e-mail pitches, tell you you're crazy to try to make it as a writer, or ask when you're going to get a real job. If you don't have the confidence to deflect all that like Wonder

Woman with bulletproof bracelets, you'll be bounced out of this pursuit dejected.

Comfortable going it alone, but amiable in social situations. This is an odd combination, but a necessary one for any kind of journalist. A travel writer, especially a guidebook or feature writer, is often traveling alone, eating meals alone, staying in hotel rooms alone, riding planes and buses alone. There's nobody to bounce ideas off of in the room.

On the other hand, the writer must be regularly starting up conversations with complete strangers: digging for information, getting quotes, asking for other contacts, finding out how things work, and getting others' opinions. The only writers who don't need these dual qualities are ones whose entire writing output comes out of group press trips. (Unfortunately, it's rare that one of those people turns in consistently great work that is refreshing or surprising.)

Observant. Do you know how many different kinds of birds are singing outside your window? Do you notice what music is playing when you enter a restaurant or hotel? Blindfolded, can you taste the difference between Chardonnay and Sauvignon Blanc, between Pilsner and Pale Ale, between Ethiopian coffee and Sumatran coffee, between Thai food and Vietnamese food? Can you tell the differences just from the aromas? Can you describe a Chihuahua to a blind person? Do you notice the characteristics of the other diners in the café where you're having coffee? Can you describe the scene in the town square where you are sitting in such a way on paper that I see the details in my mind?

Most of these skills are developed, not innate, but it's hard to be a great writer without them.

Curious. This may be the most important quality of all, but it's one that seldom gets discussed because this one *does* need to be innate. If you are a closed-minded, dogmatic person who only gets news from one source, doesn't have a passport, and never reads quality fiction, you are going to be a lousy travel writer. Sure, that's my opinion, but it's based on more than two decades of experience meeting hundreds of other travel writers. All the good ones are open-minded and very curious about the world, about other peoples' opinions, about other cultures and religions. As Maureen Littlejohn says, "The best travel writers have a unique voice, credibility, honesty, and a natural curiosity."

As a travel writer you are constantly diving into subjects you previously knew nothing about. If you can't investigate these stories and places with an open heart and mind, it's nearly impossible to do a good job and it will show. Being a stubborn pundit with rigid beliefs works fine if you're a political columnist, but it's toxic for a travel reporter.

You also have to go beyond your assumptions, your stereotypes, or even drop everything you now know about a place in order to be open to new angles. As Kim Foley MacKinnon says, "No story is too small. Every single person and place has something fascinating to tell if you just look hard enough."

Passionate. Every good travel writer I know is passionate about travel, just as every food writer I know is passionate about cooking. You don't see someone who seldom watches sports become a sports writer. I'd rather get poked in the eye with a knitting needle than to write about crafts, so of course I'll never cover that subject. If you think it would be fun to be a travel writer because you had a great time on your last vacation—which was three years ago—this is probably not the right subject for you. If you haven't gotten away every chance you had, travel is not your passion. Become a mommy blogger, a music reviewer, or a gardening writer instead.

Before going down any of the various paths available to writers, it's important to reflect on whether travel itself is truly a subject that gets you excited. Not the highlights of a great vacation, but the entire experience: the bus journey, the strange food, different languages, finding your way in a foreign land.

Just as an artist becomes a painter for reasons other than the associated income, the tough slog of becoming a successful travel writer requires an above-average level of interest in the subject. Be sure too that you have the skills and tenacity to turn this passion into income. As a business writer friend of mine likes to say, just because you love to drink doesn't mean you should own a bar.

If someone dear to me wanted to become a travel writer, I would advise that they look deeply and see if it is really their passion. Contrary to what the travel writing schools advertise about earning six figures a year, doing it for the money alone is a sure way to fail. If it is your love and passion push ahead!

~ John Lamkin, freelance travel writer and photographer

Traditional Earning Opportunities as a Travel Writer

While this book may be called "Travel Writing 2.0," the rise of one media does not mean the automatic fall of another. The first time I put out this book more than half the travel writers I surveyed were still making the majority of their income from print. Now that has dropped to below 35%, but that's still significant.

To ignore these outlets, especially considering their still-higher pay, doesn't make sense for those who want to expand their income streams or step up their visibility. For me the print world is a very small percentage of my income, but I'd be lying if I said I didn't get a special thrill from seeing my name on a big article splashed across two magazine pages. And the checks are good. So I'm still not completely turning my back on print.

As some of the examples in the previous chapter illustrate, few freelance travel writers are one-trick ponies. Though most have a defined niche, which is incredibly important in terms of standing out from the pack, they have multiple income streams deriving from different kinds of work.

Writers like Tim Cahill and Pico Iyer have done well taking features they wrote for magazines and packaging them as chapters in a book.

Some magazine feature writers are able to take one trip sponsored by one magazine and get paid enough to justify all the time spent on that trip, but this is rare. Most writers need to hustle more than this, turning each trip into multiple stories.

Here's an extreme example of how that works when it works well. Many years back I took my first trip to Peru and spent two and a half weeks on the ground. Even though my wife was with me and I was in vacation mode part of the time, here's what eventually came out of that trip over the course of several years:

1. 28 hotel reviews for a trade publication
2. 9 hotel reviews for LuxuryLatinAmerica.com

3. "Through the Eyes of a Porter" article for *South American Explorer* magazine

4. A different slant on the porter article for *International Travel News*

5. "Saving Machu Picchu" for *Transitions Abroad* (when it was a print magazine)

6. "The Coca Plant Paradox" for *Transitions Abroad*

7. A front-page destination story for the *St. Petersburg Times* newspaper

8. "On the Pisco Trail in Peru" feature story for *Imbibe* magazine

9. "Inca Trail 101" for Backcountry.com's web magazine

10. "Slow Roads to Machu Picchu" in the *Boston Globe* (with added material from a second trip later)

11. Multiple Peru posts on the Cheapest Destinations blog

12. Chapter updates for The World's Cheapest Destinations

Granted, not every trip generates a few grand in income and 20,000 words of copy like this one did, and if I hadn't spent sufficient time there traveling independently, half of this would never have come to pass. That's one disadvantage of press trips, which we'll cover later: you don't control your time or schedule and these trips are often too short, too frantic, or both.

I've had a similar output on several other trips, however, with articles continuing to trickle out years after I left the place. I've placed articles from a two-week trip to Hungary and the Czech Republic in a dozen outlets, give or take, from a hotel website to a drinks magazines to a blog run by a tour company. Some of them were pure service pieces, others were damn fine narratives if I may say so myself. I never wrote some editor or tourism person saying, "I want to do a story about Hungary." Instead my pitches centered on the history of Hungarian wine and the biking greenways of Moravia. These were commercially viable but unusual and they lent themselves to branching off in multiple directions for different outlets, print and online. My revenue flowed from many taps, some print, some online.

In this section I'll break down the different revenue streams coming from traditional outlets and explain how to go about earning income in those areas.

Magazine Print Writing

This is what most people daydream about when they say, "I want to be a travel writer." You jet off to some far-flung place on a fat expense account, write up a story on the fabulous time you had there while lounging around the pool, then open your mailbox soon after to find a four-figure check in an envelope. Ah, the life.

Unfortunately, living that scenario on a regular basis and making a great income from this work alone is incredibly rare—the equivalent of being drafted into the NBA or England's Premier League. For every long feature story in a major travel magazine, there are a thousand short little articles that make up the bulk of a writer's work. After all, even if you are successful enough to manage to net an average of $2,000 per feature, getting one of those plumb assignments every month will only earn you $24,000 a year before taxes.

Let's even assume you get assigned longer pieces or a double now and then and it averages out to $3,000 per month, or $36,000 per year before taxes. If you live in New York City or London, good luck living off that.

> *My keys to success have been luck, the Travelclassics conference, more luck, and not being afraid to rewrite something 300 times if that's what it takes to get it right. There's also no one who writes like me, either in style or content, so if an editor wants the kind of thing I do, I'm the only option.*
> ~ Edward Readicker-Henderson, freelance writer

Most freelance writers try to land as many assignments as they can from as many outlets as they can, hoping it all adds up to a decent income over time. It's not unusual for a busy freelancer to be juggling interviews and research for five assignments at once, writing until midnight on one article after checking out the city sights and hotels all day for another. The only freelance writers who can manage that stereotype of sipping piña coladas by the resort pool while "on assignment" are those who have someone else actually paying the bills at home. Or they are retired.

It's hard to generalize about print pay rates because they are really all over the map. Big famous magazines that everyone has heard of will pay $1 to $2 per word, sometimes a bit more for the right high-profile writer. There's a tier of quality magazines, top newspapers, and trades after that paying a bit less, then there's another tier of regional magazines and smaller circulation pubs that get into the 10 cents to 25 cents range. The local equivalent of that $1 to $2 per word range is rare in Canada, the UK, and Australia, partly because of lower potential circulation—and advertising. In all countries there is then a whole range of barely-hanging-on magazines and newspapers that pay you a pittance, assuming you manage to actually get paid.

Some publications will openly list their pay scales in guidelines or in reference book listings. Others treat them like a secret handshake, only revealing them when they give you an assignment. In those cases it may be open to negotiation, but only if you have any real leverage on your side.

Now that we have that out of the way, assuming you still want to pursue this route, here are the steps.

1. Come up with a unique angle that is perfect for a specific publication's style and content

2. Send a pitch e-mail (a query letter) showing you know the publication well, why this ideas is right for them, and why you are the person to write this piece.

3. If you get rejected, go back to No. 1. Re-slant the pitch and try elsewhere. If your idea is accepted, get the terms in writing and go to work. (They may pay expenses, but often will not, so keep the ideas focused on places you can get to easily or are already visiting.)

4. Study the publication again as you are writing and make sure your content, style, and tone fit in well with what's already there.

5. After multiple drafts and polishing edits, turn in your story on time or early.
6. Make any requested changes or follow up after a reasonable time to see if any other edits are needed.
7. Eventually get paid.
8. If possible, see if this trip or research can be applied to other articles. Pitch those to different publications.
9. Pitch the editor with another idea while he/she still remembers who you are.

This is the way it has been done for generations, though at least e-mail has sped up the rejection process. It hasn't made most editors any faster or more considerate, however, so you'll still do lots of waiting and you'll still encounter plenty of "pocket vetoes" where the harried editor never gets around to responding to you. (This still drives me crazy, by the way, and I've been dealing with it since the days of mailing completed stories and slides by post from Bangkok. As an editor, I personally respond to every query.)

You need *lots* of patience for this path.

There are entire books written just on the query part of this process—overkill if you ask the editor in me—and I've listed some of them in the resources section. Obviously I've just simplified this process to the bare essence. You can learn plenty more on this subject by reading other books, visiting writing websites listed in the resources, and hanging out in the right forums. But sooner or later you just have to get out there and get bloodied.

Here are some factors that will help your odds.

Develop a portfolio

Like many editors, when I get a pitch from a writer I look first at their credentials, second at their idea. I know a terrific writer can make almost anything sound interesting, while a bad writer can take the greatest trip in the world and turn it into a dead-boring story. I want to see what you've written already to see if you and your style are a good match. I want to know your area(s) of expertise. This matters far more than what you've put into your query letter. Other editors feel differently, but better safe than sorry on the way you project your image.

So develop a portfolio of articles before you go pitching to the big boys. These days there's not such a stigma about articles written for the web as there was when I started doing online articles more than a decade ago. So get in where you can, print or web, and start writing unique things that are worth noticing. Then put up a portfolio page that only requires a link in your pitch to see what you've accomplished. (In cases where the article only appeared in print, you can convert it to a PDF that can be opened in a browser.)

In theory you could limp along without this by linking to your blog, your LinkedIn site, or some other substitute, but I wouldn't advise it. You may get a cranky editor like me who thinks, "If this person can't be bothered to create a portfolio, how hard are they going to work on this article they're pitching?" Turn off the social media streams for a while and go make something built to last.

You can set up a portfolio site using simple "what you see is what you get" (WYSIWYG) templates without having to know any HTML. You can do this through the likes of Web.com, GoDaddy.com, Bravenet.com and others, but if I were doing this tomorrow I would probably go with iPage.com. They're only $3.50 a month and they throw in a lot for that amount.

See examples of good sites and more tools to accomplish this in the Next Steps to Success section.

Really study the publication you're pitching to

Whether your target publication is print, digital, broadcast, or sent by a medium that hasn't been invented yet, this part is *extremely* important. Most magazines and webzines publish writers' guidelines somewhere: on their website, in MediaBistro, or elsewhere. Nearly every set of guidelines will tell you to study past issues and articles to see what works for their publication. (Even if they don't publish guidelines, assume this is a requirement.)

As any editor will tell you, however, far too many writers ignore this advice and send terrible, badly targeted queries. As an editor myself, I'm flabbergasted at some of the awful pitches I get that have nothing to do with what Perceptive Travel is about. In some cases it is obvious they have sent the same pitch to dozens of editors at once, hoping some fool will bite. (In a few cases they've even blasted it to 50 editors at once, putting all of them in the "To" field.)

There's no excuse for this and if you start off on the wrong foot with an editor, you will probably never get a second chance. If I get two dud pitches in a row from a writer, no way I'm ever going to open a third. Instant delete. That may sound harsh, but others won't even give you that much latitude.

Before querying a publication, *really* study what they are about. For print, dissect at least the current issue, but preferably a few issues if you can find them in a library or can access them online. Read the letter from the editor. Study the table of contents. Figure out which section of the magazine is right for your idea. Get an idea of word counts, writing style, point of view, and tense—the mechanics of the publication. Look at the story array, travel budgets in the informational sidebars, and what kinds of ads are there to get a sense of the target audience. If they have a media kit on their site, sometimes posted under "Advertise with us," then study that to see how the magazine wants to be perceived. If you're lucky there will even be an editorial schedule there for coming issues.

"Gosh Tim, that's a lot of work," you may be thinking. "Why would I do all that for an idea they probably won't accept?"

Well, do you want your chance of success to be 5 percent or…zero? If you don't take the time to match your slant to the publication, you have almost no chance of getting an assignment. Go bet on some horses because your odds will be better.

There are some shortcuts out there that will help this process even more, like the pitching tips available to paid Avant Guild members at MediaBistro.com or editors' panels at conferences run by SATW or NATJA. Follow the advice to the letter when it comes from the editor's mouth. Craft your query with specific references to the publication—showing you've done your homework—and make the subject line relevant to your idea.

After all this, you'll at least have a shot at getting noticed. Ignore these steps and your query will be lucky to even get a form letter rejection.

> *It's worth the $50 a year for Media Bistro's Avant Guild membership solely for their How to Pitch section, which comes complete with assigning editor's e-mails. Get out and get to know people. I get assignments now from editors I've met in person. We're all just people, and we like working with people we know and like.*
>
> ~ Dana McMahan, freelance writer

Some people who do all this correctly may get a great break right away—it can be done. Sheila Scarborough's first real travel piece was in *National Geographic Traveler* magazine. She says she did it "by reading a bunch of books on freelance writing, paying careful attention to the content of magazines that I subscribed to, and pitching a story to them that I thought might fit based on reading the magazine for years. It worked."

Aim appropriately

As I mentioned earlier, there are certain rules in place for print magazines, more of them than with the less structured web. Only the very smallest will hire you to do a feature story unless you a) have a fantastic track record b) know the editor well or c) are the indisputable go-to expert on that subject. Otherwise you need to pay your dues and break in with something smaller.

An editor will typically give you a few small assignments of 200 to 400 words first to see if you are dependable and can conform well to their style. It gives the appearance of meritocracy, but it's really not. Even if you've done five major features for magazine A, the editor of magazine B still probably won't assign you a big feature if she hasn't worked with you. Relationships matter a lot.

So if you keep trying to hit a home run without ever getting a base hit, you will get very frustrated. Start off sending queries to smaller publications that hire lots of freelancers before you even think about querying fortresses like *Travel & Leisure* or the *New York Times*. Otherwise it's the equivalent of wanting to try out for the Yankees without ever playing in the minor leagues. You are wasting your time and that of an editor—who will not appreciate it in the least. If a big glossy is going to assign a short piece to an inexperienced writer, they'll just give it to one of their junior editors or interns and do it in house. They don't need a freelancer for that.

Even when you are pitching those smaller publications, think small and focused. For every big feature story in a magazine there are at least 20 to 40 pieces taking up a page or less. Unless you are a masochist, go for where the work is and come up with bite-sized story ideas that can be explained in a paragraph and will run a few hundred words in print.

Like it or not, this is what most editors really need from you. And editors are your customers in the print world. If they don't want to buy what you're selling, you will not get any assignments.

> *Consistency is the most important key. You have to pitch. You have to follow up. You have to keep going after the markets you want. If you sit back and wait for the work to come to you, you will be a hungry want-to-be writer. It's not a hobby, not a way to get free trips. It is a job and you are 'on' more than you are 'off'.'*
>
> ~ Susan Lanier-Graham

Thinking about what the editors are buying and publishing regularly is important too. Most of the glossy travel mags really sell themselves to advertisers as "lifestyle publications," which is why they are filled with ads for luxury cars, jewelry, watches, and perfume. Flip through them month after month and you'll notice that the pretty pictures are what matter the most. Often the words seem to be there merely as an accessory to the photographs. At least half the contributor credits in the front of the publication are usually photographers, not writers.

The magazines are selling a fantasy world and that world does not include grotty destinations that are really hard to reach. It does not include huts in the woods and days without showers. Other magazines' readers eat that stuff up, so go pitch to them instead.

Once you target correctly and actually get an assignment, don't pop the bubbly until you've got something in writing—preferably a contract, but at the least an e-mail spelling out the terms on pay, deadline, and rights. The scope of all that will put you to sleep if I cover it here, but these are the things you want to be concerned about:

- How much you'll get paid
- When you'll get paid
- What is required of you (word count, photos, specific information to be included)
- The deadline
- Who owns the various rights to text and photos
- What happens if they don't use the story (a "kill fee" promises you a percentage of the pay if they don't use the article.)

The best publications pay "on acceptance," which means when they accept the article they send you money, or they at least send it prior to publication. More common is for you to get paid "upon publication" or "x weeks after publication." This is the main reason the idea of trying to support yourself as a travel writer when you set off on a round-the-world trip is pure fantasy for a new writer. If you're writing for print, most of the checks won't arrive until after your journey is finished and you're back home. In some cases, they don't arrive at all—the magazine goes under before you get paid.

For the rights part, ideally you want to keep the rights to what you produce so you can resell the stories elsewhere, but I personally don't care about this as much as some writers do. If it's "work for hire," meaning the publication owns all the rights, I just adjust my effort accordingly. For example I'll make sure I'm not sending something that I'd be duplicating elsewhere or sending my best photos. For a hotel review, for example, they can have the rights to my prose and pictures if the pay is appropriate. I'll be on to something else and probably wouldn't sell that review elsewhere anyway.

If you're a prolific writer and photographer with lots of assignments, rights aren't such a big deal. But if you've put together a masterpiece that's unique and you could conceivably resell it to multiple outlets (or use it later as a chapter in a book), you don't want to give up all the rights.

If you're principally a photographer, you probably don't want to give up *any* of your photo rights unless you're being paid handsomely for it. So you want to sell "First North American Rights," "First Electronic Rights" (often with a certain exclusion period), or something else that's restricted to a single instance. "All Rights" means they can do whatever they want with it in any media for eternity.

Once all that is worked out, do a great job. Make your first assignment as fantastic as it can possibly be. Edit, proof, and then edit some more. Have at least one other person edit it again. Then hand it in early, exactly as requested. Make any changes requested and furnish any additional information requested with a smile.

When you eventually get that paycheck, now it's time to celebrate. Parlay that article into more assignments. Then do it all again.

Newspaper Writing

This type of media is in trouble, no doubt. There's one advantage to new writers when it comes to newspapers, though: the editors aren't as hung up on your track record.

"In the United States, newspaper travel editors don't want to receive queries for stories; they want to get the already written story for them to consider," says David Farley, an author who teaches travel writing classes at New York University. "This is good news for newbies: it means you don't have to have a list of already published clips to show off with your query. Instead, you can just send in the finished piece and the editor will consider it by the piece's own merits and not necessarily what you've published (or haven't published) in the past. This is how I first broke into travel writing. I submitted a story on Rome to the *Chicago Tribune* travel section and they published it. After I established a working relationship with the editor, I could then start pitching."

Unfortunately, the *Chicago Tribune* is one of the few papers that still has a viable travel section on Sundays. Many of the others are now just collections of wire service stories with maybe one feature written by a staffer who went on a press trip. My own lame paper in a city of one million people has a single page of travel stories most weekends, none of them written by anyone in the area. *USA Today* has a good weekly travel section, but it is almost all staff-written. Travel stories in the *Wall Street Journal* are mostly written by regular columnists or those working in a foreign office as news reporters. Breaking into the *New York Times* is almost as tough as bagging a feature in a major magazine, with the added annoyance that they have lower pay and what may be the most restrictive freelance contract on Earth.

In 2010 there were fewer than 20 newspaper editors handling nothing but travel at US newspapers and I think we're down to about one-fourth of that now. Do your homework and aim carefully. The UK is faring better than the US, so maybe there's another five years left in the system there, but the future doesn't look bright. If appearing in a newspaper travel section is one of your life goals, you had better get on that pronto.

As David Farley mentioned, most newspaper editors don't want to see queries. Send them a finished piece or send the first two or three paragraphs of it—that's usually all they're going to read before making their decision anyway. Newspaper editors know what they want and they can tell in a flash if you've got what it takes to meet their requirements. If your piece is not in AP style, if there are typos, or if you take too long to get to the point, you're out in five seconds flat.

Many newspapers still cling to a "no sponsored trips" policy, but then lower their pay rates each year, adding insult to injury. Plus the pay was already pretty crappy before. To be frank, this is the most dead-end option in this chapter. If you are a religious person, put newspapers in your prayers because we really need for them to stick around if we want to keep getting relevant local news and investigative reporting. Unfortunately, they're already last century's news when it comes to travel.

Writing for Trades

Business to business magazines are more stable than consumer ones because they have a more predictable readership and revenue stream. Whether it's mining or footwear or travel, the readers are people who live and breathe that business. The advertisers are companies who want, or must, reach those readers and create a favorable impression. With many trade magazines, there's no such thing as a "Chinese Wall" between editorial and advertising either: you spend a lot of money on advertising and the editorial coverage will follow.

So writing for the trades can be a more lucrative and dependable pursuit if you can get your foot in and then deliver on a regular basis. There are travel trade magazines like *Travel Weekly, Meetings & Conventions, Hotel & Motel Management*, and *Travel Agent*. There are also online-only publications, plus some others that are sold by subscription only to travel agents, such as *Star Service Online* (reviews of top hotels) and *Weissmann Reports/Travel 42* (in-depth destination guides).

Ironically, there is often less competition for slots in these publications as there is for consumer magazines. Most writers don't take the time to research them, you won't find them on newsstands, and there's no glory in it—often you don't even get a byline. Writing for the trades is much less of a roller coaster, though, and if you get in good with one of them, you can probably parlay that into assignments from others run by the same company. Two publishers in particular—Northstar and Questex—have the majority of the big travel trade imprints.

At first I wanted the high-profile bylines in magazines and newspapers. Now I'm going where the paychecks are, and increasingly that's working for companies/corporations: blogging and writing for websites, as well as print custom publishing (i.e. brochures for tourist boards or travel agent magazines). It's not strict travel editorial, for sure, but I still consider myself a "travel writer." I envision continuing the same mix of income streams I have now: a combo of print editorial and custom advertorial or corporate gigs.

~ Kara Williams, freelance writer and blogger

Pitching to the trades is more of a pull than a push. Your goal is to get an assignment, not to sell them on your idea. They have their own very clear ideas about what they need and the best bet for success here is to meet those needs competently and on time. Obtain a copy of their writer's guidelines and editorial calendar by calling the editorial office if they are not published online. When you approach the editor, your letter should focus on where you live (for local assignments), where you'll be traveling in the next six months or year, and your qualifications. They may want to see your résumé or c.v, so have one ready in case.

Guidebook Writing

Guidebook writing is as much about researching, project management, and time management as it is about actual writing, and the day-to-day job is frequently far from glamorous. As the guidebook competition has increased despite lower overall sales, pay has decreased. To make the numbers work, most new writers have to work 12-hour days for weeks on end, researching all day and writing much of the night. After all that, they are lucky to earn more than minimum wage after expenses and they wake up one day wondering what happened to the last three months of their life.

In the good ole days, these guidebook writers received royalties on top of their fee payment, so the writers who did successive editions could end up with a nice ongoing income stream. Those contracts are becoming rare, however, and most publishers now do some kind of straight "work for hire" agreement with expected expenses rolled into the total amount.

The day-to-day work involves inspecting dozens of hotels and restaurants in each location, taking down bus and train schedule times, getting opening hours for every notable museum and attraction, figuring out prices for everything, all while trying to formulate a description of the place that doesn't sound like what everyone else has already written. Some of the better publishers furnish expenses in addition to the book advance, but others just lump it all together. Either way you will not be living the high life. Most writers either rent an apartment to have a home base or they stay in cheap hotels on the move. They rarely get to eat leisurely meals at all the fancy restaurants they are including or stay at all the luxury hotels listed in the guide. Some do get hosted along the way, but in other cases this is prohibited by the publisher.

> *It is rarely possible to visit more than five or six restaurants and four or five hotels. Those numbers go way down if you do, in fact, visit any of the sites the town is known for. The numbers go down if transportation is delayed, the weather sucks, you don't feel well, or any of the other thousand disruptions that are bound to surface in international travel. Then there's the whole issue of trying to review nightlife, already wiped out from a day's work, with the full knowledge that the next morning you have to get up and start all over again.*
> ~ Thomas Kohnstamm in *Do Travel Writers Go to Hell?*

I've never written a guidebook. It's a monumental job and frankly it scares me. I've gotten a taste of what's required when doing the Travel42 Reports—trade publications used by travel agents for their clients. After a week solid of checking phone numbers, bus schedules, and restaurant hours, I'm exhausted. Writing a guidebook is very hard work. It's the toughest job in travel writing and most people who think they want to do it have no earthly idea of how draining and time-sucking it can turn out to be.

One of the most prolific writers I know is Lara Dunston, whose name graces dozens of guidebooks and a steady stream of magazine features she finds time to fire off before she moves on to a new place. "I co-author with my husband and he's also a photographer so we pitch and sell our work as a package. We're doing rather nicely, although working incredibly hard to derive the income we're making. We work seven days a week and we only really take a few hours off at Christmas."

Some writers do make good money doing mostly guidebook work, but usually these are writers who are getting royalties from a successful guide they have researched for several editions. Or they are writers like Dunston who cram many projects into a year and work their guidebook research into major feature stories for magazines as well. After a while though, this grind can wear you out, especially if you see your earnings per project declining.

For new writers, however, a guidebook glut and low pay have combined to make guidebook writing jobs some of the easiest ones to land.

When there were only a few guidebook companies out there, they seldom had to advertise openings or hire new writers to work for them. The cream of the crop wanted those assignments. Now that there are so many guides out there and veterans have wizened up to the low pay scales, it's easier than ever to find open assignments.

Avalon Publishing (Moon Handbooks) openly publishes openings on their website. See the resources section at the end for where to look for others or just get in touch with the acquisitions director. Be warned though: it will not be a pretty picture when you realistically estimate the research time and expenses then look at what you will be paid. Go in prepared to be poor for a while.

Here's my advice to alleviate some of that: make your first guidebook assignment one for your own city or state. You won't spend so much on travel expenses, you'll already know much of the area, and you can do it all faster because you know where to look for information. Keep track of your hours so you'll know how long it all took, including edits and template inputs. Then when it comes time to evaluate the next possible assignment, you can just double the time and expenses to get an idea of whether the job is worth taking.

Guidebook writing can be rewarding work for the right kind of person, but make sure you *are* the right kind of person. Ideally, you are super organized, obsessive about getting the facts straight, detail-oriented, good at time management, and very responsible. If you're a big picture creative type who delights in creating beautiful prose, don't take a guidebook job. Both you and your editor will be miserable before it's all over.

Brice Gosnell is no longer at Lonely Planet hiring writers, but I think this excerpt from our interview before the first edition is timeless.

We need people who are able to write well, of course, because it means more editing time for us if they cannot. It's not about flowery language though; we need a journalistic approach, seeing a place or situation from all sides. We will include controversial things, but we strive to provide balance.

cont/d ...

Even more important, however, is being travel savvy. We want someone who is well-traveled, not someone who just took their first trip out of college. When we look at a writer's potential, their travel history comes first.

Expertise and experience in a specific area is very important for who we hire. If you know an area well already, you have an advantage. Also, everyone wants to write about Paris. We need someone who wants to write about Kazakhstan or Suriname. If you can identify yourself as someone who wants to go to the lesser-known spots, great. Knowing another language is a great advantage. Having a special expertise in something gives you a definite advantage too—say a degree in art history. In a case like that we may hire you for a special section.

On the ground, we want you to be observant, to give us those special moments, those things that nobody else would know. Tell us what's special to do apart from what the crowds are doing. Give us insider tips. Also, be open to feedback, which is often much harder for young writers. Remember, we are giving you feedback because we want to keep working with you. Don't ask a million and 20 questions by e-mail and annoy your editors to death. Pick up the phone and have a conversation when you need an answer that's not in your guidelines—it's far faster.

~ Brice Gosnell, Former Publisher for the Americas, Lonely Planet

Joshua Berman has written a variety of Moon Handbook guides. He got his big break after working for the Peace Corps in Nicaragua. "My coauthor and I pitched our first guidebook to Moon. We told them we were going to write the first-ever comprehensive guide to Nicaragua and we wanted to do it for them. They gave us the job, then a few years later, offered me Belize when that writer retired." Later Berman also got tapped to write *Living Abroad in Nicaragua*.

Lonely Planet tends to estimate expenses when determining your pay. With many other publishers, you are offered a flat fee that does not take any of this into account, and you are on your own to make it work. So naturally, writers cut corners and find ways to research places remotely. (Remember that the next time your guidebook leads you astray and choose accordingly in the future.) I'm not going to incur the wrath of publishers here by saying who pays terribly and who doesn't, but for overall working conditions, I've met very few authors who have bad things to say about working for Lonely Planet or Moon/Avalon, though the latter has dropped some of their long-term authors when they wouldn't take a huge pay cut. Other writers have had great experiences with each of the other guidebook companies as well. Some pay more, some less. Some are hungry for new writers; others tend to use a pool of people they trust. Research and apply to find out, but realize that there's not as much money coming into these companies as there used to be.

This is one of the few areas of travel writing where you can actually apply for a gig and get it. Nose around on the websites of the various guidebook companies and you will often find a section outlining parts of the world where there are seeking writers to fill a hole. You may find, for example, that they need someone to update a Buenos Aires guide, write the first edition of their Manitoba guide, and write the southeast section for their USA guide. If you don't see a section like that, you will at least usually find contact information for submitting a work history or proposal.

This is how Zora O'Neill got her start in travel writing. "I answered an ad! Really! I'd been trying to get into travel writing for magazines, but a friend forwarded an ad from Moon guides, about the new (at that time) Metro series and the New York guide they were hiring for. I was assigned to write the hotels section. I used that to approach other guidebook publishers and it snowballed." Now Zora has written more guides for Moon plus others for Lonely Planet and Rough Guides, on destinations from Amsterdam to Santa Fe, from Mexico to Egypt. She also got a cookbook published in the process: *Forking Fantastic!*

If you apply and eventually get assigned to cover a certain area, take a good look at the contract and carefully calculate your expected expenses. No matter how good it sounds otherwise, accepting a book contract that will take months out of your life but won't even cover your expenses on the road is probably going to make you resentful unless you have good motives for putting up with this. Many a guidebook writer has accepted unfavorable terms just to break in and get the experience. As long as they knew this going in, they were able to retain a positive attitude.

Those who have signed on without doing any calculations have found halfway through that they were going to come out poorer on the other end of the assignment than they were going in. Sometimes they get angry and get sloppy, they start cutting corners, and the guidebook is not as sharp as it should be. The writer is unhappy and is soured on the experience. The editor is unhappy and never wants to hire that writer again. The readers of the guidebook are unhappy because there are holes and mistakes that mess up their trip. Nobody wins.

> *In a guidebook writer I look for a love of the place and a genuine enthusiasm to share knowledge to make travelers' experiences more valuable. This is key because without that as the foundation, it's hard to get through as grueling a project as writing a travel guide. I also look for people who can think strategically— it's a good sign when this comes out when I haven't even asked the question yet. Finally, I look for people who respond well to feedback and suggestions. That's not to say I expect all authors to do everything I want. I feel like the best authors are the ones where we're on the same wavelength most of the time, but they speak up when they don't agree with something.*
> ~ Grace Fujimoto, Acquisitions Director at Avalon Travel Publishing

Book Writing

"You should write a book!"

Nearly everyone who has traveled around the world for a year has heard this from at least one well-meaning friend or relative. Maybe from all of them. They say this because they can't fathom that tens of thousands of people are traveling around the world right this minute and that it's really not a very unique experience anymore. Most also don't understand that writers make very little money from book sales.

I was confronted with this reality early, as a young child when we picked up a friend of my mom's one day in the car. She was a children's book author and I had four of her titles, autographed, on a shelf in my bedroom. I couldn't believe it when we got there: she lived on a rutted dirt road in a vine-covered little house with peeling. Her rusty car, which was waiting to be towed to the shop for repairs, sat in the driveway. During a conversation in the car it came out that she didn't even have a TV. None of this made sense to me. When I eventually had my mother alone, I asked why her friend didn't live in a big fancy house. Why wasn't she rich? "She's not world famous," my mom replied with a laugh. "She just writes nature books for kids. It's what she enjoys doing."

For the vast majority of authors, writing a book has never resulted in much of a payoff. The book distribution business has never been logical and there are too many efficiency leaks in the system for any one party to really do well. The bookstore chains still alive are in big trouble (sales declining 5-10% every year), the publishers are in big trouble (cutting staff, reducing the number of imprints), and author advances keep declining or disappearing completely except for a few high-profile authors who are a sure bet.

This is not a problem unique to travel writers, of course. Many famous writers were working day jobs for four or five books before they started making writing their full-time job. Faulkner was a postmaster. William S. Burroughs was a copywriter. T.S. Eliot was a bank clerk. Nicholas Sparks sold pharmaceutical products. In an article in *Poets & Writers*, a group of literary agents guessed that no more than 100 American novelists support themselves from their writing alone.

That was in the '00s though, and my how things have changed. Amazon has been a godsend for many authors, giving life to books that wouldn't have found much action in a physical bookstore, and for print-on-demand (POD) or other forms of self-published books, this has meant the difference between selling to a few relatives and selling to thousands of strangers. By being 10 times more efficient than the traditional system—not a hard thing to achieve really—Amazon has changed the game. Bookstores hate this and publishers aren't at all happy about the power Amazon wields, but for authors the rise of online sales has been a beautiful thing. With Apple's introduction of the iPad and other readers making inroads, competition is heating up as well.

I would guess that there are at least ten times as many novelists now making enough from book sales alone to be earning a comfortable living. There have even been a few "Kindle millionaires" writing genre fiction. When you move to easier-to-market non-fiction books, the number making a living from book sales expands much more. It seems that every month I hear a podcast interview with some author that is pulling in six figures a year just from Amazon Kindle royalties.

We are in a transition phase, as in many other industries moving from a physical product to a digital one. As the music business found and the movie industry is starting to find, it's hard to charge as much for digital goods as physical ones. Some publishers have embraced the difference and made it a wash by saving money in other areas, such as paper and shipping costs. Some have turned to efficient print-on-demand systems so there are no books printed that will later have to be destroyed as returns.

The obvious end step would be a world where we are all reading books on some kind of digital reader. Just as we will not suddenly see an end to CDs or DVDs, however (or even vinyl), this will not be a 100% transformation. It could be a decade before e-book readers become truly mainstream. Plenty of people who don't travel much are perfectly happy with the current form: a book is inexpensive and there's no recharging necessary. You have a huge selection at the library for free.

That isn't stopping lots of companies from jumping in with both feet, however. First there was the Sony Reader and the Amazon Kindle, and then a competing one called Nook from Barnes & Noble. Seven more were introduced at the 2010 Consumer Electronics show, but only Kobo has survived—swallowing up the Sony version too. The iPad thrived and so did a whole slew of Android tablets, ones from Microsoft, and the Kindle Fire iterations built on Android. You can bet more readers, slates, and pads will come out each year and keep getting cheaper. A 7-inch Kindle Fire tablet was on sale for $40 as this book was wrapping up.

For now, the digital reading experience isn't close to what it could be, so it is still a niche in the market. The general population still isn't happy with the price, first of all, since a reader typically costs more than $100—before you even load it with books. Illustrations don't render well, the Kindle Paperwhite is black-and-white only, and so far even the iPad can't give you the coffee table book experience with lots of large color photos. An electronic gadget is still not as pleasant to hold in bed or in a hammock as a book. You can't take e-readers to a place with no electricity for very long. Plus there's the inherent flaw that there's no such thing as a "used book" in the digital world, and the devices discourage sharing except for those who pay for a check-out kind of system like Amazon Prime. You pay full price or you don't read it. Great for publishers and authors, but not so great for readers used to loaning, sharing, yard sale buying, and checking things out from libraries.

For authors going through the traditional system, electronic books are a wash at best. Unless people suddenly start buying lots more books overall, there's not going to be any more money than before in the author's royalty check—maybe even less since the list price is lower.

For many writers, the reason to write a book goes beyond the bottom line though. For one thing, you can say and do a lot more in a book than you can in any commercial travel article. Here's how Chuck Thompson put it in *Smile While You're Lying*:

> *The stories my friends actually pay attention to never seem to interest editors, most of them emasculated by demands to portray travel as an unbroken fantasy of on-time departures, courteous flunkies, sugar-white beaches, fascinating cities, charming locals, first-class hotels, golden days, purple nights, and, of course, 'an exotic blend of the ancient and the modern.'*

When you write a book, you've got many pages to give good travel stories their due. You don't have to worry that an editor will strike something because it will annoy an advertiser, that it's "too negative." Quite the opposite actually: books about disasters and trips gone wrong sell as well or sometimes better than fantasy fulfillment books that get picked up by book clubs. (For one thing, they sell to both sexes.) Bad trips are bankable.

The main reason to write a book, however, is it still transcends every other form of printed media and gives you an air of credibility that's hard to match in other ways. Your grandma might not know what a blog is, and your 12-year-old cousin thinks having a blog is about as noteworthy as having a cell phone. Both will be impressed if you put a book with your name on it in their hand, however.

> *My first two books—Vagabonding* and *Marco Polo Didn't Go There— have been a great platform for my career, and I believe that books (more than articles) have more staying power in taking your career to a new level.*
>
> *I realize this isn't in keeping with the new media landscape, which is skewing even more towards online media— and even video—but I think that in-depth, well-written and researched projects (like books) have a way of standing out, regardless of whatever new media becomes fashionable.*
>
> ~ Rolf Potts, author and writer

How Book Authors Make Money

Let's step back though and look at the general structure of payments. Writing a book and putting it out through the traditional route is a tough way to make money, mostly because there's not much money in it for anyone. If a book costs $20, the actual wholesale cost to stores is closer to $10 before discounts and they can return it and get credited if it doesn't sell. (Despite this terrific arrangement, most bookstores still struggle to make a profit.)

So typically the publisher will get 45% to 50% of the list price after shipping, part of that naturally going to pay overhead: printing, design, marketing, sales, legal, and the nice New York or London offices they need to rent for all those support people. The author typically gets 10% to 15% of the publisher's take in the form of royalties depending on the deal and whether it's a paperback or hardback. So at 10% that means the author gets $1 per book on a $20 title, or $10,000 if 10,000 books are sold. As any author will tell you, it's not easy selling 10,000 books net—after returns are processed.

But hold on. Did you get an advance against royalties? If so, your sales have to recoup that amount first before you see another dime. If your advance was $10,000 then congratulations, you just broke even. If you sell another 400 copies net next quarter you'll rake in a big $400. That "net" number is after returns, press review copies, bookstore review copies, and all kinds of nefarious "free goods" deals that trade books for advertising or in-store positioning.

If the publisher has high hopes for your book idea and you get a fat advance of, say, $50,000 in order to enable you to go live among the natives in Papua New Guinea to write your hilarious memoir, and it's a hardback, you may need to sell "only" 30,000 or so to earn back your advance. Some manage this. But not many. In travel especially, it's not uncommon to get an advance that's $5,000 or less and never see a check after that.

Royalty rates are significantly higher with the self-publishing method known as print-on-demand books, which is attractive if you already have a following or are good at marketing. I put *The World's Cheapest Destinations* out this way and it has sold quite well through four editions. I put the paperback of *A Better Life for Half the Price* out directly with Amazon via CreateSpace and sales have been quite healthy. Authors do most of the heavy lifting anyway in terms of marketing and promotion—most publishers do little more than package and distribute these days—so it's only fair that you take a higher cut if you can get it.

There are disadvantages to this approach, however. No bookstore distribution, for a start, which means you better have something that will sell well online rather than to bookstore browsers. Some reviewers have a bias against any kind of self-published books since there are fewer barriers to entry and a lot of really crappy books that come through some POD publishers like iUniverse and Author House. Last, there's no advance and you'll have to lay out some of your own money up front for cover design, set-up fees, e-book conversion, and review copies.

Self-publishing is nothing new and some authors have had plenty of success saying, "Screw you guys" and doing it themselves. Jack Canfield and Mark Victor Hansen collected 144 rejection letters from publishers for their first *Chicken Soup for the Soul* book. We know how that turned out. Some authors have started with one self-published book and have built up a whole publishing company. Print on demand just makes the process more efficient: no stacks of books in your basement that you have to peddle and ship. Some authors are going straight to Kindle and not even worrying about print. Some have become millionaires without ever having one book on a bookstore shelf because they're keeping most of the revenue from each book sold. Even if Harper-Collins came calling now with a big advance, those authors would probably say, "Nah...I'm good."

There's still a stigma with this approach though, even among authors. Some authors think the prestige of a name publisher outweighs any revenue advantage. That's often because their book is just a means to an end, not something they're doing for a revenue stream. Be aware that you may face negativity from people who will automatically assume your book is sub-par if it doesn't have a NYC or London imprint on the inside. The customers who want what you're selling? They couldn't care less.

A big plus with the legit POD publishers is that you own your book. You can sell foreign rights, get picked up by a major publisher, sign a movie deal, and sell e-book or audio book rights if demand warrants it. The publisher I use (Booklocker) sells a load of straight PDF e-books that can be read on most any device and they'll get you into bookstores of Apple, Kobo, and Nook. They send me a nice monthly royalty check like clockwork and I sold the Italian rights to the second edition for a few grand in additional earnings. (Plus now I have an Italian book with my name on the spine—cool!)

This book you are holding in your hand went through this POD process because I thought putting a 2.0 book out through a 1.0 system made no sense. So I get five bucks when you buy it instead of a dollar or less and the publisher makes its fair cut as well. You probably didn't find it in a bookstore, but that matters less and less each month, it seems. I buy magazines and coffee in bookstores, but it's a rarity when I actually buy a book in one—even though I buy a lot of books. A shame, but the prices and selection in bookstores bum me out after shopping so long online. Even the superstores seem to have lousy travel sections when you're used to having everything in print (and then some) at a click of the mouse, at better prices too.

Are You Ready for This?

A book can catapult your career and make you an instant expert. It will open all kinds of doors for article gigs, guest posts, media attention, and speaking opportunities. Understand though that this a major undertaking that will consume your life for a while. Writing and organizing 60,000 words or more and keeping it all interesting is exponentially harder than writing an article or even 20 articles. You had better have a lot to say on the subject and be able to say it in a way that keeps the reader's interest for a very long time. I'd bet that anyone who has asked, "How hard can it be?" and plunged in before they were ready has had a rude awakening down the line.

There are two important questions to ask before writing even one word:

"Who is going to buy this?

"What's the potential market?"

As Angela Hoy at Booklocker says, "It is imperative that authors have a specific market in mind before they begin to even outline their book. Most authors now seem to come up with a book idea, write the book, and then try to figure out the market they're going to sell to. Having a firm market in mind first, before the writing process, will make the book far more marketable in the end."

Any traditional publisher or literary agent will tell you the same thing. If they read anything in your book proposal after the idea pitch it will be the marketing section. They want to know who would buy this book and why. Get the idea right first, then the marketing plan. The best-written book in the world won't make any money if these elements aren't in place first.

Ideally, you're listening to your tribe and giving them what they want. What are their pain points? What questions do you always get? What are people like your readers asking on forums and message boards? Unless your purpose is pure entertainment, the easiest path to success is to solve the problems of the readers you already have—or the ones you know very well because you're part of their tribe.

For some writers this happens in reverse. They put a book out that ends up serving a need, then they launch a blog to have a more ongoing forum for its angle. That was the approach taken by Michael Huxley of BemusedBackpacker.com. "I was an author and novelist first, then published my own series of backpacking guidebooks, then started my blog."

If you do it right, this expertise that you have packaged up without a middleman can lead to at least enough income to cover a few monthly bills. As veteran writer Mike Gerrard says, "In the last few years most of my income has been coming from websites and our own e-books, and much less from guidebooks and print publishing."

Selling E-books Direct

E-books are not really new, so I've kept them in this old media section. They're still just electronic versions of what we're used to in printed form. They've been out in some version since we could first read text on a computer. What has changed is that the market for them is expanding exponentially and they have become easier to market. At the beginning of this decade their high growth was coming from a very low base—more than 95% of books sold then were still in physical form. The situation has changed dramatically since then. Kindle sales for my books are now five or six times what the paperback versions are. The devices to read them are getting better, the prices of a Kindle, Nook, or Kobo reader have dropped to a range more people are willing to meet. The popular iPad and various Android and Windows tablets have given some consumers a reason to experiment with e-books for the first time. (On those you can simply download the Kindle app and read whatever you buy on Amazon, for instance.)

Right now you can buy electronic books in a multitude of formats for a multitude of devices, from plain Adobe PDF files you can read on most computers and smart phones to proprietary formats that work on one device only and can't be shared. The thing is, an author can now bypass the whole publishing establishment and get their book on all these formats relatively easily.

I sell a lot of e-books, but they are just electronic versions of my print books, either directly from the publisher's site with a link from my blog or through Amazon's Kindle store, so the marketing is the same. I split the profits with either my publisher or Amazon depending on the format. Either way the earnings are several times what I would make from a traditional publishing house---with not much more work.

Some bloggers have had some success selling e-books only, never even bothering with paper. There are big advantages to this if you have a big enough following: no distribution, no printing, and very high royalties—100% even if you're selling PDFs direct and not through others. (A big advantage of selling direct is that you can set any price you want.) Royalties generally start at 45% and climb from there. For most markets you get at least 70% of the list price. That's a pretty sweet deal for piggybacking onto the platforms of Amazon, Barnes & Noble, or Kobo.

> *Most of my income has been through my books and itineraries. Over the past year I've taken the approach of trying to standardize my books into three main sets of offerings: 'Intro' books, which cover a country in broad brush strokes (think 'Culture Shock!', but 50 pages long instead of 250); Itineraries, which offer a 3-7 day plan to a city or region; and Guidebooks, which are aimed at the independent travelers that needs good directions to get there themselves.*
>
> ~ Chris Backe of OneWeirdGlobe.com

The usual way this works is that someone who is known as an expert on something puts out a book of "insider knowledge" or something that compiles his other scattered writings into one central and easy-to-read document. The e-book could be on scoring frequent flyer miles, living in Costa Rica, traveling on a shoestring, or many other topics. Ironically, the ones that seem to have the most success are "how to make money on the Internet" kinds of books that advise you to, among other things, write an e-book. And around it goes.

I am more encouraged about this area than any other, because e-books offer a chance to move old media to new without losing much in the process and actually making life better for the creators. True, reading a book on a Kindle or iPad is still a second-rate experience compared to reading it in its physical form, but it's close enough. For round-the-world travelers, it's a godsend. It's certainly a far better transition than going from a magazine to a web page— especially a web page on mobile. The information is still digested in a form that your brain can process easily for hours on end.

Corporate Writing

As I was finishing this book I dissected one issue of *Condé Nast Traveler* page by page and discovered an amazing breakdown. Out of the 240 total pages, 116 of them were actual editorial pages (including a fashion spread with almost no text). But 55 pages had "special advertising section" at the top: they were paid advertisements meant to look like articles. This means that for approximately every two pages of real editorial, including pages with just a one-sentence caption, there was one page of copy written by someone hired by an advertiser rather than by Condé Nast Publishing. Somebody got hired on the outside to write all that material, project by project. Based on what I've heard from many writers, those ad copy page jobs probably paid better too.

That's just one type of corporate writing. I'm using that phrase as a catch-all here for anything meeting a company's needs and paid for directly: website copy, brochures, sales pitches, direct mail copy, corporate blog posts, or press releases. There is also a whole big sub-industry called "custom publishing," which comprises magazines and newsletters put out by a corporation. You probably get some of them in your mailbox from the likes of Sony, GEICO, or your bank, whether you ask for them or not. Some of these magazines can be pitched like ones on the newsstand; others require getting to the right person and applying. Once you're in, you'll usually get regular work from them on an ongoing basis.

This is generally not glamorous work and it comes with its own batch of headaches and ethical issues, but it pays well. It's also a whole lot easier to get paid on time by your state tourism board, a hotel chain, or a custom publishing company with sound finances than it is to get paid by a consumer magazine teetering on the edge of bankruptcy. No nagging required.

> *For my freelance writing, I'm doing more content creation for tourism boards and ad agencies and less destination features for travel glossies. I actually prefer this route, as it's a much more lucrative way of staying in the travel industry.*
>
> ~ Kristin Luna, freelance writer

It's hard to systematically go about finding this kind of work though; often the work finds you. The person with the need starts asking around and your name comes up. I once got an assignment on the spot at one of my wife's work parties where the hiring guy was the spouse of my wife's co-worker. Some writers get work by being available when the regular person is on vacation or sick. For these jobs networking matters—a lot.

Besides happenstance, writers often get into this kind of work by either cold calling companies, by posting their credentials and bidding on sites like Upwork, by keeping an eye on Craigslist, or by watching sites where writing jobs are posted regularly. (See the Resources section.)

> *Writing is a craft, freelancing is a business. I make a good living at this because I don't see myself as an "artist." Instead, I see myself as a small business owner—someone who does what he must do to minimize overhead and maximize profit. This is why I do corporate work at all—across my "line" of "products," it is the cash cow.*
>
> ~ Matt Villano, freelance writer

These corporate writing assignments need to come with a budget, so be prepared to state your fee right off the bat. I prefer an hourly fee if it's something with an uncertain time frame, but the person doing the hiring may need a total project number. In that case you have to do your best to estimate how much time it will take, pad it a little to be safe, and put that into a proposal.

Be willing to negotiate, but don't give away your services for cheap unless you're really desperate. If it's a reputable organization, you can bet they're paying market rates for tech support, printing, janitorial services, landscaping, payroll, and every other contracted service. So charge the market rate for the service and your experience. My rate is $40 to $50 an hour plus travel expenses depending on the job. I've seen some writers charge as little as $15 an hour and others charge as much as $100 an hour if they were a clear expert in a given area.

If you're good at ghostwriting books for celebrities or CEOs, you can charge even more after you've got a track record. I've billed my regular hourly rate for the six business books I've worked on as a ghostwriter, but if I signed on with someone famous getting a $200,000 advance, I'd certainly bargain for more.

Corporate writing may be a one-off gig now and then, or it may become your main source of income if you get in with a company that needs a lot of output on a regular basis. It's a hard thing to predict and plan for, but definitely worth pursuing once you have some experience and contacts. Much of it can be done from behind a desk, which may not be your initial goal in "travel writing," but that does keep your expenses low. In other cases a company may pay your expenses to have you report from a conference or convention.

There's no denying that if you're comfortable with this kind of work, it can do wonders for your bank balance.

> *My writing income has grown significantly over the past year since I started devoting more time to freelance writing. I am writing more for web outlets, but I am also being paid as a copywriter and a blogger for travel campaigns.*
>
> ~ Yilin Wang, freelance writer

Digital Opportunities for a Travel Writer

My skill set is a combination of web programming, travel writing, and a deep-seated desire to stay away from a cubicle!
~ Stuart MacDonald, Publisher, TravelFish.org (based in Bali)

I like the idea behind the Indian god Shiva. Besides the legend he supposedly lives atop a mountain smoking hash, he is interesting because he is the god of both destruction and creation. He can be a mean bastard when things need to be blown up and destroyed, but then he can create something better in its place.

Many cultures have deified this idea that you can't have creation without some kind of destruction and we see it in the real world when a hurricane or tornado leads to a rebuilt city with better infrastructure and safer building codes. In order for a company to reinvent itself, it often has to scale back or destroy the product that has been its main cash cow—a very painful transition. Many just can't do it and they just stop growing or they go bankrupt.

We are clearly in a transition phase right now with media and there are two sides to that story. On one hand the destruction side, where the print and network broadcast world we've known for more than half a century is crumbling down around us. Jobs disappearing, magazines folding, TV networks struggling, and newspapers getting thinner and thinner. That is making many travel writers scared, depressed, or sleepless. It's driving others to quit the business altogether because it's gotten too difficult.

Some see a threat in this transition; others see a huge opportunity. While the old ways are working less and less, many writers are finding tremendous success following a new path. The travel writers I surveyed for this second edition of the book were upbeat overall when it came to their finances and the average earnings were significantly higher than when I surveyed people for the first edition. I find that incredibly encouraging.

My experience is only anecdotal, but I know more travel writers making a consistently comfortable living from digital media than I ever knew making a consistently comfortable living from print writing in "the good old days." These people are also more confident, more relaxed, and more optimistic about the future. Let's take a look at how to get there.

Blogging for Yourself

"Start a blog and write what you want."

That advice has turned many a head and pulled in many subscribers for "How to make money on the Internet" types. And why not? It's as enticing as fat-free frozen yogurt or the promise of speed-reading. No query letters, no editors to please, no editorial calendar to fit into, and no style restraints that will hold you back. What freedom!

Remember that the root word of freedom is "free" though. That's what you'll be working for day after day, week after week, for six months to a year until your shiny new blog gets some traction—if it ever does. Instead of putting together articles for a set fee, you are putting together articles that will hopefully "be monetized" someday through advertising or other means. Your pain, your gain—if it works. Unless you have good traffic and a following, however, those ad earnings will be next to nothing. (See the next chapter for where that ad money comes from.)

For many, that's okay. They are blogging to promote themselves or their expertise, not as a moneymaker. It's their mouthpiece to sell consulting, sell books, or get noticed by the media. If you're doing this as an income generator though, be prepared for a long slog.

Like many bloggers in the early days, I started the Cheapest Destinations Blog without even thinking about whether it could ever make money. I just set it up to promote my book and to give journalists a taste of what I had to say. It was purely a promotional vehicle and a place for me to float out ideas for articles. Then Google AdSense and easy affiliate ad programs came along and I stuck some ad code on my blog. Just like that, from then on when I sat in a Wi-Fi bar and wrote a blog entry, I could rationalize that the blog was paying my bar tab. Sweet! Eventually it started making enough to pay my mortgage and I was shocked. Who knew? But this "instant success" was years in the making: the blog already had a big following by the time I started monetizing it.

Some very popular blogs today are still ad-free, however, including the one from marketing godhead Seth Godin that I referenced earlier. You can also add lots more examples from people who make money from products or services, such as John Jantsch (Ducttapemarketing.com), Gary Vaynerchuk (garyvaynerchuk.com), or Brian Clark (Copyblogger.com/blog/). These people make most of their money from speaking or selling something online so they don't really need to care if their blog itself makes money. It's a means to an end, a talking billboard, or a place to form the thoughts that will later go into more lucrative works.

It's important to remember that stance when grousing about people who write for free. For a lot of very successful people, writing is not something you do to make money: it's something you do to communicate with your potential customers and followers. Writing is not a vocation for them, it's just a conversation, or a regular speech through typing. For many, the "free content" is just a way to get people into a sales funnel and try to sell them something later after some trust has been built. In fact you could say the whole site is really an ad. There are just no *outside* ads for services or products they don't sell directly. Everything they're promoting is all theirs.

It is clear that the right person can turn a blog into a real job and a platform, leading to success on their own terms. I say "the right person" though because it takes a certain skill set (which can be learned) and a certain mindset (which cannot). If you run your own blog, you own it. That means the technical side, the advertising side, the administrative side, and yes, the content.

So if you're the type that likes to get marching orders and then complete the task as outlined, this is not a good path for you. If you get flabbergasted when a software program doesn't do exactly what you want it to do and you call your brother, sister, spouse, or best friend to fix it for you instead of figuring it out or reading the help screens, this is probably not your ideal medium.

WordPress upgrades have gotten less problematic over time and it has been years since I had to rebuild a blog after an upgrade snafu. Still, you have to do those upgrades, keep the plug-ins updated, delete spam comments, make sure your firewall is keeping out attackers, and do the right things to keep the site from slowing down. One slash mark in the wrong place can screw up your whole design and leave you frantically combing every line of code to find the one tag that wasn't closed properly. Throwing up a blog and writing is easy. Maintaining it and making a living from it are hard. (Hint: have a regular person who knows the tech side better to lean on, even if it's just a regular on Fiverr.)

> *Browse other up-and-coming travel blogs, assess your competition, and establish your niche early on Network on social media, or through groups like Travel Massive, and find your tribe (you will need the support) If possible, find a mentor Have patience: success will take time, dedication, and a slew of hard work Last, don't try to enter this field if you've never traveled outside of your native country!*
>
> ~ Kristin Luna

Still, many bloggers consider this a more secure path for making *some* money at least and not being so dependent on print editors. Nobody took blogs seriously at first, but now the income potential is clearer for those that succeed at it. Many travel writers have skipped the whole freelancing for others route and are making more money than the average freelancer without having to go through any gatekeepers.

There is plenty of advice out there on getting you on the path to income in months instead of it taking you years of trial and error. Here's the main problem with trying to make money as a blogger though: ten bazillion other people are trying to make money as a blogger. If you believe some of the stats you read, there are almost as many blogs as there are readers. So once again we get into the same Darwinian struggle that exists in writing for magazines or getting a book deal: for every person making a living with their blog, there are probably at least a hundred just middling along, hoping to generate the equivalent of minimum wage for their efforts. And it's hard work on top.

I can just imagine what you may be thinking. "Hey, I bought this book for answers, Mr. Buzzkill, not a dozen reasons why I can't be a rich blogmaster of the universe! Give me the magic formula!"

If you want a shortcut, here it is: go read every recent and popular post on the likes of ProBlogger. Fizzle.co, and CopyBlogger, then follow their links to more great advice. Keep following the paths where they take you. Add any others run by podcasters you like that are covering this subject. It'll require a few days or weeks of bleary-eyed, non-stop reading and listening, But after all that you'll know close to everything there is to know about making money from a blog, including the fact that "there's no magic formula." Sorry.

For best results, here are the initial steps. Take them and understand it's the start of a journey, not a weekend building project.

Where's your sweet spot?

Be on the lookout for voids that you can fill with your own efforts, no matter how bad they are at first. Don't worry, for now, about how you'll make money or a career off it. Share what you love and the people who love the same things will find you.

~ Austin Kleon in *Show Your Work*

The crucial first step is to ask yourself a serious question: What can I cover better than anyone else out there?

I can't emphasize enough how important this is. If it takes you days of contemplation or the time it takes to walk the whole Appalachian Trail to figure this out, it'll be time well spent. There are a ridiculous number of generalist travel blogs out there that are pretty much interchangeable. "Here's where I went last week. Here are a few pretty photos. Here's what I did there."

Yawwwwnnn.

If that's the best you can do, don't even start. That path has been walked, forged, paved, and pitted with potholes. Unless you started down that path six or eight years ago, you're too late. The same goes for a whole slew of barely-more-differentiated general categories such as family travel, food travel, travel hacking (loyalty points and miles), and backpacking around the world.

There are people out there who already own those categories and are doing a very good job at it week after week. They are guests on CNN. They get quoted in *USA Today*. They have 20,000 people on their newsletter list. They come up #1 in Google for a dozen keyword phrases like, oh, "family travel blog." So unless you have a suicidal streak, don't go there.

Did you know there's a whole convention for mommy bloggers? Or that there's one for travel bloggers on three different continents from TBEX and another from PTBA? That gives you some inkling of how crowded the field is.

So think differently. Or at least think smaller. "Niche it down" is the operative phrase.

I've now started five blogs and in each case I filled a hole that nobody else was filling. Or at least not filling well. By the time anyone else could have figured out what I was up to, I had too much of a head start for them to ever catch me. I just sold one of them for mid-five-figures and three of the other four are solidly profitable each month, despite me not asking any contributor to write for free. That's not because I'm so brilliant at marketing. It's because in each case I saw a market need and filled it. There may be fewer of those holes to fill each passing year, but other new ones pop up—partly because of new tech developments, new travel trends, and newly rising destinations. The opportunities are always there if you look around with a creative eye.

If you really keep coming up empty on your brainstorming, hire me for a short consulting session. I see a dozen holes every week in my research for articles. If I could clone myself I'd start blogs on them myself. I can sit down with you any day and find a dozen categories that come up close to empty in the search engines, with little in-depth content anywhere.

It wouldn't be hard to find one that aligns with where you live or what you're passionate about. You have the power to fill these holes yourself without waiting for permission. It's not a matter of applying for a job and hoping someone else will hire you. Put on your Nikes and just do it.

Unless you live in London, New York, San Francisco, or the Pacific Northwest (hotbeds of travel writers), there's probably nobody doing a really good job of blogging about what's worth seeing and doing in your town, or maybe even your state.

Pretend you're a tourist who has never been to your area. Can you find really good, authoritative information just by doing Google searches? Try it. You may be aghast at how bad your potential competition really is, especially compared to what you can find in a $15 guidebook.

> *Remember that the world is your audience. You do not need to leave home to be interesting. Write about your backyard, your dinner, write about someplace nearby and why you love it.*
> ~ Lisa Niver of WeSaidGoTravel.com

Unless you like to be Sisyphus, forever pushing a ball up a steep hill, you should find a niche that nobody else is covering well and own it. Otherwise you are relying on your network, your personality, and sheer force of will to make things happen. It can still be done this way, especially if you're the popular girl everyone wants to hang out with, but you'll probably be more successful following the path of less resistance, one that you can dominate in the search engines.

In the not-so-distant past, the most popular blogs were often written by groups—ones like Jaunted, Gridskipper, Gadling, HotelChatter, Brave New Traveler, and Uptake.com—which are all gone or absorbed now. This often makes sense because they can throw up more content day after day and snag lots of search traffic. It's easy to dominate by sheer volume.

Conditions change fast though and now most of those on that list were either swallowed up by a corporate media company that then sent them to the gas chamber after passing them around boardrooms like a hot potato.

A few like TravelDudes and TravelingMom are still making this work, however. I run a few blogs with multiple contributors and there are some major advantages to that in terms of scheduling and promotion. Things get interesting though when you look at some of the most popular travel blogs written by just one person, since these now often reach as many people as blogs funded by a billion-dollar corporation.

Here are some of the top independent, one-person or couple-written travel blogs as of late 2015, based on cross-checking several "most popular travel blog" lists published online that rank them based on Google Analytics traffic or other third-party measurement factors. I put them in alphabetical order and they should *not* be considered a definitive list because different methodologies are flawed in different ways. It's a rough sampling from Q4 2015, not a proclamation.

Adventurous Kate
Alex In Wanderland
Cheapest Destinations Blog
Everything Everywhere
Expert Vagabond
Green Global Travel
Have Baby Will Travel
Johnny Jet
Keep Calm And Travel
LandLopers
Leave Your Daily Hell
Legal Nomads
Migrationology
Never Ending Voyage
Nomad Revelations
Nomadic Matt
Nomadic Samuel
Our Awesome Planet
Pinoy Adventurista
Solo Traveler
The Blonde Abroad
The Everywhereist
The Expert Vagabond
The Planet D
The Poor Traveler
The Savvy Backpacker
Travels of Adam
Twenty-Something Travel
Uncornered Market
Wandering Earl

Wandering Trader

Y Travel Blog

You can find links to all these just by putting "most pouplar travel blogs" in Google and finding the sites that do these rankings quarterly. If you do you'll see that it's a pretty diverse lot. Most of them are tied to one or two personalities, but for subject matter it swings from shoestring to luxury, solo to family, food to adventure. Some are heavy on photography or video, others big on tips and advice.

There's not a whole lot of commonality there except that all of them built up a following and are fairly good at SEO and self-promotion. You can run into the people behind a lot of these blogs if you attend conferences where they gather. These four are the most popular: TBEX (Travel Bloggers Exchange), SATW (Society of American Travel Writers), PTBA (Professional Travel Bloggers Association), and NATJA (North American Travel Journalists Association).

There are many other popular one-person blogs that are probably just as popular or more so than the above, but are part of a corporate site that bundles everyone together, like the Frugal Traveler blog at NYTimes.com, or the various frequent flier blogs bundled together at TheBoardingArea.com. Some travel resource sites also have a blog (like at my Perceptive Travel site), but it's just part of the mix, not the main entry door. A whole slew of others are more about lifestyle design than travel, such as the blog from *4-Hour Workweek* author Timothy Ferriss. He writes about travel now and then, but it's not the main focus. It's the same for others about food or booze or the life of a touring musician.

I put that list up just to show who is getting loads of traffic and to encourage you to find a different subject matter than what they are already covering. Note also that some of them are pretty general, but that generality is backed up by a person who has become a brand name. Or a traveling couple. They're big enough to attract and keep readers now no matter what they do, so they can widen the scope. If you drill down even on the personality blogs though, there's usually a core focus that drives what they do.

> *Make sure you have a clear vision of what you want to write about and what service you want to provide. It should be about travel first and what you can do for your readers next.*
> ~ Dave Bouskill of ThePlanetD.com

Blogging can be a rewarding path, but take the time to think through these following key questions before you launch. Once you can answer all of them clearly and with vision, you're definitely onto something.

1. What can I cover better or more thoroughly than anyone else?
2. What niche am I passionate enough about that I can write hundreds of different short articles about it for years on end?
3. What can I write about for 6-12 months that won't require going into the hole financially?
4. Do I want to be known as the expert on this subject or destination? Can I credibly become a media resource?
5. Am I willing to stick with this subject or slant for years on end in order to enjoy the payoff? Or am I willing to hire and pay other writers once it gets going?
6. Can I explain what my blog is about in an "elevator pitch" of a few sentences?
7. Could this subject area lead to other revenue sources in terms of articles, books, speaking engagements, or tours?
8. Is it something that would eventually generate advertising interest and text ad click-through from readers?
9. Am I truly helping people with this slant or am I just looking for a way to talk about myself?

Many people have given the following advice before and I think it's the equivalent of Star Trek's prime directive: "Write about something you are passionate about."

What can you stay interested in forever? Commercial considerations matter a lot and you need to find a way to differentiate yourself. Some famous business gurus think the whole passion requirement is bad advice, that you just need to like doing things well and making money. But if you pick a subject or destination just for the earnings potential, it probably won't last and you will waste a lot of time and effort.

On the other hand, just finding your passion won't cut it either if there's not a market for that passion Find the balance and you'll be in the sweet spot. Persist in that sweet spot and you will profit.

Passion + Customer Desire = $$$$

This self-blogging path is not for everyone though. Almost every blogger I know has had their blog come crashing down at some point from a server glitch or getting hacked. (You haven't seen real panic until you see a blogger who can't log on to their dashboard or pull up their site on the web!) You've got to learn basic HTML commands, how to use plug-ins, how to edit a template, and how to edit photos and maybe even video. You have to be at least somewhat promotional and be willing to learn the basics of search engine optimization. You need to get links back from other people too, which doesn't happen by magic

I also can't emphasize enough that blogging is a real commitment. Maybe not quite at the level of having a kid, but definitely up there with owning a dog. Some weeks it feels like all I did was write blog posts. Sure, you can pop out some posts in a half hour, but the good ones often take several hours when you factor in the time spent on photo editing, link insertions, SEO tweaks, tags, and formatting. Some posts I've spent the equivalent of a whole workday and then some writing and tweaking. There's no way around it: making money from a blog takes real work.

Besides all that, it's harder and harder to get away with crappy writing over the long term. Unless all you do is write clickbait articles and post pictures of your hot body in a bikini, it's hard to build an audience without either giving them solid information they can't get elsewhere or moving them emotionally through great writing.

> *My number one goal has always been to improve my writing skills. I've done that, year after year, so I call my blog a success. It's nice that I also have strong traffic and social media followings, but I would not have been happy if I'd built that following with poorly done list articles that are written for the purpose of ranking highly in Google.*
>
> ~ Barbara Weibel

From idea to implementation

If you want to forge ahead, here's how you get started.

You can get set up quickly on an existing service like Blogger or WordPress.com for free, but I would strongly recommend installing WordPress on your own hosting service with your own domain. If you don't, you may find you need to do so later to get to the next level and then it's a real pain and a loss of traffic while you relocate. Better to be on your own domain to start with so you will establish the brand. The domain provider and hosting service don't matter much as they're all reasonably priced now ($5-$20 per month unless you have huge traffic), so pick the one offering the service and interface you're most comfortable with. I've used a bunch and find it hard to recommend one as being far superior to the others. See the resources section on TravelWriting2.com for a few ideas.

WordPress is free. Typepad requires a monthly fee, but some users like it and are willing to pay. Follow the blog software instructions carefully for the install or better yet hire someone else to do it for you. You'll find plenty of people on Fiverr.com or Upwork who do it every day. Pick an off-the-shelf free or premium theme and don't worry about getting everything perfect at first. It's easy to make adjustments later: change the theme, add a logo, change the header, or adjust the colors.

Once you're installed, the posting is simple after that. Figure out how often you want to post and go at it. Assume few people will be reading in the beginning, but act like a thousand people are because those posts will be indexed by the search engines later. I say "later" because there's this thing called the Google Sandbox which puts you on hold until the company determines you are for real. It takes time to crawl out of there and start walking, no matter how good your content may be.

Remember that the actual set-up and writing is only the beginning. Consider this wise quote from Corbett Barr, who now is one of the partners at Fizzle.co: "If content is king, promotion is prime minister."

The greatest content in the world won't break through the clutter if you do nothing to promote it. Shy wallflowers are not successful bloggers. You will need to network, to promote, to get inbound links, to get media attention. When it's your own show, it's all on your shoulders. I'll discuss that more in the self-promotion section.

Make your blog as clean and clutter-free as possible in the beginning. Pick a template that will accommodate ads later, but use them very sparingly at first. You won't make much money the first six months from them anyway, so don't clutter up your site with visual distractions and code that slows down the load time. Concentrate first on saying something worthwhile and building up an audience.

Blogging for Others

If starting your own blog from scratch and writing for free for half a year at least sounds too scary, you may want to start out writing for others. Or do both. For most of the time I've had my own blogs, I've continued to write for several others as well as a freelancer.

The main advantage of writing for someone else's blog is that they will often get far more traffic than you can generate yourself. There is definite strength in numbers: multiple people are doing promotion, there is more content for the search engines to index, and there is usually someone else (not you!) taking care of the back end tweaks and upgrades. Somebody else is worrying about the revenue side. You just do your thing and get paid—a little anyway. You can concentrate on your passion without doing all the extraneous work not related to writing. You'll get better at the craft as you go along.

Very few blogs that hire writers pay a whole lot though, with $5 to $20 per post being where most of them seem to fall. If you spend an hour on crafting each blog post that's pretty lousy money. If you spend a half hour, you're at least above minimum wage. If you're quick and earn $30 a post, it starts to look like something that will really pay some bills. It's great experience though no matter what, and experience makes you a better writer. It makes you good at self-editing too, which is a valuable skill that editors love. Plus some of them lead to nice perks, such as press trips, hosted hotel stays, or travel gadgets to review and keep.

Some blogs will only require a post a week or so, but the requirements below, from a real ad on Craigslist, are more common.

Small publisher with two part-time, freelance writing opportunities to produce 6 to 8 blog entries, or 2 to 4 web articles, per week.

Writers should have online experience and be comfortable writing for affluent readers, ideally with professional background in some aspect of leisure travel. Must be able to create intelligent, well-crafted pieces. Must be adept at online research and produce original work.

Work independently from your home; your hours. We retain all rights to the content you produce. Ideal second job for extra income. Experienced only; no beginners or interns. Anticipated duration: 3 months, with a possibility of extending.

Please reply with your contact information and attach or link to a few relevant writing samples. All replies kept confidential.

* Compensation: $90-$200 per week depending on experience and volume

See a few red flags in that ad? It says "experienced only" but doesn't pay very much. On top of that, they retain all rights to what you produce, meaning you can't use any of those sentences ever again in your own work. That's not necessarily a deal breaker and I've accepted that arrangement in cases where I knew I couldn't reuse it elsewhere anyway. They didn't get my best work, of course, but they didn't pay for my best work either. Everybody (sort of) wins. But take that deal with trepidation.

Figure out how much total time is involved in any blog or webzine job before deciding whether it is worthwhile for your particular situation. I have a rather dim opinion of Internet writing sweatshops and content mills such as Demand Studios and Examiner.com. So do most other editors and full-time professional writers. They have also fallen out of favor with Google too, to the point that one of the biggest (Suite 101) went belly-up a few years ago. So I would only advise taking a job with one of those companies if you really have no better option and you need the practice.

There are some writers on those platforms who are happy with the arrangement, but for every one of those you'll find many ex-writers who say, "Never again!" Before you sign up with any of them, carefully read the terms and conditions of what you are getting yourself into and ask to speak to others about how much they are really making each month and how many hours they are working for that amount. If it's less than a burger flipper at McDonald's—which it usually is for a year or so—it might be better to move on. With patience and a long view, however, it can be a good match eventually.

There is another set of content mills that are a bit higher up on the food chain, like the ones that fall under the About.com umbrella and the sprawling AOL universe. These pay bonuses based on traffic, but they have a higher editorial standard and publish articles more meant for humans than for search engines.

I've written for multi-writer blogs about hotels, first for HotelChatter.com (bought then shuttered by the Condé Nast empire) and the Uptake Lodging Blog (bought then shuttered by Groupon). Neither fattened my bank account much, but the postings kept my skills and knowledge sharp for hotels and gave me an additional outlet for placing reviews of places where I was staying when out on other assignments. When Uptake went under though, I started Hotel-Scoop.com and now run that show myself, bringing some of my former fellow contributors with me.

I've also written for a tour company's blog, a car rental company's blog, a personal finance company's blog, and two hotel booking sites' blogs. For those I've gotten $150 to $400. That's in the range of typical pay for a print article, but these were longer and more in-depth posts. The pay for others' blogs is all over the map, but most group blog sites that publish frequently pay $25 per post or less, though some pay bonuses for traffic or revenue targets on top.

For this kind of money, you don't want to take just any blogging job. Find a good match. The idea is to put yourself in a position that is good for your profile, your niche, or the area where you want more practice writing about a subject. The money is never going to come anywhere close to meeting your monthly living expenses—unless you live in Guatemala.

The ideal situation is where you are willing to put in a lot of time and effort and in return you get a decent flat fee. A revenue share or traffic bonus is nice, but understand that it's a long time coming on those after your article starts getting search engine hits.

The main problem with any group blogs that pay extra based on page views or Google AdSense clicks is you end up writing for the search engines instead of writing something that sets you apart. You write things that people click on, read for 15 seconds, and then click away from. That means posts with lists in the title and posts with "best" or "worst" in the title. As Stuart MacDonald of TravelFish says, "Don't get caught up in 'Top 10 writing' (The 10 Best beaches/backpacks/bars). This type of writing is asinine and totally forgettable—even if it may pay a few of your bills. Write good quality, engaging material and people will read it and you'll perhaps develop a following."

It's hard to do that when your compensation is based on page views of individual posts. If you're going to write about The Best 10 bars or beaches somewhere, at least do it for your own site or for a print outlet (they're in love with "listicles" too) so you can make some decent money from it.

Be advised too that there are a few popular blogs out there that pay absolutely nothing to most freelancers. The Huffington Post is the highest-profile one, but you'll find plenty of travel ones too. Why in the world would anyone still write for them? Because the writers want the high profile, or the traffic to their own site, or the links in to their own site, or they have a business to promote. Or they're getting some perks out of the deal like trips or hotel stays. PR people don't care if you're getting paid or not—they just want results. As I'll say several times throughout this book, compensation takes many forms.

I personally think a travel content website that can't afford to pay writers is broadcasting that quality content isn't a priority—unless it's a user-generated model like TripAdvisor—but that's just my opinion. There's no rule saying people can't keep trying to make it work if they can keep finding writers willing to work for free.

I only ask that if you consider yourself a pro, or someone who wants to go pro, to turn down these offers when they come from an organization that could pay, but doesn't. It's one thing to do volunteer work for a solopreneur to get links and exposure. It's quite another to do it for a corporation paying everyone *except* the contributors. I got an offer from *USA Today* as I was finishing this book, asking me to be a subject expert researching and picking 50 blog nominees for one of their silly 10 Best faux contests. Despite a three-day turnaround deadline, my inquiry about pay got the response, "I understand it's a short turnover, and unfortunately we don't have a budget for our category experts at this time." You know the editor sending the request was getting paid, and the people designing and maintaining the site were getting paid. So were the people selling ads to run alongside that content. Just not the person creating the content.

Just say no.

Writing for Webzines

Sometimes it's a fuzzy line between online magazines/webzines, travel content sites, and blogs, but in general for the non-blog sites you would be writing articles meant to be entertaining or resourceful over the long term and there's less pressure to crank out words to feed the daily beast. Some of these sites are narrative publications with good stories and destination features (World Hum, Perceptive Travel, GoNomad, The Literary Traveler). Others are service-oriented sites with lots of great advice on travel and overseas experiences (BootsnAll, the Matador network, Transitions Abroad, TravelFish, and Yahoo Travel). Others are extensions of a print magazine, with assignments made specifically for the online part, such as Outside Online and National Geographic's Intelligent Traveler. Still others are good content sites that are an extension of a booking service, such as EuroCheapo.com.

> *It's easy for me to say "No thank you" to writers who obviously haven't taken the time to become familiar with the types of stories we publish. Successful freelancers know their target publications. They're familiar with the kinds of stories published, the various sections, the tone. They also are clear and concise in their writing, both in their pitches and stories. They demonstrate a professionalism and a level of writing that signals that I won't have to go through too many edits. Successful freelancers also understand that edits are part of the process. They're willing to work with editors to fine-tune stories.*
>
> ~ Michael Yessis, co-founder, WorldHum.com

For the webzines trying to put out lasting content of value, the requirements are not all that different from comparable print publications, though in some ways you have to be even better—you can't rely on huge photo spreads, charts, and sidebars to grab casual browsers. As with any publication, the easiest way to blow your chances is to fire off a query without reading a good selection of what's already been published.

Pitch the best online publications the same way you would pitch the very biggest, most established travel magazines—like a professional.

Be advised, however, that there are a lot of hucksters out there running travel content sites. Not as many as there were before Google started penalizing the content farms, but there are still a lot of them cropping up every month. After a while you start questioning the intelligence of people who start up these new projects and wonder how in the world they can find anyone anywhere to work for what amounts to a fraction of minimum wage. Here's a real ad that ran as I was putting the first edition of this book together, just so you can see how ridiculous it gets.

Looking for detail oriented, super-accurate, geographically savvy writers that are able to produce quality content in short time frames to work on an existing Vietnam Travel Guide website."

The ad continues, demanding *"flawless grammar"* and command of the English language, then finally gets to the pay part.

"Project details: 5 Articles each month, 1200 - 1500 words. Payment: USD 40 per month."

That's right: 6,000 to 7,500 words of flawless prose each week for all of $40. Most people can't even *type* fast enough to make that pay off, much less write something that's not complete gibberish. I will say throughout this book that sometimes you need to work for nothing or close to it to build up experience and a portfolio, but this is not the way to do it, by being a slave to an exploitative start-up. Run away!

Web Publishing

To rank well, build a site so fantastic that it makes you an authority in your niche.

~ Matt Cutts, Principal Engineer at Google

When *Vanity Fair* puts out a list of the top-earning individuals in Hollywood, the people making the big bucks from the movie business, all the people in the top 5 are usually producers or have "producer/director" as their title. It's the visionaries behind the scenes—the ones taking the big risks—that are making the real money, not the faces you see on the screen.

Likewise, I'll say this many times and in many ways, but the most successful travel writers I know—and almost all of them that manage to put six digits on their tax return—don't really think of themselves as just travel writers. They run a site or a network of sites they turned into a business. Most like the sound of "travel writer" just fine, but their business cards often have titles like president, CEO, founder, or publisher.

These people have parlayed their passion and abilities into authority websites—not merely blogs—that have become key destinations for readers who want to get information on where they are headed or what they plan to do with their life.

There are lower-profile sites such as Tom Brosnahan's TurkeyTravelPlanner.com that earn plenty of revenue by being the top place to go for info on a specific subject. PriceOfTravel.com isn't all that sexy—it tells you what things will cost where you're going—but that's information a lot of people want to know.

To be a web publisher you had better have a very clear vision of what sets your site apart and what need it will fill. If you get it right, you could be headed to more money than you have ever earned before. If you get it all wrong, you could be the proverbial debt-laden small business owner. A resource site is a bigger commitment than a blog, especially on the front end, and requires more factual research. Once it is established, it can dominate the search engine rankings and earn good money without constant daily additions. High reward, high risk.

The good news is, starting a good content website is far cheaper than it used to be, especially if you do all the writing and posting yourself. The bad news is, it's cheaper for everyone else too. So once again, you had better pick a subject, niche, or destination that you can cover better than anyone. EuropeForVisitors.com has already been done and the site has got a 15-year head start on you. Ditto for anything general about Hawaii, New York City, family travel, or cruises. When it's your own baby, you need to think like a mix between an inventor and a marketing maven. Where's the hole in the market?

> *If I were starting out now, I'd do pretty much what I've done: I'd pick a strong topic and build an "evergreen" editorial travel-planning site that would bring in traffic and revenue month after month, year after year.*
> ~ Durant Imboden of EuropeforVisitors.com

Digital Corporate Writing

I know one travel writer and blogger whose day job involves a very different kind of writing: she's a ghost blogger. Getting a nice paycheck instead of byline glory, she takes business leaders' ideas and puts them into a form that works online. The business leader gets his or her thoughts out on a regular basis online, but writes a check instead of spending hours toiling away at it.

There's also plenty of corporate travel writing going on. Someone has to fill up hundreds of pages of content on all those official tourism bureau websites and more often than not there's nobody on staff with the time and talent to get it done. So the tourism bureau farms out the writing work to a freelancer. Many hotels and attractions—if they're smart enough to realize they need good content to show up in the search engines—will also hire freelancers to beef up their pages. (Search engines like pages that have 400 or more words of text on the page, not swirling Flash sites with lots of pretty photos and no info.)

Most of these jobs are not advertised, partly because the organizations doing the hiring don't want everyone to know they can't do it in house, partly because they'd rather hire someone they know already or who has been recommended. So play nice with your local tourism bureau because you never know what jobs are being discussed in meetings. Join any local writing groups that may exist in your area and network with other freelancers. Often the first question a writer gets when they turn down a project offer is, "Do you know someone else who would be good for this?"

Other times the organizations don't know they need someone until it's pointed out to them. Some writers with the right cold calling temperament have had success in pitching their services to tourism boards, independent hotels, and attractions with terrible websites. To do this, you need to clearly illustrate where the deficiencies are (outdated information, poor search engine placement, not enough content to draw visitors) and clearly show how you can remedy the situation. Be ready to discuss what you would charge—per hour or per project—and be ready to illustrate what kind of return on investment they should see in six months or a year.

Still others get steady work writing e-mail newsletters, writing a tourism board's blog, or handling a thinly staffed organization's efforts in reaching out through Twitter and Facebook. Even if the organization has a full-time public relations person, that person is probably plenty busy just writing press releases and interfacing with media on stories, interviews, and press trips. If you can ease the writing burden without costing them a fortune, many organizations will see you as an answer to their problems.

Online Income Streams

I've alluded to the fact that most of the real success stories out there in the travel writing world are creators who own what they publish, not the hired guns writing a feature or two a month for the glossies. For the uninitiated though, the whole idea of advertising creating a sizable income seems dubious, ambiguous, maybe lacking in substance. "I wouldn't even know where to start when it comes to selling advertising," is a common refrain. That's understandable. We're trying to be writers here, not sales reps.

Anyone who has been to journalism school has had it completely and repeatedly jammed into their brain that the revenue side of publishing should be strictly separated from the editorial side. That "Chinese Wall" has always been full of holes—note the correlation between advertisements and content in your typical glossy travel magazine—but at print pubs with a staff of 100, this was relatively easy to pull off most of the time. They could at least pretend that the editorial staff didn't talk to advertisers. The low-overhead web is a different story. When a successful site is a one-person operation, how do you split the commercial from the creative? Both functions fall on the same shoulders.

Fortunately, this advertising process has become so automated now that you only have to do any real selling if you're booking direct ads for your site. The rest of it can be as simple as pasting in some code and working out the payment details. That won't make you rich, but it's a start and it's certainly no sweat to implement.

Here are the general buckets into which most ad revenue streams fall.

Google AdSense

This advertising system is probably the most common and it's what is most likely to be the first thing to take blogging from a hobby to a moneymaker for most people. You install a piece of code where you want the ads to run, Google serves up text or display ads relevant to what is on the page, and you get paid each time someone clicks on one of the ads. Every month you pass $100 in earnings (previous balances are rolled over), you get a check or direct deposit. It's dead simple and effective, which is why Google has thrashed every other Internet company when it comes to earnings: they're getting a big piece of every click and advertisers love them because they can clearly track the results.

The earnings on your end are mostly beer money at first though and are never worth quitting your day job for until you get traffic in the hundreds of thousands of visitors and have a high click rate. If we assume you earn an average of 20 cents per click, it takes 100 reader clicks on ads just to get to $20. To make $100 you would need 500 clicks. If your click-through percentage is 1%, which is actually pretty good now that mobile surfing is so common, then you would need 50,000 monthly page views to earn $100. If you managed to earn 60 cents per click because of your subject matter, those 50,000 page views would earn you $300. Better, but still barely enough to make a car payment. And only a small percentage of travel blogs get that many hits a month. So you probably need to have traffic in the millions to live off Google alone.

As a rule of thumb, most bloggers and webmasters make between $10 and $40 from every 10,000 page views—the high number coming from making the ads as prominent as the content or blogging about a subject that generates high keyword prices. Getting just 10,000 page views a month is a challenge though, so this alone is not going to cut it for a while.

Besides that, the ads are ugly. That's part of the reason they work so well—they blend in with the text and are matched to the content—but slapping a bunch of Google AdSense blocks up is a sure way to kill the aesthetics of your site or blog. Keep in mind too that people leave your site when they click on one of these ads. In the early days, can you afford to lose all those readers?

The key is finding the right balance between the best placements for earnings and managing to keep from annoying your readers and looking cheap. It's hard to avoid AdSense because it's the simplest and most effective ad tool to integrate, but only a few sites depend on this as their main revenue stream.

Aggregated Affiliate Advertising

Companies such as Commission Junction (CJ.com), LinkShare, and AvantLink are also a godsend for individual bloggers and publishers. In one spot you can sign up for the affiliate programs for multiple companies and you get payment for combined earnings. So if someone clicks on an Expedia ad and books a $200 hotel stay, you may make $8. If someone else buys a suitcase from eBags, maybe another $5. A few more transactions and let's say your total is $55. You haven't made a lot from any one vendor, but a couple of months later Commission Junction makes a bank deposit for the combined amount—all $55. This allows you to match the ads to what you are writing about, choosing from the integrated dashboard that presents all the banners and text links from the different programs you've joined in one place. You can even link to individual products or hotels in the text of what you are writing.

The main disadvantage of this, as with all affiliate ads, is that you are doing all the work but only getting a fraction of the purchase as commission—typically 3% to 10%. If nobody purchases anything from that REI ad you had up for two months, REI just got lots of branding exposure without spending a cent. You only get paid if you deliver a paying customer. So you have to experiment and test to find out what works for your readers.

The other disadvantage is that you need to be accepted to each program within the aggregator individually. So Travelocity may approve you and Hotels.com may reject you, or vice versa. There's no explanation as to why this happens. I have sites with huge traffic that are #1 in Google for key travel phrases that still get rejected and I have no idea why. Some sites approve everyone; others are very strict. You won't know until you start applying.

Some websites have great success with affiliate programs, and for others it's a complete bust. Often this depends on the subject matter. If you write about Las Vegas or Orlando, it's very easy to get bookings by integrating hotel program ads. If you write about some kind of product regularly, such as cameras, then it's easy to tie in camera model links and earn a commission from photography accessories. Not so easy is earning money from a straight travel or destination site, especially if you cover an obscure destination with no chain hotels and only one airline. Or you write for budget backpackers. A few months of experimentation will tell you whether these ads are a waste of time or a godsend.

> *"59 Things I Leaned on the Road" could get huge traffic but won't make much money. "59 Best Value Hotels in XYZ City" is a different story.*
>
> ~ Roger Wade, niche website publisher

Another reason to consider them is the future: these are about the only ads that pay off when someone is reading your blog from a mobile device like an iPhone. Those tiny screens don't render banner ads or Google text ads very well. But if you have affiliate links in the actual blog post, as you would when reviewing a product, the text is normal size and readers are far more likely to click through and buy that book, CD, or backpack.

Direct Affiliate Advertising

Some companies are not set up through the big clearinghouses and you need to join up with them individually. This is more of a hassle to keep up with and you need to hit a higher minimum to get paid, but it can be worth the trouble for the right company.

Amazon is the most obvious case and in some ways they invented the whole idea of affiliate advertising, using it to grow rapidly in the early years and leave everyone else in the dust. When I first started out with Amazon I had trouble hitting the minimum of $25 in commission in any fewer than six months. I still earn almost nothing from their UK and Canada versions. The US one rocks for me now, partly because the more items you sell, the higher your commission goes. In some months I'll hit the 7% commission level and will earn a few hundred dollars in 30 days. They'll pay you in gift certificates at a lower minimum than cash. Amazon seems to sell almost everything too, so almost anytime you mention a product you can insert your own affiliate link and potentially make a commission.

Others that run their own programs include World Nomads travel insurance, the Agoda.com booking site, AirTreks round-the-world tickets agency, and lots of smaller players. If a company like this is a great match and your site is ready for prime time, get in touch and apply. If you're not getting big traffic though, I'd start with Amazon and the aggregate sites. Otherwise you could be waiting a year to hit the minimum payout and get your earnings.

Once you get established in a specific niche, you can reach out to potential partners directly and set up affiliate deals. These will generally pay a higher percentage because you're an obvious partner instead of a faceless blogger coming through a matching platform. The couple behind MyTanFeet.com covers their home base of Costa Rica extensively and they're connected with a local car rental company, hotels, and a tour company, effectively doubling their income by funneling readers to these partners.

> *My income sources have totally changed. Thanks to better traffic and good ranking, affiliate income has shot to the number one source of my income, where previously it was the lowest source.*
> ~ Corinne McDermott of HaveBabyWillTravel.com

Network Display Advertising

Network advertising is a waste of time unless you are getting thousands of visitors a day. Otherwise the ones that will accept you are a "race to the bottom" group that will pay you somewhere around 50 cents to $1.50 per 1,000 visitors. That is known as the CPM rate and it can go to $5 or more for a really good targeted network, but that's still not all that much. Serve up 50,000 banner ads at a $5 CPM and you earn $250.

That's for a good network. Unfortunately, most of the networks are just serving clients trying to get as many eyeballs for as little money as possible. On top of this low rate, they probably won't fill 100% of your ad space. Let's say for argument's sake that they fill half. If you get 1,000 page views per day, or 30,000 in the course of a month, with a $1 CPM and 50% fill you've earned a grand total of...$15. Selling just one direct ad at $30 a month would double your earnings for that space. Or putting up an ad for your own book.

This gives you some sense of why magazines and newspapers are not finding much salvation on the web. Those banner ads are no replacement for what they're running in print. Networks can make sense for filling remnant space on a popular site with big traffic, but if you're just starting out it's not worth considering. You're better off in the long run putting up an ad to get newsletter subscribers than putting up something you don't control that only earns you $15 a month.

Paid Display Ad Listings/Sponsors

This is what most people think of when they imagine running their own site or blog. "I'm terrible at selling. How can I cold-call people and ask them to buy ads?"

In reality, you're very lucky if you can pull in any of this advertising at all for quite a while. You either need to be very specialized or have really high traffic. At that point you may be able to sell some direct ad blocks, or companies may even contact you. (So always have an "Advertise Here" page with rates or contact info just in case.) This is generally the most lucrative kind of advertising you can get since the companies are paying to reach your specific audience and you set the price.

It takes work to make it happen though. There is more sales work involved in this kind of advertising than with any of the others mentioned in this section. Nothing is automated and it's not for the timid.

If you manage to make some sales, you could get anywhere from $25 to $250 a month from a single ad on the home page. If your site is really popular, several times that amount. You may eve be able to package social media mentions, editorial coverage, and other services to hit four figures. So get popular and the money will follow. It may even land in your lap. I don't really sell all that many ads: I respond to inquiries about advertising. There's a big difference.

I do have someone selling the largest packages for me though since my primary job is creating content, not chasing down marketing people. I pay her a fat commission and we both win.

Text Links and Sponsored Posts

Many bloggers and web publishers make a significant amount of their income from text links and sponsored posts, though not as much as they did before Google went through the Panda and Penguin updates earlier in the '10s. These are links to another website, usually a commercial provider, which is paid for on an annual or permanent basis. Some companies buy these for the "native advertising" content marketing aspect. Others buy these ads for SEO purposes, to aid their search engine positioning. Google rankings are partly a popularity contest: the more inbound links you have from authoritative sites, the higher you'll probably show up in searches for key phrases. This is a way for these companies to gain more inbound links and they're willing to pay a sizable sum for the placement.

This is yet another reason to specialize: the companies and agencies that buy blog content placements of some kind want to buy them from sites that rank very high in search engines themselves. If you can dominate a niche, you'll get more of these contacts knocking at your door.

The danger in selling text ads is it's a practice Google, otherwise known as Big Brother of the Internet, isn't at all fond of. The cynical say the company doesn't like the ad competition. Google sees it as people trying to game the system. So while there's nothing illegal or (in my opinion) immoral about selling text ads, it has the potential to get you slapped on the wrist by the self-proclaimed boss of the web. Some high-flying websites got hit so hard by Google penalties at some point that they went out of business. Others had to spend years cleaning up their link profiles, undoing all the underhanded promotion they had paid for in the past. Some bloggers got hurt in the process as well, especially ones that got the double-whammy of losing their main source of ad income and getting search penalties at the same time

You can do this in the right way directly yourself or you can offer legit sponsored posts on matchmaker sites. I am using text links and sponsored posts interchangeably here but in the end the main difference between the two is that the latter usually have a disclosure statement at the end and "no follow" designation in the links themselves.

The matchmaker agencies are bound to come and go and there are probably at least 30 of them just for mommy bloggers. But at the time of writing some of the established ones included Izea, TapInfluence, TheMidGame, Influencer Orchestration Network,

Contently, and Cooperatize. Dig around and you'll find plenty more—including some that pay for mentions on Instagram or Twitter. The fee for mentioning a brand or service and disclosing that it was sponsored typically falls in the range of $30 to $700 for a blog depending on traffic and social media reach. If you're a superstar on YouTube or Instagram though, it could be higher.

You need to be smart about this and have some integrity though unless your intention is just to be a whore for hire. If most of what you write is meant to puff up someone else's product or service, you're just a copywriter, not a travel writer.

> *All those sponsored posts...so awful. Seems bloggers are just the right hand of tourist boards and are producing nothing but crap content.*
>
> ~ Matt Kepnes of NomadicMatt.com

To avoid the kind of sponsored posts that make readers cringe, take the offers that get you and your readers excited. Is this a product or service they use—or should? Do you already love what you're promoting so it's easy for you to talk it up? If so, then you've made a match that works for everyone, hopefully as a long-term partnership.

Free Stuff

If you are influential in any field, companies and PR agencies will start offering you free stuff so you will publicize their brand. Movie stars have designers begging them to wear their clothes. Rock bands have musical instrument companies begging them to use their guitars and drums. Athletes not only get free clothing and equipment: they get fat checks in return for wearing and using it all.

To a less lucrative extent, this phenomenon exists in the writing world as well. The most obvious example is a hotel or visitors' bureau sponsoring a writer's trip, which leads to press coverage for everyone. People who blog about theme parks seldom pay to take the kids on a theme park vacation. Music writers don't pay for concerts. Auto writers drive a different car every two weeks without paying for anything but gas. Fashion writers have great wardrobes draped upon them by clothing companies. I can pack a whole suitcase with travel apparel people sent me to review for Practical Travel Gear before I sold that site.

There's a whole ethical spectrum to all this, with some writers recoiling from the whole idea and some editors banning the practice. At the other end are people who will write gushing praise about anything landing in their lap, whether the product or service was great or not.

Most of us reside somewhere in the middle, accepting freebies when it makes sense but still writing about them with honesty. I think it is also fair to put some kind of blanket disclosure statement on your site or blog saying that you receive these trips/rooms/shoes or whatever on occasion. Some sites (and brands) ask for a disclosure at the end of each post because if you follow the FTC disclosure rules to the letter, virtually everything you received without paying should be disclosed in every post, picture, or tweet. Whether that's really feasible or sensible I'll leave up to you. My opinion is until the TV shows, movies, and magazines are held to the same standard, I'm only doing what the readers or paying clients demand.

It seems to me that the ethical arguments about this have become less of an issue as the gatekeeper press has faded in significance. If people don't trust a writer, they'll go elsewhere with one click. Most magazines don't disclose anything about advertiser influence or whether they sent back those shiny gadgets after reviewing them and frankly I couldn't care less anyway as long as the review is accurate, balanced, and well-supported. Just be advised there is potential for conflict whenever you get something for nothing. Be honest and true and you'll sleep better at night.

Sponsored Social Posts

If you have a huge social following, someone will ultimately want to pay you to tap into that and reach your fans. This can look totally natural if it's something you would normally rave about, or quite sleazy if not. If it doesn't make you cringe when hitting "send," then you're on the right track.

As mentioned earlier, the matchmaker companies trying to put brands with influencers (and take a cut) are proliferating like crazy and you have to sign up with a multitude of them to get a few offers worth pursuing now and then. Once you get big enough, you'll get direct offers too or you can put this service into an ad package. If you have huge numbers or engagement, you don't have to wait for them, of course. Start sending out your own proposals.

Product Sales

One of the best ways to really make a decent living as a blogger is to sell something your audience wants to buy. The most obvious ones are e-books or guides on a subject where your followers are experiencing pain, want to improve, or just need travel guidance on something particular from someone they trust.

For most bloggers, this is an easy step that can earn more than the usual advertising revenue methods. As Johnny Ward of OneStep4Ward.com says, "Don't reinvent the wheel—find a sexy wheel and use it "

You can put out a physical book, as discussed in the traditional section, but some people get far more sales out of the electronic version. Others skip the paperback altogether and go straight to Kindle. In 2009 e-books were less than a billion-dollar market in the US. Now they're heading toward $9 billion in sales per year, plus another $1.5 billion in the UK alone. In those two countries, e-book sales have surpassed print overall. The mix seems to have plateaued, which is probably healthy, but in many genres the advantage definitely goes to bits and bytes over printed paper.

Amazon gets at least half that business even by the most conservative estimates and the company estimates that at least 25% of its sales are for self-published books. Think about how significant that is: more than $2 billion worth of Kindle books are sold each year that completely bypass the traditional publishing system. There are some hot authors (mostly in genre fiction but with some how-to book writers too) that have become millionaires by leveraging that platform.

I'm no top-100 author, but every month Amazon sends me at least $650 in royalties for book sales, and this doesn't even count what goes through publishers. Sometimes it tops a grand if I've launched something new. My latest book isn't even available as a Kindle purchase, though: I do direct e-book sales through my own site so I can both capture e-mail addresses and offer premium packages. If you want that one, you have to come to my own purpose-built site.

This is the approach taken by several successful writers and bloggers, including Chris Guillebeau and Nomadic Matt Kepnes. Both have traditionally published physical books you can buy on Amazon or in a store, but they make much more money from the higher-priced direct sales ones that are more focused on a niche. They're not limited by the de facto cap of $9.99 that is in place for Kindle books on Amazon. (You can sell it for more there, but then your royalties get cut in half, a not-so-subtle penalty.)

Do your readers keep asking you the same questions? Do they keep complaining about the same things? Have you noticed search trends that are leading new readers to your blog? Take that information and serve it up as something you can sell. Yes, this takes work and commitment, but the margins are great after your sweat equity goes in and this can be a recurring stream of revenue that doesn't require daily attention.

There's also the audiobook option as well, selling through Audible or Audiobooks.com. This used to be an expensive endeavor, but now it's possible to produce one professionally for a grand or two by outsourcing.

Keep in mind that selling your own e-book or course requires you to switch your focus from social media to e-mail marketing if you haven't done that already. You can only get so far marketing something like this through social. If people have voluntarily given their e-mail address to hear from you regularly, they'll be a lot more receptive to a product that meets their needs.

I haven't seen a lot of success stories of bloggers selling physical products, but in theory you could be drop-shipping Tshirts, custom backpacks, or other items ideal for your traveling readers. Experiment and see what works. The tools to do projects like this remotely are cheaper and easier than ever.

> *If the goal is to create a sustainable business then eventually you'll need to have a product or products that will bring in income vs. selling content. That could be a membership to the site, or something tangible, or consulting, etc. In my case I've opened an online shop with work I commissioned, so it's a subdomain of the site with products for sale there. That's the newest part of the income streams for the last few years.*
>
> ~ Jodi Ettenberg of LegalNomads.com

Courses and Membership Sites

I didn't even include this category in the first edition of my book because there were very few people in the travel space having much success with it. This has changed quite a bit though as better software, better landing page builders, and more people giving good advice about how to do it have made things easier.

Online courses and membership sites are a massive business, in the multi-millions, from direct sale models to gathering places for teachers like Udemy.com. These are not to be confused with online degree or certification programs that are accredited. Rather these are very specific courses on how to solve a specific problem. If, once again, you've established yourself as an expert on some subject, you can then likely get people to pay for your advice if you deliver results.

> *Historically, I've made the majority of my income since 2007 by selling various forms of advertising. Much smaller sources have been ebook sales and affiliate marketing. In the last few years Travel Blog Success, an online course and community I co-founded with Michael Tieso, has grown substantially.*
>
> *cont/d ...*

> *In 2015, my earnings from Travel Blog Success eclipsed everything else combined, therefore it will be the business I focus on going forward. I'll continue to run my blogs, however, I no longer want to be dependent on advertising from them as a way to support myself.*
>
> ~ David Lee

This is not easy work and you need to have a following of people willing to pull out their credit cards. This is substantially easier if you've been focused on a clear subject and you have built up a good e-mail list. You also have to be able to solve a pain point or improve people's lives. Giving students a step-by-step road map to earning good money teaching English overseas to pay off their student loans is a valid course idea. Showing people how to travel around Thailand by bus is probably not. (That might be a worthwhile lead magnet or $1.99 e-book, however.)

Membership sites are like a course that never stops, usually with some form of regular communication between you and the members: a message board, a private Facebook group, or regular webinars or hangouts. The participants are the most motivated people and the most interested in implementing the advice, so this group is usually smaller than the number you can sell a book or inexpensive course too, but they'll pay recurring revenue instead of buying something once and being gone.

If you want to amplify your earnings with my group or just see how I've set up the program to get an idea, see RealMoneyWriters.com, which I launched following the book release. There are two levels: the first runs mostly on its own, while the second involves a mastermind group where I am heavily involved in leading and coaching. There's peer feedback and advice from others in that (higher-priced) premium level.

I will sell thousands of this book you're holding, but I don't need to sell thousands of mastermind memberships. Just 10 or 20 can mean the difference in having a good year and a great year if done right. Naturally I—or anyone else doing this—has to deliver great value to justify a price that's 10, 20, or even 50 times the price of a book, but when you're a real expert that can change lives through your advice, you can make people thankful to keep paying.

They'll even send you gushing thank-you letters you can use as testimonials.

Tours and Trip Planning

When online travel booking really got going, most people predicted a complete demise of travel agents. Most of the generalists did indeed disappear, but the ones who became "travel specialists" focused on a specific niche are doing quite well. Some travel writers and bloggers who have covered one area or type of travel extensively have organically gotten business as travel advisors and some have turned that into a major income stream.

If you're the expert on Italy and people keep asking you for recommendations, try asking, "Would you pay me to set up an itinerary and pick the best hotels?" There are probably plenty of your readers who have more money than time and they'd be glad—and highly relieved even—to hand over some cash for the waving of your magic wand. If they're spending $10,000 on a family vacation to Italy, giving you $500 of it to make sure they're seeing the best of the best is money well spent.

The higher up the scale the travel is that you cover, the more potential there is as an advisor. But even if you're a backpacker covering a cheap country, you could get hired as a tour guide, a consultant, or a trip planner just because of your demonstrated expertise. Several guidebook writers I know have made more money from these opportunities than they did from sweating away for six months on the guidebook itself.

You could also sell local tours, as many bloggers are doing in places around the world. I've got a small street food tour business in Guanajuato, Mexico that generates a nice steady income even when I'm not there. Amanda Ponzio-Mouttaki went further and established Marrakesh Food Tours, now a six-figure business. Beth Whitman has parlayed her Wanderlust and Lipstick travel site into an adventure tour company that does tours to Bhutan, Papua New Guinea, Bali, and other spots.

If you're based somewhere and know that city better than most others, could you turn that knowledge into another income stream? Could you do historic walking tours? Pub crawls? Food tours? Gallery tours? How about family scavenger hunts? Never underestimate what people will be willing to pay to come away with a unique experience.

Also realize that your writing and blogging skills can serve you well in getting that tour noticed in search engines. It took me just one year to get my street food tour site (MexicoStreetFood.com) to No. 1 in Google and on TripAdvisor for the phrases I was targeting. Not bad for something I started as an excuse to get out of my home office now and then.

Developing a Niche

It is impossible to produce superior performance unless you do something different than the majority.

~ John Templeton, legendary investor and mutual fund company founder

There was a popular business book out last decade called *Blue Ocean Strategy*. The core point was that you can get all bloodied trying to fight in a crowded market, but if you can create a whole new market that didn't exist, you're sailing in your own blue ocean. The successful examples of this are around you every day: Apple, Google, CarMax, Netflix, Twitter, Dropbox, and GoPro for a start.

It's hard to create a new market in this travel field, but it's not all that hard to focus on one thing and do it better than anyone instead of trying to be a generalist pen for hire. Just being a general "travel writer" puts you in a bloody pool and you'll have a hard time getting higher wages than anyone else doing the same thing.

Becoming known as the expert on independent boutique hotels in Italy is a different story. You can count your competition on one hand. The same goes for single-track biking in New England or kayaking in Belize.

Brad Olsen of CCC Publishing has published four books with *Sacred Places* in the title. He *owns* that market. Joan Petersen of Ginkgo Press has a dozen *Eat Smart In____* books that cover Mexico, Peru, India, Sicily, Brazil, and other great food destinations. She certainly doesn't have to prove to anyone that she's an international cuisine expert.

While being a jack of all trades can make sense for some people, especially part-time writers, not having at least one specialty can be detrimental in the long run. If you write about anything or any place, you are putting yourself into a very big sea of similar writers and the only way you can stand out is to be a far superior or more professional writer. I know a few successful feature writers who get away with this because they are so good at what they do and have such a great track record that they are able to be generalists. Whatever assignment comes their way, they can cover it well: luxury Caribbean this month, budget Bali next week, the architecture of Barcelona next. They are curious enough and observant enough—and talented enough writers—that they can make any of these stories sing. Even for them there are some assignments they just won't take because they'd be too bored with the subject matter. They know their skills, but also the limitations of their interest.

Many beginners make the mistake of looking at the most popular blogs, some of them very general, and thinking that's the model they should follow. But those popular ones are personality blogs that were started years ago—in some cases 10 or 15 years ago—when the field was less crowded, and they have 10,000 hours of work put into them already. They're the General Electrics and Coca-Colas of our world. Do you want to compete on that playing field?

For most of us, we need to be identified with something specific to get assignments from editors, to sell books, or to build up a following on the Internet. This can be as general as European train travel or as specific as wine tourism in France on the destination side, as general as family travel with teens or as specific as kite surfing on Lake Tahoe on the "how to" side. The more general the subject, though, the harder it is to stand out.

> *To be successful you have to know the subject matter your audience wants to read. You just can't write about everything in the world without a focus on some aspect of it.*
> ~ Jim Ferri of NeverStopTraveling.com

As the media gets sliced and diced more ways and also gets more competitive, editors are increasingly looking for writers who have something special to offer. As Sean Keener, CEO of BootsnAll says, "Find a niche that you are passionate about. Don't follow the crowd. Define what makes you unique."

This doesn't mean that the wine tourism in France person can't write about B&BS in Vermont or the Lake Tahoe windsurfing person can't write about Ecuador, but neither one can switch specialties every two months, continually ditching the old one for good. I can write about luxury travel just as easily as budget travel at this point in my life, but with books out about cheap travel, I have a much easier time getting noticed and quoted in the media for the latter. Editors actually call me with assignments sometimes, solely based on my visibility in this subject area. If they want an article about kite surfing, they're going to call that specialist instead.

> *If you are second—and you are smart—you can learn from the first person's mistakes. But by the time you are the 15th or 16th, you probably cannot add much that's new. If you do something for the 15th time and do it dramatically better, that's incredibly rare.*
> ~ Ester Dyson, venture capitalist, in Inc.

So, what are you an expert at, or in what area could you easily become an expert? Think long and hard about this and make sure it's a subject or place that you care enough about to cover in detail for years on end. Turn off the electronics and take a hike—literally. Get out of the office and find someplace quiet to think. Take a lesson from Pixar: they didn't come up with all those terrific movie ideas sitting around a conference room. They always headed to a cabin 50 miles out of the city to do their most important creative thinking.

This thought process is important because the focus needs to connect. There's no sense in becoming the European river cruises expert if you don't like ship cabins or hanging out with retired people. You don't want to become the Minneapolis travel specialist if you hate the cold and want to move south as soon as possible.

Specializing is especially important in the blogosphere. Starting one today about general family travel or restaurants in Paris would be an exercise in futility unless you already have a huge following as a book author or TV show host. It's too hard to stand out from the pack. Find a niche that's not so crowded already or choose a truly unique way to cover that place/subject. For Mariellen Ward it has been solo female travel in India and that continues to pay off no matter which way the media winds blow:

> *My income has changed drastically. Previously, I made most of my money from freelance writing and editing contracts. Today, I make most of my money from work related to my blog. In the future, I think I may make money as a brand ambassador and consultant.*
> ~ Mariellen Ward of BreatheDreamGo.com

Darren Rowse, who runs the popular ProBlogger site, succinctly explained in one particular post why a niche is so important. I'm paraphrasing a bit here, but these are the key reasons:

1. **A niche blog attracts more readers naturally.** People come back because they care about the subject and want to learn and interact.
2. **A niche blog is easier to monetize.** Specific topics draw specific advertisers and those ads get a more favorable reaction from readers.
3. **Niche blogs do better in search engines.** If you're all over the map, Google doesn't know what your site is about. If you specialize, it's more likely to be seen as authoritative.
4. **Niche blogs build credibility and profile.** Experts draw attention from the media, from people who want to hire experts. Who has ever said, "Get me a generalist on the phone"?

In its most obvious form, this can be about a place. Search "Jim Cheney" at TravelWriting2.com and you'll see our interview with a guy who only writes about the U.S. state of Pennsylvania, on UncoveringPA.com. Almost every blogger I've quoted in this book comes up short when compared to the traffic generated by the niche blog DisneyFood.com.

ModernHiker.com is a popular site that's mostly about hiking in and around the major cities of Los Angeles and San Diego. National Parks Traveler covers—you guessed it—traveling in U.S. National Parks.

Some get even more specific than that. There's a blog about traveling with autistic children (AutisticGlobetrotting.com) and some very successful ones covering a specific island or town block by block..

How do you know if you're onto something? Try the old entrepreneur's trick of condensing that specialty or blog into a short "elevator pitch." If you can summarize your specialty or your blog's slant in a couple of sentences at a cocktail party, you're probably on the right track. If you search variations of that on Google and have a hard time finding good information, you know you can zoom to the top of the rankings rather quickly. Do a test and see if you can build an audience. It's low risk but could have a high reward.

What would you like your future bio to say? Could you explain *that* during a short elevator ride or a cocktail party introduction? Figure it out, then find a way to make it happen. Work hard to dominate that subject matter by putting the readers first. Then you just have to worry about the imitators.

> *There are now a ridiculous number of people starting blogs in my niche every single day—and deciding to write a 150-page book on the subject. You have to be able to prove you care MORE about your subject than everyone who shows up hoping for free travel. Becoming a profitable business that can write off (at least a portion of) the travel you choose makes you more trustworthy and authentic than everyone who showed up yesterday.*
> ~ Shelly Rivoli of TravelsWithBaby.com and related book

The Part-Time Expert?

It's perfectly fine to develop your niche as a part-time freelance writer. Many well-known bloggers have a day job. Many guidebook writers don't depend on that pay to cover their annual expenses: they lead tours, they have a flexible office job, they work for an NGO abroad, or they do seasonal work of some kind the rest of the year.

Plenty of the travel writers you see on press trips or at conferences are not full-time writers. If you attend a Society of American Travel Writers meeting, you'll find that a large number of the people there are of retirement age. They don't need to do this for a living. They're doing it because they enjoy it.

More power to them. They might only make $25 writing an article for a low-paying web publication or a small weekly newspaper, but they're traveling around southern France or the Caribbean for a week on somebody else's tab, so that doesn't faze them. Telling them they shouldn't work so cheap is going to fall on deaf ears. They're having a blast.

If this really bugs you, find another profession to pursue. It's the reality of the marketplace and it's only going to become more common as print work dries up.

If you are in a position to be a part-time travel writer, with no concerns about the financial payoff, then in a way you are the ideal candidate for a happy career as a freelancer. You can get more assignments, take more trips, and enjoy yourself more while traveling than someone who actually has to make it all pay the bills.

I don't have any hard data on this, but I'd guess from experience that the majority of travel writers going on press trips regularly are either supported by a working spouse, have another job that pays the bills, or are retired. So if you are one of the above, join the club. It's a happy club to be in.

For part-timers with no money concerns, breaking in is pretty easy. There are a zillion small print publications and websites that pay nothing or a nominal amount that may as well be nothing. Some of them actually have a sizable audience. You may not earn money, but you'll earn some form of glory. The coverage may be enough to get the interest of a media relations person handing out press trip spots or at least some local party invites.

On some other sites you'll toil away in obscurity, especially if you join up with one of the content sweatshops cranking out listicles and listbait multiple times a day. These are good for writing practice and the occasional bottom-feeder press trip invite, but not much else. If you're going to crank out as much content as they usually want, you're much better off in the long run starting your own site and owning the content forever.

You may find, however, that being a part-time blogger is tougher than it sounds. There's much more to it than writing the text, from adding media to WordPress administration to interview calls to trip coordination to social media promotion. As Heather Cowper of Heather on Her Travels says, "It's tough not having enough time to do everything I would like while holding down a full-time job as well as blogging." There are a lot of sad travel blogs out there on life support, barely hanging on, because the owner hasn't really put much of their heart or muscle into it and postings just show up randomly now and then.

Photography and Video

Traditional travel writing books spend lots of time discussing photography and selling photos. I'm only going to spend a few pages on photography because now it's a given. For most of us, photos are table stakes. When writing for the web, a story without photos is a half-done assignment. In the digital age, photos aren't something that are going to earn you much extra cash—unless you become an Instagram star and organizations pay to tap into your audience. Or you're able to eke out some bucks from selling stock photos.

Think of photography like a college degree in the 21st century. It's nothing special like it was half a century ago. It's something you're expected to have if you're a person trying to get a good job. If you're a travel writer now, you're expected to be able to take decent photos.

Note that I said "decent," not "fantastic." When you're writing a feature story for a major magazine, they want fantastic, so they're going to hire a professional photographer. They want a pro who will give them beautiful shots that can dramatically cover two pages. In magazines with smaller budgets, they'll either use photos you submit or they'll pull stock photos of some kind. They want something that looks good in print, but they can't afford to hire a photographer and pay expenses. So they compromise.

When you get to articles on the Internet, the visuals matter a lot, but not as much as in print. There was hope that tablets and hybrid laptops would produce digital magazines that made better use of graphics, but it turns out few consumers will pay for that. Plus, half the time people are viewing articles on something tablet-sized or smaller.

Since web publishers can't assume that everyone has super-fast bandwidth and Google counts load time as a search factor, most avoid large photos with a high resolution. These shots slow down the time it takes a web page to load, plus the dimensions and layout of a web page don't allow for the kind of "spreads" you get in a magazine.

Photos just don't have the same impact visually on the web or the phone and they certainly don't have much impact on the bottom line for content sites. For better or worse, readers are just in more of a hurry online. They love photos for sure—look at the popularity of photos on social sites—but for a quick armchair travel fix or a laugh most of the time.

The other problem is, photography really has been devalued in the digital age, the same way routine writing has been devalued but worse. The reasons are similar: anybody can do it, we're awash in far more images than we need, and there's no scarcity. Every year, the entries in amateur travel photography contests get better and better. Cameras and filtering programs on phones keep getting better too. If nothing else, there's a lot more good stuff to choose from. Everyone's got decent equipment and everyone can take 100 shots of the same subject or scene to get it right without spending any money for photo development like the old days.

> *If you can learn to take good photos—and it's really not rocket science—that gives you an edge. My photos are a big draw for readers. After all, we live in a visual society where people look at photos and skim content, usually only stopping to read when a photo gets their attention and draws them to the subject.*
> ~ Jim Ferri of NeverStopTraveling.com

So it's a rare case that a web editor will pay much extra for photos. Usually they are a required part of the package. Required to the point that they can make or break your submission. When I asked GoNomad editor Max Hartshorne what freelancers do wrong the most, he went straight to photos. "They don't send good photos, or they send just a few photos when we need at least 20-30 to choose from. They don't put it all in one e-mail with a link."

I deal with this every month as an editor at Perceptive Travel. Part of the submission process is making things easy for the person on the other end. That means getting the whole package right, not just the Word document.

Here are some tips on making the photo piece of the package more attractive and easier to use, whether you are writing for someone else or illustrating your own blog.

Camera Options

It seems like I shouldn't have to mention this, but you need a good camera. I still see writers walking around with the inexpensive small camera they bought five years ago or relying on their iPhone to try to take pictures of a subject 20 meters away. It's hard to take good photos without a good camera. Fortunately the definition of "good" has gotten more fluid. With some skill, it's possible to get good photos with a simple point-and-shoot automatic, as long as the light is good and you're close to the subject. For bloggers who just upload images to social media, a camera phone might be enough.

Taking one step up will make a noticeable difference, however. There's a category of cameras called "super-zoom" that are better than a basic point-and-shoot but not as heavy, bulky, or complicated as a digital SLR camera. With these you have a long zoom, a larger lens, and manual override controls. For most situations, that's plenty. You can pick one up for between $200 and $500 depending on the zoom length, the model age, and the bells and whistles included. Some will even shoot in RAW format. They're not compact enough to fit in your pocket, but they take better photos, especially when you can't get right up close to the subject. I've published two-page spreads in print magazines from photos shot from this kind of $300 camera and more than 1,000 on the web.

Go up another step and the compact mirrorless cameras allow you to take professional photos without the bulk. The drawback is you still have to carry more lenses—especially for zooming—but the camera has a bigger sensor than a superzoom but is not as bulky as a full-blown DSLR. Some bloggers known for their photos have gone this route so they're not so loaded down.

If you have more money to spend and don't mind lugging around more equipment, a DSLR camera will provide the most control, the best lenses, and the most features. I personally don't think it's worth it for most people unless they're shooting for print regularly, but plenty of other writers strongly disagree. If photography is your main focus, then compromising is probably not the best path. Just go for what the pros use and suck it up on the bulk and weight. But read the manual and learn to use all the functions you're paying for.

A small travel tripod can be a big help, especially in low light situations. You can use this with a video camera as well. For a pittance these days, you can also load up on other accessories such as a standing lightweight travel tripod, polarizing lenses, or reflector circles for interviews.

Of course it's not all about still images these days. If you're going to shoot video frequently, a GoPro and maybe even a drone would be a good investment. If you're going to shoot videos with your regular camera, pay attention to the mic and see if what you're considering has an audio external mic input. If you're going to do video interviews regularly, it might make sense to invest in lavalier mics you can pin on someone's clothing, just as a news reporter would.

Learn to Take Interesting Shots

If you have never taken a photography course in your life, you might want to sign up now. I've met travelers with great equipment who come back with collections of boring photos. I've met others who use their phone and come back with stunning shots. The first never developed an eye for photography or the skills to compensate for less-than-ideal conditions. The second learned and improved. The first type takes photos when the light is all wrong. The second type takes advantage of periods when the light is just right. The second person overcomes an equipment deficit with an artistic eye, patience, and better framing.

There are some basic skills that can be easily learned and applied. Sure, the pros spend a lifetime honing these skills and developing their own bags of tricks, but for the writer who is not trying to get into *National Geographic*, a basic level of proficiency will do it. So take a class, do online tutorials, read some books on the subject, and get advice from others with more skill and experience. As with writing, after you know the basics, the rest of getting better is all about practice and continual improvement.

There are some key strategies that help when taking travel photos for publication, however.

1. **Get some color in the shots.** Travel is about adventure, fantasy, relaxation, fun, excitement, and exploration. Five drab gray shots won't convey any of that.

2. **Mix up the composition.** Leaf through a bunch of magazines and you'll see this aspect over and over again. Some wide scenery shots from afar, some close shots of details. A crowd, then one face. A night shot, a bright beach shot. Think in terms of opposites as you shoot.

3. **We like people!** A travel story with no people in any of the photos looks kind of strange. This can be local people or it can be travelers having fun, but landscapes and monuments alone don't cut it.

4. **Show us something different.** The best photos tell us a story or at least intrigue us enough to make us stop and ponder the image. Don't take the same postcard shot everyone else has taken a million times if you want it to be worthy of publication. Look for a unique angle.

5. **It's not all about you.** Sure, if you have a personality blog that's your personal mouthpiece, now and then it's appropriate to make yourself the focus. But in general, a sea of selfies is usually a sign of amateurism. (And an oversized ego.)

Find the Drama

There are some situations where you are limited in how creative you can be. The obvious one for travel writers is hotels. I've probably published 1,500 hotel photos and have edited a few thousand more. There's a limit to the variety and it's hard to make any standard room shot dramatic without manipulating it. But still, there's a lot you can do just by shooting from a different angle, framing things in an interesting way, and grabbing images that capture the Golden Mean in design—especially outside of the guest room.

The same principle can be applied to other difficult cases like river rafting trips, hiking trips, rainy days, or visits to iconic monuments. It's a challenge, but the answers are usually right in front of you if you wander around surveying the scene before snapping away upon arrival. A tour company I traveled with in Peru had this advice for travelers in their instructions, but it's great advice for travel writers too: "When arriving in a new place, wait 15 seconds before snapping any photos. Take in what you're seeing first and really observe."

See a new place with your eyes first instead of through a viewfinder.

Learn to Edit

On an almost weekly basis, I'll get a writer sending me giant five-megabyte photos by e-mail, which is a royal pain in the rear for a web editor. These are photos coming straight out of the writer's camera, files that are so large they could be blown up to wall-covering poster size. For the web, it's like sending me a novel when I've asked for a one-page story. You can bet it bugs other editors too. Do you want to risk an editor not hiring you again just because you can't be bothered to figure out how to use simple photo editing software, or figuring out how to upload your shots to a cloud service so you can send one link?

Take the time to learn how to crop, how to reduce the resolution, how to sharpen. You don't need the big learning curve and expense of Photoshop for any of this. The software that came with your camera can probably do it. If not there are some free shareware programs that are easy and effective. See the current options at CNET's download.com. There are also online services like PicMonkey and Canva that will let you take it further and size/design for multiple needs like Facebook covers and custom YouTube slides.

A so-so photo can be made to look great with the right cropping, and a lot of composition problems can be fixed with a few simple tweaks. Learn this stuff so you can turn in decent photos or you can post interesting images on your own blog.

Shoot some video

Only some sites want video. It hogs bandwidth and doesn't produce much income, but for others it is essential. Few need anything from you that's going to win a short films competition though. A clip of a minute or two is plenty and it doesn't need to be film festival quality. (Even with high-resolution videos, most of the viewing is now happening on a phone.) Some bloggers use a lot of video because it can tell a story or bring a place alive. Some also like to have their face on camera, so they can function like a travel show host.

Doing this used to be a major expense and hassle, but not anymore. The camera or phone you're already using is "good enough" and is dead simple to use. Most quality still cameras now have built-in video capabilities and some super-zoom point-and-shoots take impressive HD video—starting at a price tag under $300. You'll get better quality if you buy a dedicated digicam and a GoPro will work best for outdoor action. If you've watched much on YouTube though—especially if you've watched with a teenager—you've probably realized viewers aren't too concerned about professionalism when viewing video on the web. The subject matter is more important.

There's a second step to the shooting though—editing—and it's not as quick or easy as editing a photo. With a few hours of practice you can get it down, with software that's already loaded on your Windows or Mac laptop. It's time-consuming though, something best done when you've got a sizable block of time on your hands, like when on a long flight home.

If you're serious about doing this on a regular basis, you may want to invest in an external microphone. People are used to putting up with low-quality video, but they don't have much tolerance for low-quality audio. Some portable cameras and digicams have shielded mics and some have an input for an external one, while with a phone you can attach an external one through the headphone jack.

The Craft
of Travel Writing

Easy reading is damn hard writing.

~ Nathaniel Hawthorne

Anyone can claim to be a writer. Most aren't good enough at it to make a living from that assertion.

There are plenty of courses, books, and seminars out there that will teach you how to be a great writer. Some are decent, some are great, and others are a waste of time.

I have to admit I've never taken a writing course or workshop of any kind, apart from the usual high school and college courses that seemed to give me enough to get started. Mostly I learned by reading a lot and writing a lot, on a wide range of subjects. This takes longer and I probably could have benefitted from a few intense workshops in the beginning, but in my opinion practice is more valuable than just learning techniques. You need a good base of knowledge, you need to have at least a modicum of talent, and then the rest is a matter of getting better and better at the craft.

> *No matter how smart you are, you're not going to be very good for a few years at least. I don't know why exactly this is true, but it is. Everyone's a little cheesy at first, a little overwritten, a lot cliché. It takes a tremendous amount of practice not to be. Most people never get there.*
>
> ~ Lena Katz, freelance writer and author

Some people get a lot of value out of courses and seminars, though, because if nothing else they provide dedicated writing time with no distractions plus valuable feedback from the instructor and peers. In these courses writers learn to drop some bad habits and pick up some new good ones.

Some writing courses and seminars are taught by respected editors and writers who have proven beyond a doubt that they know what's great writing and what's not. You can find out more about these in the resources section at the end.

There are also some really fine books out there on becoming a better writer. Some are focused on travel, like the highly-recommended *Travel Writing* book out on Lonely Planet, edited by the legendary Don George. Others cover creative non-fiction in general and provide inspiration and instruction for going from average to terrific.

The one drawback to these books and courses is that they mostly focus on feature writing: on long magazine narratives where the author has plenty of space to let loose and be creative. That's all well and good, but since this book is about the commercial aspect of writing, I have to warn you that this is only one slice of the travel writing pie and it's not one that's getting any bigger.

Can You Write Better Than a 5th Grader?

I always thought editors were exaggerating when they talked about off-target pitches, query letters punctuated with spelling errors, and god-awful stories they had to sift through week after week.

Then I became an editor.

Man, oh man are there some bad writers out there. Setting aside the problem that way too many writers are lazy about reading guidelines (or think the guidelines apply to everyone but them), plenty of people who call themselves writers should really sign up for one of those writing seminars or buy a few books on how to write. Some of them appear not to have passed even a high school English class.

As Pam Mandel of Nerd's Eye View says, "Learn to freaking write. It's the least you can do."

So before we get into the finer points of craft and skill, do you have the basics down? Can you spell? Do you understand subject/verb agreement and the difference between an adjective and an adverb? Do you know the difference between active and passive voice? Do you understand when to use a colon and when to use a semicolon?

If not, please go get schooled before you send off a single query or start a blog. Get *The Elements of Style* and study it cover to cover, then read *The Elephants of Style* for some more tempered advice. Read *Eats, Shoots, and Leaves.* Figure out the differences between British and American English in spelling and punctuation if you want to submit stories to editors outside your home country. Ask for the *Chicago Manual of Style* for your next birthday present or reference it in the library or online.

When you have a spelling or grammar question, don't just guess. Look it up so you'll know. We're spoiled rotten for information now: you don't have to drive to the library to find the proper uses of racked, wracked, or wrecked.

So if you send in a sloppy query, it broadcasts that you're just plain lazy. Game over.

First, learn the basics of writing. Make sure you are using proper punctuation and have no spelling mistakes. Learn how to write in an active voice rather than a passive voice, and how to "show" rather than 'tell." When you think you are done, re-read your article and eliminate any extraneous words. Edit, edit, edit.

~ Barbara Weibel

A Strong Work Ethic is the Best Asset

Don't expect to receive much value until you've proven you create value.

~ Chris Backe

I learned a secret long ago that may have been the biggest factor in my success: showing up and doing what you promised impresses people more than virtuosity. Those who do the hiring in any industry love finding someone they can depend on.

Don't think you have to be the most talented, the most outrageous, or the most technically gifted to be a successful writer. Often you just have to be reasonably good at what you're doing and be able to meet the requirements, whatever they may be. There are lots of actors making a good living without being "movie stars." They show up on time, they know their lines, they hit their marks, they get hired again.

It's a similar scene with most creative endeavors. Movies love to glamorize the strung-out manic-depressant tortured artist and there's some anecdotal evidence that being a genius and being unhinged go hand-in-hand, but the unhinged often die young. Keep living and be merely great instead. Strangers won't cry at your grave, but you'll actually live to see kids or nieces who know you.

Want to get hired again after your first freelance gig with a publication? Do what's required. Turn in what the editor asked for, in the style she needs, with all the outlined requirements, on time, after checking for errors with spell check and human eyes.

This is obvious, but do good work. Understand the assignment. Give the editor what they need. Make their job easy. Be reliable. Respond to e-mails. Stay in word count, and never miss a deadline. This is a real job, as fun as it may look from the outside sometimes, so treat it like that.

~ Dana McMahan, freelance writer

Beyond the fundamentals, to say what's good or bad writing we first have to look at the changing definition of what "good writing" even means. First it means considering the intermediary customer (who is hiring you) or the end customer—the reader.

Narrative Feature Writing

A magazine that speaks to readers, transforms them and transports them either to a place they'd like to live or like to travel, that's the best of print journalism. Solving a problem is good, but transporting and transforming is the goal of all good editors.

~ Eleanor Griffin, former Editor in Chief, *Southern Living*

Narrative feature writing is what most everyone imagines themselves doing when they hear "travel writer." All those multi-page features with beautiful photos that are splashed across several pages, your byline in bold type at the top, right under the title. Creative, evocative writing that brings a destination to life and explores characters who glide across the stage of that glorious week you spent in the region.

Well, good luck with that. Those assignments are out there, but for magazines especially the assignments mostly go to veterans with a long track record. Narrative feature assignments are like starring roles in a movie: sometimes they go to unknowns, but usually the editor wants a proven pro. Nobody gets in trouble that way.

It is a little easier to get narratives published on the web since there are far more outlets—some quite prestigious now, some visited by only a handful of readers on a regular basis. Gregory Hubbs of TransitionsAbroad.com hosts an annual narrative travel writing contest that pulls in some surprisingly great features from relative unknowns. He says, "A travel narrative which is well-written is inspiring and interesting, especially when it rises to the level of literature or universal experience, and the web offers many the opportunity to contribute substantive thoughts and work."

Learning to write well along the way over time will get you ready for these assignments or contests when they come, so jump at any chance you get to do these kinds of stories. Write for small magazines, write for webzines, write without worrying about the money. Then by the time you graduate from the minor leagues to the majors, you'll be ready to hit a home run.

I'd say 99% of published travel writing is complete garbage: pointless rambling, no story, and far too many adjectives. If you don't actually have something to say, beyond "gee, it's pretty/interesting/rustic/a land of many contrasts," stop writing now. As VS Naipaul put it, perhaps you'd be happier playing piano. Tell me a story. Write something I haven't already read a thousand times.

~ Edward Readicker-Henderson, freelance writer

To get good at this kind of writing, you need more talent than for any of the other types that follow. You need the tools of a novelist, the eyes of a journalist, and the general knowledge that comes from a never-ending education. You need a natural curiosity about the world around you—and its history. For this type of writing, you can't just fire off a draft you wrote in one sitting.

I've won quite a few awards for my narrative writing and I choose stories for Perceptive Travel that often show up in "best travel writing" anthologies, so I think I have a pretty good sense about what's required to be good at this. I couldn't have put out the stories that won these awards when I started out as a freelance writer, though. I wasn't good enough yet.

Study. Read everything. Write every day. You get better by doing. Those who are successful recognize what's popular, what sells, but that they need to keep their own voice and be human in their stories, and to be responsible journalists. Short cuts may be exciting, but overall, those who focus on quality do well.

~ Jill Robinson, freelance feature writer

Some writers have more natural talent than I do and success comes faster. Catch them in an honest moment, however, and every one will tell you they edit and re-edit, they still get advice from others, and they still occasionally get the feeling that what they've put on the page is sub-par. One of the writers I respect the most once said quietly, "I still feel like a hack sometimes."

If you don't feel that way sometimes, you're probably not stretching enough. Writing a compelling travel narrative that will keep people reading for 2,000 or 4,000 words takes real work. Don't let any writing course come-on that promises great success after one weekend tell you differently.

I want a writer who can grab me from the beginning of a pitch or story, with a vivid image or a compelling scene or wordplay. I want a writer who can keep me hooked, who can bring me deep into a story. I want a writer who understands how to structure and tell a story, who knows what to put in the story and also what to leave out.

cont/d ...

> *I want clarity. I want a writer with an eye for detail, someone who can bring me into a scene or a place. I want to be entertained. I want a writer who, by the end of the story, has made me feel something or taught me something that I didn't know.*
> ~ Michael Yessis, co-founder of WorldHum.com

It's not hard to find good examples of narrative writing, so I'm not going to take the usual page-padding route of posting examples in this book. You can find them in annual travel writing anthologies or compilations. You can find them in travel magazines that strive to rise above the rest (especially *Outside*), or in non-travel magazines like *Esquire*, the *New Yorker*, *New York Times Magazine*, or *Men's Journal*.

Usually there's at least one good feature in the best-known travel magazines themselves, such as *National Geographic Traveler, Wanderlust, and Afar*. You can find them in webzines that include good narratives on a regular basis, such as my Perceptive Travel online magazine and the BBC's travel section.

You can also see the elements of a good narrative article by reading the ones that win contests. It's all up to the whims of the judges, of course, but see what came out on top and compare it to what you just wrote.

Is yours as gripping, as wrenching, as exhilarating, or as funny—whichever one applies? If not, keep editing.

Short F.O.B. ("Front of Book) Features

Flip through any magazine on any subject at your local newsstand and you'll find that there is a far larger market for short capsule articles of a page or less than there is for long stories. The average magazine story is now well under 500 words, with that average dragged down by all the cutesy little one-paragraph nuggets that have only become more common as attention spans have shortened.

This is where the work is. If you want to break in as a freelancer at a magazine, get good at saying what needs to be said in 400 words and then getting out. If your idea can't be captured in a capsule story like this, then rethink the angle. If you can come up with ideas that fit into small boxes over and over again, you will get repeat assignments. Do it enough times for one editor and you build trust. With trust you can finally pitch those full-blown ideas that require spending a week in the Andes or rafting down some obscure river on the other side of the world.

The writing for these short pieces is very different than for long ones. This is where you really need to study the publication to get a feel for its style. In general though, you're required to be crisp, efficient, and have a bag full of puns at your disposal. What you write will often sound much like what every other person writes in that issue—or more correctly, everyone ends up sounding like the editor. It's a formula and it's annoying, but apparently it works.

For these articles, the idea is to catch someone's eye as they're flipping through the magazine and to present something in bite-sized form. This may be something new, something noteworthy, something odd, or something funny. In any case, it's an article that gets the point across without a lot of exposition.

This is probably the only kind of writing I can think of where being good at Twitter is actually useful for something. If you can get your point across in short, catchy sentences, you'll be a good match for this kind of work.

Service Article Writing

The columns that people are likely to rip out of a magazine to reference later or copy from a web page are ones written to provide advice or information. There are a lot of these "service" pieces in every issue of almost any kind of magazine. For travel the articles are meant to inform and guide vacationers or business travelers. They are articles designed to eliminate hassles, save people money, get better perks, or help them make good decisions.

As much as we writers get thrilled about big sweeping destination stories, most readers are checking out travel magazines and websites to learn how to travel better or cheaper. Service articles are where it's at, in magazines that cover nothing but travel and magazines that only cover it now and then. The latter would include magazines like *Smart Money, Real Simple, Every Day with Rachel Ray, Women's Day, Men's Journal, Money*, or a hundred others that only cover travel as another lifestyle aspect.

In print or on the web, this is where the bulk of the assignments are. So while many travel writing articles and books seem almost obsessively focused on the craft of capturing the essence of a place and engaging the senses, what most travel writers *sell* on a regular basis has nothing to do with all that. People read magazines for enjoyment and escape, yes, but more often they read them to learn something or get ideas to make them richer/more attractive/more successful/happier. Editors know this and therefore they cram the front third or half of the magazine full of service articles. If you don't believe me, start making a list of how many pieces in any magazine you pick up start with some variation of "How to..." "Where to..." or "Tips."

This is even more true on the web, where people land on pages after a search meant to answer a specific question. "What are the cheapest hostels in Prague?" "How do I catch a bus from Cancun to Merida?" "How do I get a visa for India?" "How much will it cost to rent a house for a week in Myrtle Beach?" The people doing these searches want an expert to give them definitive answers to their questions. They don't really care about the fluff.

If you run your own blog or website, answering these questions over and over builds an audience. Let's say someone lands on your site to find out an answer to the Google search, "campground costs Smoky Mountains." If you provide that information and your site seems both authoritative and in line with their interests, that reader may stick around and keep browsing. The person may bookmark the site or recommend it to others through social media. Over time, this builds up subscribers and followers. A long blog post talking about your boring camping trip near Gatlinburg does not.

Service articles are the heart of travel writing. So become an expert on some topic or destination and you'll get work telling readers what you know.

Web Feature Writing

Feature writing for Internet sites is different than writing for print media, mostly because the attention span is even shorter on the web. Numerous studies have shown people read faster and with less attention as soon as they go on the web. Also, much of the difference depends on word count. Perceptive Travel, World Hum,

Transitions Abroad, and GoNomad publish relatively long articles. They toss aside the idea that everything has to be in easily digested chunks and they have differentiated themselves from the crowd by doing so.

Most websites aim for shorter pieces though, rarely topping 1,000 words. For search engine optimization purposes, they would rather have a focused story of 400 to 600 words clearly utilizing specific keyword phrases than to have a long murkier narrative with subplots and characters. (This is a rule to break now and then for your own site, especially in posts for the people really diving into a specific subject. Some of my most popular blog posts are more than 3,000 words!)

In general, the higher the pay, the harder it is for a newcomer to break into a given web publication, but it's still easier online than in print since the publishing constraints come from available budgets, not from issue thickness or the ratio of full-page ads to articles.

Short Web Article Writing

See the blog section below for blog posts, but there are many travel websites out there that pay for short articles on a specific subject. These are sometimes meant to offer complete destination coverage on a specific region, so the editor will assign short pieces on each town or attraction and will put each one on its own page. Or a site may require unique hotel reviews, unique restaurant reviews, boutique store rundowns, etc.

More often than not, the editor cares more about the uniqueness and the presence of the right keywords than about how well you have crafted the story. Punctuate properly and use good grammar and you're set. In other cases (such as the hotel reviews assigned at LuxuryLatinAmerica.com), the editor wants what's on the page to be better and more detailed than anything else out there. Again, study the publication and guidelines carefully to turn one assignment into many.

For these stories, you may be required to submit them in HTML-ready text as well, or be required to post them through a dashboard and manually insert all links and photos. I advise you to learn all this anyway, as you'll need the skills in the future.

Blog Writing

There's a fine line between travel content sites and blogs (originally called "weblogs"), but a blog is expected to be in a specific format of current posts on the front page and others accessed by category and/or tag links.

There are two kinds of blog writing: what you write for your own and what you write for someone else. For your own, you make the rules, so I'm not going to tell you how or what to write. It pays off in the long run to look like a professional: edit, proof, spell-check, and don't use others' photos without the proper permission or attribution. Be unique instead of copying or commenting on what others have written. Offer something worth returning to. Write around a certain theme or point of view instead of regularly posting about your cat, your husband, politics, and your weekend getaway all on one blog (unless you are a celebrity and people really care). Write on a reasonably regular schedule.

Most people visit blogs to be entertained, to learn something, to get advice, to improve their lives, or to keep up on a specific subject. If you don't meet one of those needs, your traffic will probably never take off. If you're writing for someone else's blog—especially a corporate one—they will have very specific requirements and a typical style.

Writing for blogs is very different than writing articles that are for a newspaper or magazine (print or online). Blog posts are expected to be less formal and more conversational, with shorter and fewer paragraphs. This doesn't mean you can't write a 2,000-word diatribe now and then, but don't make it a daily habit. On your own blog you can write things that nobody would publish—and you might get a lot of traffic.

You can drill down to a level of detail that wouldn't get past an editor's desk at a magazine. I've done posts on water purifiers, the south Florida Tri-Rail system, and what ships pay to go through the Panama Canal on my Cheapest Destinations blog. On the Perceptive Travel blog, the writers there have done posts on a village in Armenia, the Hutchinson Kansas Grain Elevator, a specific street food stall with a story in Bangkok, craft spirits in Chattanooga, and the Neon Boneyard in Las Vegas. Your editorial limits are far broader on a blog, so go nuts.

> *For the most part I think blogging will continue to be a slightly less digested form of writing than formal journalism or essay writing. In most cases, including mine, it bears as many similarities to letter writing as it does to journalism. And just like authors from years past approached letter writing with a different focus than essay writing, there's a similar difference with blog writing. There's simply less rewriting and polishing to be done with a blog entry.*
>
> ~ Rolf Potts, Author of *Vagabonding*

If you're getting paid to write for someone else's blog, naturally you need to adhere to their requirements. They all have specific content needs and unique dashboard interfaces, plus an editorial style of their own that you need to match. Guest posts for others' blogs need to blend in with their existing style and format.

I love writing for blogs more than other formats because it's where I feel I can say exactly what I want. I like the immediacy of it and the ability to follow any whim in terms of subject matter. When readers stop by, it's because of content I've created, not because of what an army of editors and writers has collectively put together. But don't be fooled: it's still a lot of work, especially if you're doing multiple posts every week—or every day. The nice side effect? You get a lot of practice with coming up with ideas and writing about them.

Trade Writing

Writing for trade publications essentially means writing for a non-consumer audience. You are writing in a factual and comprehensive style for people in the business. They are reading what you wrote because they need to for their job, not because they are spending a leisurely afternoon being entertained.

Over the years, I've done a lot of work for two publications sold through subscription to travel agents. One specializes in detailed hotel reviews and the other in mini-guidebook reports that summarize a destination and give travel agents info they can package into a report for customers.

One of my first real gigs as a travel writer was one of these, writing reviews of 79 top hotels scattered around Turkey. I did well on that, so they hired me to do Israel, Egypt, Jordan, Korea, Guam, Saipan, Nepal, and India within the next three years. I went on to cover Peru, Argentina, and parts of Mexico and the US.

I still work for them now and then. I love these jobs because the terms are clear, the pay is decent, and they pay on time. Business to business writing is often like that—more professional and more stable.

I know other writers who get most of their income from trade magazines such as *Aviation Week*, *Travel Weekly* or *Meetings and Incentives*. In general this kind of writing requires more industry knowledge than most beginners have, however, so this is one of the few freelance jobs where the editor may ask for a résumé or a rundown on your work history.

Trade publication writing is more journalistic than most travel writing. Business readers want the facts and supporting quotes without a lot of fluff. They won't look at your byline and don't want your opinion. The hotel and destination reports I've written didn't even provide a byline at all: I'm anonymous. Writing for the trades is about the paycheck, not about getting famous or building up a following.

Guidebook Writing

Are you obsessive about the facts? Detail-oriented? Super-organized? A fast writer? Let's hope so on all counts if you want to be a guidebook writer. This is a Job with a capital "J." I get stressed out just thinking about all the work that goes into creating a guidebook and my wife has standing orders to talk me out of it should I ever be offered a contract to write one.

I admire guidebook writers because they have serious dedication. One project requires months to a year of their life and in order to make the finances work, they have to do it quickly, thoroughly, and efficiently. Every time, they have to defy the old handyman question of, "Do you want it done quick, cheap, or well? Pick two."

How far you can flex in the writing depends greatly on the publisher, but in any case your verbal skills take a back seat to a guidebook's core purpose: supplying information. You can embellish the descriptions and add a dose of humor, but not until you've got the current bus schedule worked out in detail, thank you very much. Apart from a few boxed sections that allow you to tell a story about some specific site or historical event, you barely have time to write full sentences before moving on to the requisite restaurant listings and museum hours.

Some writers thrive in this environment and are masters at getting everything just right. Others quickly get into the right mode for a guidebook, but then branch off and do wonderful narrative articles or other books.

There are very few courses or books for this kind of writing. Your best teachers are other writers, the publisher's instructions, and stacks of guidebooks studied in detail.

For the dark side of the story, read Thomas Kohnstamm's book, *Do Travel Writers Go to Hell*? Then go read all the rebuttals from other guidebook writers by searching the name of that book on Google.

Travel Book Writing

Not all travel books are guidebooks. Some of the best-selling ones are something else: narratives from the likes of Bill Bryson, J. Maarten Troost, Paul Theroux, Frances Mayes, or Tim Cahill. Some are informational books on a specific subject, such as traveling with children or gaming the frequent flyer system. Others are reference books on niches such as responsible travel or are coffee table books filled with gorgeous photos.

So it's impossible to generalize except to say you need to know enough about that subject to sustain a whole book's worth of text. You need to be an accomplished writer with plenty to say. And if it's a narrative book, you had better be able to tell a great story and have a good following on top of that. Otherwise an agent won't sign you and you're stuck putting it out yourself—a daunting prospect for something that's not informational in nature.

If you have aspirations of writing a book, do your homework on how to put together a good proposal, outline your book, and lay out how you'll promote it. Even if you're self-publishing, this is time well spent. Then make the magic happen for 200+ pages. I'll just emphasize this one point: before you decide to write a book, make sure you can write a lot of good articles or a few years' worth of blog posts. The book—and the marketing—will come much easier after that.

Writers must first be good writers, they must know their subjects, and if I'm going to consider them for writing or editing a book they have to be personable and flexible. Life is too short to work with someone you don't like or respect, especially on a creative project that requires collaboration. They also need to be responsible and reliable, so I know they're going to do what we've agreed they will do.

~ Larry Habegger, Executive Editor, Travelers' Tales Publishing

---

In the end, my advice for any kind of writing where you have control over the outcome is "be unique." Aim to do what nobody else is doing, not to forge the same path. Here's a quote from the famous novelist John Updike that I love:

"Professionalism in art has this difficulty: To be professional is to be dependable, to be dependable is to be predictable, and predictability is esthetically boring—an anti-virtue in a field where we hope to be astonished and startled and at some deep level refreshed."

Self-promotion

In reality, the ONLY thing you need to do is this:

Step 1: Build an audience
Step 2: Sell them stuff

~ Derek Halpern of SocialTriggers.com

Mastering a niche and being an expert at something is essential now, but that still only gets you halfway to success. Like the proverbial tree falling in the forest when nobody is around, you'll still toil in obscurity if a few key things don't happen to raise your profile.

Making those things happen isn't magic: success requires a concerted effort and a self-promoting mindset.

Many writers hear "self-promotion" and cringe, the same way many indie rockers and struggling painters do when they're starting out. Without some smart self-promotion, however, it's almost impossible to create any sort of income from your art. Someone who's noisier and more visible will get that income instead.

Promoting yourself doesn't mean you have to be a loudmouth jerk who dominates every conversation and bores everyone around. It doesn't mean steering every conversation subject toward yourself, online or off. It certainly doesn't mean putting up 30 tweets or Facebook status updates every day. After all, many of the most successful nonfiction writers are, by all accounts, self-effacing people who are quite pleasant to be around. (Who has ever called Rick Steves or Don George a self-absorbed jerk?) They've found a way to be visible without being aggressive about it.

There are a lot of successful bloggers out there who are terrible schmoozers at parties and lots of book authors who never brag about their accomplishments. I'm not very active on Facebook or Instagram and many successful writers think Twitter is the clearest evidence yet that the movie *Idiocracy* is coming true before our eyes.

Most writers who make real money at this are visible somehow, though, if not on one of the social media methods, then something else instead. They have picked a few paths to recognition and are promoting themselves actively on a regular basis by doing the right things for their situation, week in and week out. Maybe it's reaching out to media weekly, sending a regular e-mail newsletter, or doing regular speaking gigs. They seek out opportunities instead of waiting for things to fall in their laps.

If they have something to sell, they're also asking for an order now and then. They're building an audience and then meeting the needs of that audience. By doing that, they're earning an income.

Each method outlined below is involved enough to warrant its own book or workshop, so learn more about each as you go and figure out what's best, but here are summaries of a few key visibility tactics. Some are more important to bloggers or webmasters than they are to pure freelancers, but consider each a tool that can be employed at different levels of commitment depending on your own situation.

Keep in mind that different methods work better for different people. You need to do something regularly to make it in the digital age, and a little discomfort comes along with that for many, but doing three things well beats doing 30 things in a half-assed way.

Your own blog

For some people this is a great vehicle to promote their work. For some it's the foundation of their whole business.

For others it's a waste of time: don't assume it's an automatic need, especially if you're primarily a freelance writer who is not entrepreneurial.

A blog works best for a defined niche that lends itself to lots of ongoing content and reflections on changes in the environment or marketplace. If you intend to be seen as an expert on something or someplace specific, by all means forge ahead. If you are likely to build a following by bringing new material to your tribe every week, then a blog is essential. It's a great mouthpiece, a search engine magnet, and eventually something that will get you media attention and writing assignments.

But what if you're a guidebook writer covering different areas every few months? Or a feature writer with no specific beat? Or a regular columnist or blogger for someone else who has a hard enough time coming up with ideas each week? In those cases, a blog is probably not a good idea. It will just suck away more time and energy without accomplishing your goals or making you more money. Many writers should be bloggers, but definitely not all of them.

Keep in mind that a blog can turn into an all-consuming endeavor that takes up more and more time as it grows. Diving into this commitment without clear goals and expectations is a big mistake. You may need one of these, but if you don't at this particular moment, there's no point in doing it halfway. Even between the first edition of this book and now, many bloggers I highlighted have abandoned that body of work and it's sitting there. It's like an abandoned puppy who wasn't cute anymore, so the owner lost interest. That's just plain sad.

Your own website

A blog can be a good promotional tool or platform, but when it comes to self-promotion for freelancers, a portfolio site is essential unless you never want to write for anyone else. This is the first thing I, as an editor, seek out when I'm deciding to hire someone, no matter what they've said in their query letter. It's also what I expect to see pop up on the first page of Google when I search their name. If, instead, I get their Facebook page with shout-outs to their friends, drunken selfies on Instagram, and a blog about their cat, I start questioning their status as a writer.

Even if you do have a travel-related blog, either build a portfolio site as well or make a really good "About Me" page on your blog, with links to your best work. This is as close as you'll ever get to free advertising for your services and thus the easiest return on investment decision you'll ever make, even if you spend some money on a designer. See the Resources section for a few ideas on where to get started—including a site I like where you can just plug in your links and it generates a pretty portfolio.

Search engine optimization (SEO) knowledge

If you build a portfolio site or blog and then neglect to include the keywords relating to your niche, you are invisible to anyone searching for that niche. The basics of SEO are elementary: figure out how you want people to search for you or your site and make sure you have done the right things to get your site high up in those results. Google ranking is complicated, but it's primarily a popularity contest. You can't win that contest for "cheap flights," but with some work you can win it for "best New York sidewalk food carts," "northern England barge tours," or "spelunking in Missouri."

If you are the foremost expert on urban hiking in the mountains around Los Angeles (as one blogger I mentioned earlier is), then obviously you need to have things like "urban hiking expert" and "Los Angeles" in your title or description and in the words of the actual text somewhere. Each separate page or blog entry needs its own set of keywords and phrases. These go in the text and they also go in something called "metatags" that are instructions to the search engine bots.

In the next phase, you want to get people to link to you or you put your own link in things you write elsewhere on the web, preferably using those key phrases that describe your expertise now and then. Links to your name don't hurt either, especially if your name is not really unusual and you want to rise above the others with that same name. (On that note, if you do have a really common name, find a way to differentiate yourself, like adding your middle name, a nickname, or an initial.) Writers who are easy to find get assignments, get interviewed, get noticed, and get book deals. Those who are hard to find online will struggle more and more as the years go on. In a world where social media and search are everything, being low-profile on both means you're practically invisible.

There are ways to build up many of these links naturally, through message board signatures, profiles on sites where you're an active member of some kind, or blogs where you make a comment. Writing material worth linking to helps a lot, as does having good friends and alliances. Don't sweat the keywords so much anymore. It's actually advantageous now to have a "natural looking" variety of them pointing to your site(s).

Physical networking

One of the best time-tested ways to raise your profile is to widen your network of friends and associates in your field. If anything, the digital world has enhanced the power of personal connections. A link from a high-profile blog can mean more than a quote in a major magazine, and all you had to do was get in touch with a friend.

Join local writing groups if that's an option and attend a conference now and then where you can meet other travel writers and editors. When people know who you are, they're more likely to read what you write, recommend what you write, and hire you or recommend you when the opportunity comes up. I'll take five contacts I've met face-to-face over 100 new Twitter followers any day. There's a stronger bond that's longer lasting.

The good news is, those social media platforms have made finding and meeting the right people easier than ever. When I'm in a new city I'll look up a writer or two and get together in person. Before the web it was really hard to track people down and meet them. Now it's done with a few clicks. No excuses anymore: get out from behind the laptop, put the always-on distraction devices away, and have sustained discussions.

Many organizations are out there that will formalize this networking. See the resources section at the end for the web sites of the Society of American Travel Writers, North American Travel Journalists Association, American Society of Journalist and Authors, Professional Travel Bloggers Association, and others. As the print world some of these organizations are inextricably tied to fades in importance, the organizations themselves are at risk of being less relevant. Still, for a couple hundred bucks in annual dues, they can be worth it for jump-starting your contact list and access to PR people and press trips. Many of the people I've hired to write for me over the years, I've met at conferences.

Other ad-hoc communities, however, are free and are more relevant to non-print writers. Check out the MediaKitty.com community and the Travel Blog Exchange—or find Facebook groups tied into your specific interests and goals.

Message boards

You don't hear as much about these as you did before people started sectioning themselves off in Facebook groups, but message boards are as powerful a place as ever to create a presence and build your credibility. Whether your expertise is Tuscany, barbecue joints, or skiing in Idaho, there's probably a message board somewhere with people interested in that subject. Find it, join it, become a part of it. Put a link to your site in your signature and you'll find people following that to your site. Link to an article you've written now and then (make sure it's useful) and people will click on that. If you're really an expert, over time you'll build authority and you'll learn a few things you didn't know as well.

If you ever plan to write a book, hanging out on message boards can give you a good sense of what people are curious about. Before I put out my first book, *The World's Cheapest Destinations*, I spent a lot of time reading questions from soon-departing around-the-world travelers on Lonely Planet's Thorn Tree. The questions that came up over and over again (and still do) were, "How cheap is it to travel in [insert country]" and "Will my budget of [insert amount] be enough to last six months in [insert itinerary]?" I didn't have to do any market research beyond that. I knew there was no book out there answering these questions and if I created one that was good it would keep selling year after year. After four editions and more than 15,000 copies sold net, I think I can safely say I was correct.

New places to share information keep cropping up all the time. There are paid forums with limited numbers, like Fizzle.co or Dynamite Circle (tropicalmba.com/dc/) for entrepreneurs. Then there are open free forums like Quora.com where people pose questions and answers for anyone to see. Many industries have their own forum somewhere, via a trade organization site or one run by some authority in the field.

If you want to become an expert on some place or subject, first figure out what needs to be known. Then when you have all the answers, you're at least halfway there. Now share them.

Following others' blogs

Similar to being active on message boards, most successful bloggers are those who are actively in touch with other bloggers. They have related blogs set up in their RSS streams or their Twitter feed, they read them, and they comment on posts that interest them. This does two things: it creates a link back to your own blog (a "no follow" one though, so don't overdo it) and it gets you on the radar of that blogger and his/her readers. People with like interests gravitate to each other. Successful bloggers make a tremendous number of valuable contacts through this simple action. Many of those bloggers become readers of what you are writing and they link to your work when they see something they think is notable. You can also share work on social media and give it a thumbs up on Reddit or Stumbleupon.

Like many of the best self-promotion methods, this is painless and free. As usual, just keep it reasonable—being annoying will have the opposite effect than the one you intended. Spending too much time on this and not enough on content creation becomes futile past a certain point.

Guest Posts

One surefire way to expand your profile and get a valuable link back to your site(s) is to write a guest post for someone else's blog. Sure this is another "writing for free" opportunity that some will frown upon, but it's a powerful tool. You preferably want to look up and not down when pitching a guest post to a blogger: aim for a site that has far higher traffic and more followers than your own.

Drawing from your expertise, craft a short article that's a great fit for that blog's readers—preferably in plain text or HTML to make it easy on the host. A guest post is often welcome because it saves the host a day of filling the blog with her own material and it provides an outside perspective. This action can create a valuable new inbound link or two (which helps your search engine positioning), bring in new subscribers, and help cement your status as an expert.

Very few bloggers take the time and effort to do this: I probably only average two or three legitimate requests a year for this, even though I run a blog that gets 80,000 unique readers a month. I also get very few requests to be featured on the blog associated with this book you're holding, even though it's clear that the format is to interview writers and editors about what's working for them.

Show some initiative and it's easy to stand out from the pack.

Email Marketing

Just as I said many bloggers spend way too much time on social media and not enough creating good content built to last, most of them also don't spend nearly enough time on building an e-mail list. I know bloggers who have 30,000 Twitter or Facebook followers and zero people on an e-mail list. That's just plain idiotic. An e-mail list you own. You don't own anything that's on a third-party platform like Instagram or Twitter. You're building a house on rented land.

As we've seen with Facebook, one algorithm change can cut the number of people who see your posts down to a tiny fraction of the total. With e-mail, on the other hand, typical open rates are between 20 and 35 percent. And people spend far more time reading an e-mail than they do reading individual social media posts. The click-through rates are also exponentially higher for the links contained there. Like 10 to 20 percent compared to click-through rates for Twitter of 0.05 percent and falling. Instagram doesn't even allow links except on your profile page, so click-through there is essentially zero.

Email offers the best way to intimately stay in touch with your readers or fans, in a medium where nearly everyone is paying attention. As I've heard several people say, nobody "catches up" on their social media after a vacation. They do plow through all their e-mails, though.

There are whole books and courses devoted to e-mail marketing, but here are the basic steps for bloggers or subject experts:

1) Offer a "lead magnet" or "ethical bribe" to your readers to get them to sign up to your list. This can be a special report, a checklist, an e-book, or something else digital, or it can be a big discount on something you sell. Or a chance to

participate in a big giveaway. Experiment and see what works.

2) At the least, send a thank you autoresponder that then sends them back to your website or blog. Better yet send a series of autoresponders that gets them familiar with you and maybe puts them into a sales funnel. Most e-mail newsletter programs like Mailchimp, Aweber, Benchmark, or Constant Contact offers the option to do this with any paid plan.

3) Send out a regular newsletter (frequency up to you) that highlights new posts, gives people useful information, and maybe has links to your products or has affiliate ads. If you're going to launch something, use this list to build anticipation and engage your fan base.

4) Keep repeating this process and guiding people to your sign-up page, possibly even using paid Facebook or Google ads to bump up your total numbers by reaching people who don't know you already.

I use a paid program called LeadPages that creates nice sign-up pages and lets you link to a signup box from text in your blog posts. If you don't have the budget for that, there are cheaper plug-in versions that aren't as robust, but will cover the basics.

I also use a plug-in that puts a bar at the top of each page with a newsletter signup link. Two of the best-known plug-ins for this are FooBar and WP Notification Bar. I've grown one list to more than 7,000 people in a year and a half just using that and LeadPages. You can go all-out and use a pop-up box, but be advised that will turn a lot of people off and make them leave your site. They may never come back. There are other options that are less intrusive, like boxes that fly in from the bottom after a certain amount of time or ones that pop up in the sidebar instead of covering up the content. Try OptIn Monster or PopUpAlly—the latter only pops up as people are about to leave. If you don't like those, search the WordPress site and look for ones described as "not annoying."

If you use the paid Feedblitz service for RSS and e-mail, you can also collect addresses that way and keep in touch in a more automated way. Those readers will get every blog post in their inbox or you can set up a weekly digest. You can also send a regular e-mail newsletter blast to them that's apart from what you're putting on your blog. See the Resources section for links.

Social media presence

I saved the most obvious one for last because there's a whole chapter on it following this section. Social media is a great weapon but also a loaded hand grenade. It's an easy—maybe too easy—way to communicate with a group of others at once. Some very successful writers I know pooh-pooh this whole phenomenon and think it reflects the decline of both the written word and civilization itself. Others think Twitter is the greatest invention since the microphone. They can't wait to get up in the morning and tell everyone who will listen what they ate for breakfast and what their cute kid said on the way to school.

Some have found a way to profit from this oversharing, getting thousands of visitors to their blog every day and turning that into enough income to fund their travels around the world. Some actually get paid to post to Instagram incessantly when they travel so the destination is in front of all those followers for a flash.

Others do nothing or close to it on these platforms and still get plenty of work writing for others. It's a powerful tool, but for most of us that's all it is—another tool.

As multi-millionaire business owner and small business coach Ramit Sethi says, "When was the last time you read someone's Twitter page, fell in love with them, and wrote them a check for $2,000? NEVER!"

I'm somewhere in the middle in this social media debate. Obviously I owe much of my success to blogging, but I try to write informative or entertaining posts that have lasting value instead of perishable drivel. I'm on all the major social platforms, but reluctantly for some of them. When I got to the point where I was spending more than a half hour a day on them—part of that from ad package obligations—I hired an assistant to take over much of the posting. That's because I've found anything over 20 to 30 minutes a day has a diminishing return. After that point, my time is better spent on high-value, high-leverage tasks that will earn me $60 or more an hour.

I can't tell you what will work for you, but for many people blogs are a proven moneymaker. Twitter, Facebook, Instagram, Vine, and whatever the next flavor of the year turns out to be are only moneymakers for an elite few.

In general they can be good networking tools and one or more may help you build a tribe of followers or connect with a few editors or key PR people. For others, it'll just waste time they could use instead to create something that people will still be reading a year from now. As a study quoted in *Wired* magazine said, "Media multitaskers are suckers for irrelevancy: We are training our brains to pay attention to the crap."

Use these tools as judiciously as you would any other time commitment and they can pay off if you have a plan and measurable metrics. Spend half your day on them because they distract you from real work, and it can be quite counter-productive. Remember, being busy isn't the same as getting things done.

Also remember that while Facebook, Twitter, and Pinterest seem invincible now, so did AOL, Yahoo, and Myspace at different times.

Put your most important work on sites you own, not on platforms that could fade away, go into decline, or make their privacy policies so invasive that they're practically committing identity theft. People often have compared social media platforms to a giant high school, so it's important to remember what happened to those most popular kids in your own high school 10 or 15 years down the line.

Remember, these social media platforms are a means to an end, not an end in themselves. As Jason Fried, founder of 37Signals, said in an *Inc.* interview, "It really bothers me that the definition of success has changed from profits to followers, friends, and feed count. This crap doesn't mean anything. If a restaurant served more food than anyone else but lost money on every diner, would it be successful? No."

Social media seems here to stay, and you ignore its potential at your own peril. Learn to leverage without a huge time commitment and you can accomplish great things. Read on for a more detailed breakdown.

A Whole Damn Chapter on Social Media?

Of course don't let sharing your work take precedence over actually doing your work. If you're having a hard time balancing the two, set a timer for 30 minutes. Once the timer goes off, kick yourself off the Internet and go back to work.

~ Austin Kleon in *Show Your Work*

It would look pretty strange to put out a book on travel writing in the digital age without talking a while about social media. It is hard to discuss blogging without discussing social media, since the two feed off each other so closely now.

Even if you're totally a freelancer, it's getting harder and harder to ignore the power of these platforms. After all, one in five pages viewed on the Internet in the U.S. is a Facebook page. Editors of online publications increasingly want to hire the writers with a following, those who will get the article in front of a wider audience.

> *The successful bloggers tell a story about the place rather than producing a log of their personal itinerary. Having said that, a whole lot of successful bloggers are just damn good at social media.*
> ~ Kristin Henning of TravelPast50.com

Social media costs very little beyond your time, has a huge 24/7 reach, and allows two-way conversations in most cases, so it can be a marketer's dream. Running a website or selling a product without taking advantage of these tools would be foolhardy, like working with one hand tied behind your back. Whether you're just launching a blog or trying to grow a six-figure business, social media is a powerful way to get eyes on your writing or sell a product or service.

At the risk of sounding like an old curmudgeon, though, most bloggers could stand to cut their social media time by 75% or more. They would make more money by spending that time on something more productive and lasting. For many people, social media is as addictive as meth and can be almost as destructive when it comes to their income and even relationships. When they don't get the dopamine rush of constant affirmation, they start displaying signs of an addict going through withdrawal. (Try being on an international press trip where there's more than eight hours without Internet access and watch how jittery some heavy social media users get.) Just as a drug high feels good but makes you less productive, the benefits of social media also come with a cost.

I see the power of these platforms and I use them regularly, but I also see the productivity-killing machines they can become. I've seen travel writers miss whole conversations—important ones— because they were looking down at the glow on their handheld screens, scrolling through messages from people an ocean away. I have blogger friends who have massive social media followings on multiple platforms but get fewer than 10,000 visitors a month to their blog. Where their real travel *writing* is. What's the point of that? They've lost sight of what would really change their life financially and are frittering away hours on content that's gone five minutes later.

"But it's free!" I can hear you objecting.

"But half my traffic is from Facebook!" someone else is probably thinking.

"But I got invited on two press trips because of my Instagram photos!"

Here's where the cost comes in. If you divide your earnings by time worked and you're making $40 an hour, then those three hours you just spent on social media came at a cost of $120 of your time. Was that worth it?

Considering that Twitter's click-through numbers are lower than one tenth of one percent and you're now lucky to reach 5% of your Facebook fans with any given status update, probably not. You could have spent $120 worth of your time writing a great guest post for a higher-traffic blog, doing keyword research that would increase traffic, or working on a great lead magnet that would grow your e-mail list.

If you studied microeconomics in university you learned about "opportunity costs," which always need to be factored in. If you could have spent those three hours working on a freelance article that would net you $250, you didn't just waste $120 of your time. You also gave up the *opportunity* of earning $250. Instead of a profit of $130 for those three hours, there's a loss of $370. Ouch! Still feel like you needed to post photos of your lunch and those selfies in front of the monument?

The key is to have a social media *strategy*, a plan for what you're trying to accomplish each time you go on. "To grow my followers" is not an objective, because your number of followers is just a vanity stat unless it's producing solid income on a repeatable basis. If you have 50,000 social followers but only 8,000 blog readers, you are clearly not reaching the right followers. If you have 100,000 social followers but made only $300 from your blog last month, then you are addicted to a very expensive hobby. Facebook, Pinterest, and other platforms can be a method for really accomplishing something, but you have to know what you're trying to accomplish for them to work.

I spend about 10 to 20 minutes a day on social media and outsource the rest. I have a terrific assistant in Mexico who works 10 hours a week for me at a cost of $6 per hour. Since an hour of my time doing real work that produces income is worth nearly 10 times that amount, it's a no-brainer. I use my time for the real "social" part of social media and let her do all the posting for my sites and my clients. Now keep in mind I'm a guy who runs five websites and blogs, so I have multiple accounts on each social platform. If you're just running one blog and your income isn't rising, here's the first place to start making adjustments in how you spend your money hours.

With that warning out of the way, let's look at how you can use these platforms to reach your goals and then figure out which ones can best get you there. In some ways it makes sense to have a presence on all the major platforms, but in reality it's difficult to be really active on more than a few. You have to prioritize according to what you're good at or what works.

What's Your Plan?

If your only goal is to get invited on press trips and you have sizable follower numbers, just keep pumping out the pics and updates. As the importance of social media grows for destinations and travel brands trying to sell a dream, those considered influencers on Twitter or Instagram will probably score more trips—even if they're terrible writers. Some of them even get paid a few hundred or thousand dollars for posting a brand's message or taking over a destination's Instagram account. So in the past few years this has become a valid monetization stream for a few at the top of the heap. For hot young travelers who love to post photos of themselves in skimpy bathing suits, the odds of this working increase quite a bit.

But sooner or later even those people who are getting paid for posts are going to realize they've got bills to pay and a future to plan for. Just being an iPhone photographer for hire probably isn't going to ever amount to enough to support a family and save for retirement except for the very elite few you hear about in breathy news stories. The big money (for now) is in content marketing programs and integrated programs where social media is just one element.

This view that social media is just another tool and that it can do more harm than good if it's a time-suck is blasphemy to some. It makes people who have earned a few bucks off social sharing to say I'm just out of touch. But everything I'm sharing is based on real stats, tests, research, and dollar counting, not on hunches and anecdotal evidence from a single blog. I've been publishing online since 2003 and have run seven websites and blogs in the years since.

Plus, I see the stats for all the bloggers in an ad alliance I run, which has had a couple dozen participants, from family bloggers to adventure bloggers to personality-based bloggers. I also get hired as a consultant and the first thing I do is look at the ratio of social followers to real readers. Often that's the first big red flag: I see what leads to real earnings and what doesn't.

Take a look at the following chart, with real numbers but the names removed. What sticks out to you in these stats? What do you notice?

	Twitter	Facebook	Instagram	E-mail Subscribers	Monthly Readers
Blog #1	10,400	1,200	1,400	400	3,900
Blog #2	16,000	10,500	14,500	300	6,800
Blog #3	39,000	5,200	3,900	450	11,500
Blog #4	21,000	6,000	4,400	250	13,500
Blog #5	22,500	6,500	3,400	6,200	58,000
Blog #6	7,000	1,600	750	8,200	80,000

If you've got a keen eye, you probably noticed that there's very little correlation between social numbers and real reader numbers in that chart above. The person with the crappiest social media following is the one that's getting the most traffic. I can also tell you that person is making more than $100,000 a year, too, and here's how I know: that person is me. Compared to most popular travel bloggers in the top 50 or 100 by traffic, my social numbers suck. But I'm okay with that because I'd rather have a lot of digits on my bank balance than a lot of digits on my vanity stats. I've focused on what gets real results financially.

The other thing to look at is what *does* seem to have a big impact: a sizable e-mail list. Besides the fact you own that list, instead of playing on rented land, the click-through rates for e-mail are exponentially higher than they are with any social media platform. The two blogs on that list with the most e-mail subscribers are the ones with the most true fans where it matters—on the blog.

The very top travel bloggers have gotten the balance right and are totally killing it on both ends.. They have developed a huge social following and built up a real reader base. Newbies often look at those two sides and jump to a causal relationship conclusion. Sometimes there is indeed one there, but more often that blogger built up huge traffic in other ways and the social following was a byproduct. They were on TV, they got quoted in major media articles, they did 30 guest posts in 30 days, or they just wrote really useful articles that nobody else was writing. So they show up high in search queries. Don't assume a causal relationship just based on what's in front of you. Sometimes the elements grew together organically, sometimes the person just got featured for months on Twitter as "Who to follow" and now they're on autopilot. The same can happen on Instagram, and that's gotten some early adopters to six digits on their follower numbers in a hurry. Yes, a few bloggers can credit much of their early growth to social media, so it's not always clear if the chicken or the egg came first. Just don't use social outreach as the easy crutch answer and ignore other work that may have more impact.

Look at the following and understand that yes, they can positively help your traffic and your business. They can drive some traffic, help launch a product and build up your network of colleagues. Work them hard, use them for all they're worth, but remember who's the boss. Switch to something with more leverage when you hit the inevitable point of diminishing return.

Facebook

You simply can't ignore a platform that gets an estimated 20% of all Internet traffic in the USA. Nearly half of all Europeans are active Facebook users and in the USA it's closing in on one-third. According to *Fast Company*, the average American aged 18 to 34 spends just 3.5 hours a month on Twitter and 7 hours on Instagram, but more than 25 hours a month on Facebook.

It's where you can find nearly all of your friends and followers. It's where the best group boards are and where people go to catch up on what the people they care about most are up to. If you're only going to be on one social platform, this is the one that makes the most sense for the most people.

The problem is, if you have a fan/business site in addition to your personal site (which you should if you ever hope to sell a blog or create multiple blogs), then your reach has likely declined quite a bit the past few years. It's now down to an average of 4% and will probably get worse. Facebook has become a Wall Street darling and is loved by Internet marketers because it is a very effective ad platform. If you're a business trying to reach people organically, that's a tough challenge. If more than one in ten followers sees a post you've put out, you're doing well. In a trend that's surely not a coincidence, however, if you advertise with Facebook your organic reach magically goes up as well.

You need to be on this platform, but I wouldn't spend more than 20 minutes a day on it unless you're doing that in your non-money hours just for fun. It sends some traffic, but click-through rates have been declining for years and will probably keep going down as people just look at pretty pictures and pass around silly Buzzfeed videos.

Facebook is great for keeping up with friends, but not very good at getting followers to come to your website. For that you'll need to advertise. Don't dismiss that option, though. Facebook ads can be incredibly effective and targeted if you have a specific goal, such as building up your e-mail list, getting eyeballs on a contest you're paid to run, selling a course, or announcing a book launch.

There's also a secondary use of Facebook, which LinkedIn promises, but doesn't deliver very well: business networking. In a field like ours where business and pleasure mix so readily, some of your Facebook friends inevitably end up being business colleagues as well. If you're friends—even virtual ones—that person is much more likely to answer your calls or e-mails, or you can actually message them.

> *So many of my editors from my New York days are Facebook friends who have been at five different magazines since we worked together a decade ago. Each time, they've taken me with them on each career move, so being visible online has enabled me to write for a host of different outlets due to the nature of the industry and its revolving doors.*
>
> ~ Kristin Luna

Pinterest

If you ask me which platform is most deserving of your time and has the most untapped potential, this is the one I'd say to focus on. Unlike the "here now, gone a minute later" nature of Facebook, Instagram, and Twitter, a Pinterest pin lasts forever. It sits there on your boards and other people's boards with a link back to your site, sending visitors over and over for years. You can ignore her for two weeks and she won't get upset—she'll keep sending you traffic.

The other advantage of Pinterest is that it functions like a search engine, with people looking for photos on a certain subject or certain keywords. Like Google it serves up relevant results to people already interested in that subject. Hashtags don't matter; context does.

Across my network of websites and blogs, Pinterest sends two to four times more traffic than Twitter, despite far more time and effort going into the latter. For some sites it sends more traffic than Facebook too, again with much less effort. While the other platforms generate a lot of noise, Pinterest actually sends readers, which can directly impact your earnings.

Instagram

While Pinterest has less buzz and fewer users than Instagram, it can fatten your bank account. For most bloggers, Instagram will just fatten your ego. There's only one link from it, in your profile (which nobody looks at except when they can't remember why they started following you). So people breeze through, liking pretty photos, and...that's it. There's no call to action, nothing for them to do except leave a comment.

Then there are the people who *do* get paid and some of them get paid a lot. If you want to ramp up a following that will generate cash, this is the social media platform of choice. You'll need big numbers and big engagement though, in general at least 20,000 followers but more like 50,000 and lots of comments and likes.

I get the appeal of Instagram, especially for visual brands and destinations. Since destinations and some brands love it, you can't ignore it either. When you're on that press trip to Norway or Namibia, they're going to expect to see lots of Instagram posts with hashtags. If you sell an ad package to a brand that cares a lot about their image, Instagram will probably be in the mix. Not as much as you might think, though. I've done large integrated campaigns with two car rental companies, a hotel booking company, a hotel chain, a travel insurance company, and three gear brands. None of them has cared much about Instagram, and two of those didn't even have an account. Only a few small tour companies and hotels have mentioned it. For others though, it's the core of their social strategy.

Some bloggers are making real money from being influential on this platform. As in they're getting paid thousands of dollars to post photos that feature a brand or destination. It gets even richer in the fashion and food worlds. Unless you have a huge following, however, Instagram is just another tool that can turn into an obsessive time suck and dopamine rush you get addicted to.

So sign up and spend some time on Instagram if you're not active already, but don't waste a lot of time on it if it takes away from more productive tasks. Upload a photo and like some others while you're having lunch alone or waiting in line at the bank. Obviously forget everything I've said if you are an Instagram star getting paid for that influence specifically, if you are a professional photographer, or if you are able to monetize your photos in other ways. That's not "travel writing" or even "blogging" in the sense of putting sentences together; however. It's photo posting and hashtag typing for hire.

If you're a travel writer, posting selfies in front of travel scenes probably isn't going to result in bigger checks unless you're always posing in a bikini. Put the phone down and pay attention to what the guide is saying instead so you can write a better story!

Twitter

Twitter is a marketer's dream come true because it allows you to initiate a relationship with your customer. It's the only platform where you can jump into a conversation unannounced and nobody will think you're a stalker.

~ Gary Vaynerchuck in *Jab, Jab, Jab, Right Hook*

A lot of time you'll hear Internet marketers saying things like, "I almost left my wife for Twitter" or "If Twitter went away I might shrivel up and die." People who love to express their thoughts and share what they've just discovered in 140-character bursts are downright obsessed with this platform. For most travel writers and bloggers, it's incredibly inefficient if your goal is to drive traffic to your website or blog. The click-through rate is less than one-tenth of one percent, meaning that if you have 1,000 followers, you're doing well if even one of them clicks on that link you put in your Tweet. Despite all the effort most people put into Twitter, the direct payoff is minimal.

So why does everyone keep at it? Because it's easy, and free, and let's be real—it's fun. Twitter is like a giant water cooler where you can gather and chat, showing everyone how well-read you are, or how clever, or what you thought of that movie you just saw, or how great this destination is that you're currently checking out. You can give a shout-out to anyone or ask for a meeting, even if they have no idea who you are.

But if you worked in the corporate world, how much time each day did you spend at a real water cooler, just shooting the shit with your colleagues? Use that as a guide for how much time you should probably spend on Twitter. Yeah I know, someone will always say they got a writing gig through there, or a press trip invite, or found the perfect source for an article. But out of how many hours spent, week after week? Couldn't you have accomplished the same thing if you just spent more time pitching and connecting by other means, like the good ol' telephone?

I have more Twitter followers than I have on other platforms, so I obviously don't think it's useless. I've sent out thousands of tweets, after all. The main reason I like it so much, however, is that I can spend two or three minutes on there and get something accomplished. When I'm eating lunch or waiting in the security line at the airport, for instance. Just as with a real water cooler though, then it's time to move on and get some real work done.

Ignore all this if you're a mommy blogger who gets paid five grand for running a Twitter chat about laundry detergent or you've got 200,000 followers and you get paid $100 for a sponsored tweet. Then it's a revenue stream for not much work, so take it.

Google+

The social platform that almost everyone loves to hate on has been through a lot of changes in its short life. Many of its early benefits for bloggers got yanked soon after they started to work too well—for us, not for Google. This platform either will be slightly larger in a few years or yet another service killed off by Google.

I personally enjoy spending time on G+ more than Facebook because it's a whole lot prettier to look at. It isn't so buggy and it doesn't hog so many resources on my computer. I also like how every "friend" doesn't have to be treated equally and the platform lets me choose who's an acquaintance and who's a close friend (instead of Facebook deciding that through some algorithm.)

The main reason you should be on it is kind of obvious, though, if you just look at the name. There's clear evidence that blog posts get indexed faster after being posted on G+ and plenty of speculation that all things being equal, something posted several times there will rank better in search than something that doesn't appear on that platform at all. Sometimes the G+ entry about a new blog post will show up higher in search than the actual post. If "social signals" are a ranking factor for Google, there's little doubt they're going to put more stock in the social signals they can dive into in detail because they own the data.

Brands that are heavily focused on SEO, rather than what's beautiful and shiny, tend to care more about G+ than they do about Twitter or Instagram when they're setting up some kind of integrated sponsorship campaign. Others, however, ignore it completely and may not even have an account.

Like all of these, I wouldn't spend more than 10 minutes a day on G+ and for most people 5 minutes is enough. Put new posts there, share things you like now and then, give a +1 or comment to others. With so little effort required to be active on it, Google+ is, if nothing else, a good insurance policy.

YouTube

Like G+, this platform is owned by Google, but unlike that one, it's massively popular. You can put a video up on Vimeo or other platforms and a few people will watch it, but if you put something on YouTube and it goes viral, then millions of people could see it. Most of us aren't going to see that happen, but video is a powerful platform for travel content and some bloggers have leveraged YouTube to build up a fan base and leapfrog over a lot of other bloggers writing similar things. Especially if you're appealing to a very young demographic, the time spent on shooting and editing videos can really pay off.

If you're not dedicated to becoming a regular on here, it's still worthwhile to shoot some video now and then for several reasons. First of all, the PR people love it, so you'll get some brownie points with that destination, tour, or hotel person. Second, there's a clear SEO value from having a video on YouTube that points back to your site in the description. Sometimes you can toil away for years trying to get your blog on the first page of Google for a certain keyword phrase with no success, then you post a video with the same keywords and two weeks later Google has put it at #5. Last, if you do any kind of "how to" content or you have some kind of product to sell, YouTube can be a great channel for making a pitch, explaining something, demonstrating something, or providing bonus material.

YouTube can enable you to connect with your audience in a way no other platform can. By seeing your face or at least hearing your voice as a narrator, your connection becomes much stronger.

Some people build up such a large following on here that they get paid handsomely to talk about products. As with the other examples mentioned in this section though, those people are the exceptions, not the norm. The rest of us just make a few cents off Adsense and use it as a branding tool or traffic driver.

Stumbleupon

This social platform is so under-the-radar with most people that it didn't even get mentioned in Gary Vaynerchuck's excellent *Jab, Jab, Jab, Jab, Right Hook* book—the best book I've seen on how to do social media right. The people that do use it—including me—swear it's sometimes more effective than all the others added together. "Sometimes" is the key word, though, because on Stumbleupon things sometimes send 10,000 new readers and sometimes they send 3. It's really hard to predict which story will do which. But considering it'll take you about 20 minutes to set up and less than five minutes a week to look active on, Stumbleupon is a no-brainer.

Just treat it like a slot machine you would walk past every week, feed a few quarters into, and move on. Some weeks you'll lose all your quarters. But one week you'll hit the jackpot. When you hit that jackpot, you'll get more traffic that week from this service than you did from Twitter over the course of months.

LinkedIn

This is the B2B social platform, the one you use to collect virtual business cards and reach out to people you want in your circle. Ideally it would be a place to keep your colleagues up to date on what you're doing and stay in touch with people whom you've worked with, but aren't really friends with. It would also be an ideal place for business groups around a certain topic. Unfortunately, none of that has really come to pass. The groups always seem to get overrun by spammers and only recruiters seem to average more than a few minutes a month on here.

Most people aren't really sure what to do with their LinkedIn membership unless they're selling something or hiring someone. There's a book that came out a good while ago called *I'm on LinkedIn, Now What?* In a sign of how much people care about the answer, the associated blog had an Alexa ranking of only 1.5 million as this book went to press.

Reddit

This social network/message board for geeks and those with very specific interests can be a boon to those who dive in and participate fully. I'm not one of those, so every once in a while I'll see a burst of traffic from there that I had nothing to do with. It's because somebody liked something I wrote and posted it to a group. If enough people gave it a thumbs up, then it became something that sent traffic for days and brought in a few new fans. The people on Reddit are an unforgiving bunch, though, and don't like to put up with hard-sell types. Only join a sub-group there if you're really passionate about the subject and you can talk about something other than yourself in an intelligent manner.

Vine, Periscope, Blab, and Meerkat

There are lots of other social platforms that can be effective, but if you're active on all of them then you've got no time left to do what you're supposedly reading this book to do: be a travel writer. These less-used tools and platforms can be effective for the right objective, so if you see a good match at least experiment. Vine is for short videos (which you can also do on Instagram), Periscope, Blab, and Meerkat are for live streaming, If you have a rabid fan base, or something to sell, one of these could be effective for your audience. There may be 12 more by the time you read this.

This is probably going to be a big deal in the future after all the kinks are worked out and everyone has always-on, superfast mobile Internet. We're not really there yet as I write this, and unless you're a celebrity, these services don't scale very well for now.

Snapchat

All the rage with teens who don't want Mom to see their messages, this platform is making inroads with some bloggers as well. Everything you post disappears in 24 hours, though. Do I really need to say more than that?

Tumblr and Flickr

Tumblr is kind of a mix between Instagram and a blog. Flickr is the original photo sharing tool. Both of these are owned by Yahoo. Seek out experts and articles on best practices to learn more because I am not one them.

Quora

I'm not sure whether to call this a social platform or a message board, but it's a good place to hang out if you want to communicate with a specific tribe. People come on here to get questions answered and if you're an expert, you can chime in and start building up a following. If you're a book author or are planning to be one, some time on here will be a gold mine for researching what people are talking about and what the obstacles are in a specific subject area. If you're trying to establish a tribe and become the master of a certain niche, you're sure to find some of your target audience people here.

What happens if you just do the minimum on some or most of these? If I add the traffic for all of my sites together, including group blogs with lots of others spreading the word, social traffic rarely tops one-third of the total. The percentage is just slightly higher than the combination of RSS, e-mail, and direct referral traffic. Search, on the other hand, brings in 50% to 70% of the traffic depending on the site. So all these platforms can bring in readers, but they're just one subset of the total—generally not the largest one even.

> *The disturbing trend of online and social media persona counting for more than actual quality is a major frustration lately. I'm consistently amazed—perhaps saddened is a better word—by what I see when I occasionally skim through the actual (written) content by some very well-regarded writers/bloggers. It makes me wonder whether I should just stop what I'm doing, create a catchy name for myself and for my blog, go social media crazy, post tons of splashy photos, and end all of my sentences with exclamation marks.*
>
> ~ Brian Spencer, freelance writer

If search is not contributing at least half of your traffic, you're probably not writing very search-worthy material. So you might want to spend more time on great content that answers questions or solves problems instead. Then when you spread the word it'll be for things worth sharing.

Use social media, make the most of it, ride it for all it's worth. But do it in a way that won't suck up a lot of your real content production time.

After you've written unique articles that get praise and attention and you've built up a following on social media, it's time to order that mai tai. Now that you've gotten through 200 pages of work, it's time to talk about the rewards.

Perks and Profit

As many a travel writer will say, "The money sucks, but the perks are great."

Let's be real—this is why many otherwise frustrated writers stick with it. If they stopped writing, they would be forced to travel less. And they would travel in a different way if they had to pay for every aspect of every trip themselves. Goodbye pampering resort, hello Motel 6.

Working as a travel writer and having some success at it leads to that list of perks the come-on travel writing seminars tout so loudly: free flights, free hotel rooms, nice dinners, and then a big tax write-off for expenses you still end up footing yourself.

The line between "free" and "business expense" is a blurry one though, so it's not really free if you're working the whole time instead of enjoying the experience as much as you would on vacation. It's not uncommon for a travel writer to be working for 12 hours straight for days on end, running around fact-checking and typing on a laptop while everyone around them is kicking back and having fun. It's not uncommon for press trip itineraries to start at 8 a.m. and not finish until after a late dinner.

Still, a week working on a Caribbean island beats a week behind a desk any day, so most writers bitch a lot but keep doing it.

People perceived as "influencers" get lots of perks, so become one and you get showered. That's true whether you are a fashion writer getting clothes, a music writer getting concert tickets, or a golf writer puttering a cart down a new course each week. In an ironic twist, it's also true for rich celebrities, who get much of what they wear and use without paying anything.

Personally, I'm fine with all this, but be aware that some people aren't, including the editors at some traditional media outlets. Always be aware of how these offerings and their influence on your writing will be perceived. If you're a shill for hire and are not honest in your writings as a result of what you have received, you may not be taken seriously as a writer—or a person.

I feel that a travel writer on assignment is compromised in so many ways already that the various "truth in travel" variations on a slogan are mere marketing no matter what. Whether the magazine is paying your expenses or the tourism board is paying your expenses doesn't make much difference in the end. Either way, it's not coming out of *your* pocket. Plus you're not going to see a scathing negative hotel review make it past the editor either way. Good luck finding any kind of investigative journalism or muckraking in the travel press from any publication that depends on advertising from the industry to make a living. "Don't bite the hand that feeds you" is a maxim for survival no matter who is paying your bar bill.

So I have no qualms about going on press trips (also called "fam trips"—for "familiarization") or accepting hosting from airlines, hotels, or tourism boards. Most readers of my articles or books would have a really hard time figuring out which trips were sponsored and which were paid for by the publication. Or which ones I paid for myself while on vacation. If you possess things like morals, ethics, and a conscience, it's usually not much of an issue. There are terms for writers who don't possess these things: they're generally referred to as hacks, whores, or shills. Try not to be one of these.

It's hard to turn down any offer that starts with, "We would like to fly you to..." but sometimes you have to take a breath and say no. Free travel is a beautiful thing, but remember that you're trying to be a writer that earns money, not a prostitute who writes.

If we are talking about financially successful writers and bloggers then pretty much all of them that I am aware of are people who found a niche and served it tirelessly, as opposed to someone willing to write about whatever press trips they are offered. Also, it's a lot easier to make money when you write about a reader's potential trip as opposed to writing about the writer's recent trip.

~ Roger Wade of PriceOfTravel.com and
OverwaterBungalows.net

The Pros and Cons of Press Trips

"I really have no patience for RUDE journalists! I don't care how many million subscribers, you have! Rudeness is unnecessary!"

That was what a PR person posted for a thousand of her Twitter followers to see after I sent an impatient reply to her e-mail one day. I'm generally not known as a guy who is hard to get along with, but the exchange had gotten testy for a good reason.

Here's the preceding message from her, what had caused me to get ticked off enough to be rude.

"I want to let you know that if [nearby Mexican resort area] is going to be a piece of your story—then I can probably tell you that we won't be able to help with airfare, just because if [the resort area I represent] sponsors it, they won't want to be mentioned in the same article as [that other nearby resort area]."

I replied that it seemed a bit ridiculous to make that demand considering that every single guidebook already lumped the whole region together anyway, both areas are served by the same airport, and, really, um, are you kidding me?! I had offered this person five confirmed media placements and she was worried about whether I might mention her client's kid sister to the south. I ended up scrapping all five assignments—plus the multiple blog entries that would also have come out of the trip—and packed my bag for another destination instead.

This is just one example of the kind of ethical minefield you navigate in travel journalism. Just putting "travel" and "journalism" in the same sentence is in itself a minefield. Let's face it: if you were a real journalist you would be working for a news organization covering night court battles, garbage worker strikes, political corruption, or school board elections. Instead you're covering what people do with a week or two of leisure time. That's akin to writing about movies, celebrities, music, TV shows, or designer furniture. With skill you can make it verbal art worth reading, but it's not going to win you a Pulitzer Prize for great journalism.

The person who writes the exposé on the amount of garbage your average cruise ship generates or the amount of electricity wasted by your average luxury hotel is not going to get a lot of future assignments from the travel industry press. No matter how

many "truth in travel" or "honest recommendation" proclamations
the travel magazines and newspaper sections may put in their
slogans, they are clearly a mouthpiece for the industry. An always-
positive mouthpiece. (Yeah I know, they do gripe about the airlines
sometimes, but only about economy class. Most of the ads in their
pages are for business or first class. So the implicit message is, "Just
upgrade you cheapskate!")

There's a very good reason you don't see scathing negative
hotel reviews or stories about disappointing trips in these
publications. Their goal is to sell a fantasy that their advertisers will
love. Every trip is wonderful. Every place is fantastic. A place may
have been bad in the past, but now it is "on the rise" or "the place to
go this year." Free trips or not, there is no room for real honesty in
most travel publications, especially in the print world where so
much revenue is at stake. If Celebrity Cruises is paying you
$100,000 an issue for their ad placements, do you really want to run
a feature story on how cruise ships are hotbeds for viruses and food
poisoning? If Marriott is essentially paying you your nice editor's
salary, are you really going to green-light a funny story about how
the Marriott rooms in Lima have the same bedspreads as the
Marriott rooms in Los Angeles and Lisbon? Of course not. It's
career suicide. Leave that to the bloggers. They've got nothing to
lose.

Still, spend any time on any kind of travel writing message
boards and you will find heated arguments about the ethics of
accepting freebies, especially in the U.S. I find this really comical
since you almost never see the same arguments coming from people
who write about music, cars, golf, movies, spirits, wine, or fashion.
They don't think twice about getting everything they write about for
free and being wined and dined on a regular basis. "What, you
expect me to pay for all this myself? Out of my income? No way,
it's my *job*!"

When I worked for RCA Records in Nashville and New York, I
had more than a few party-til-dawn crazy nights with music writers
from the likes of *Rolling Stone* and the *New York Times*. I'm talking
limos, backstage parties, free-flowing cocktails, and drugs I'd never
seen before and haven't seen since. More than once, the bastard
would still write about how crappy our band was on stage that night.
But hey, it was publicity and nobody expected that writer to

suddenly love our overhyped band just because he was licking some kind of elicit powder off a model's tummy and got a limo ride to the show. It was the relationship that mattered. We wanted his attention on a regular basis and we got it. He had a good time and always returned our calls.

For some reason though, in travel there are more than a few holier-than-thou editors and self-appointed ethical experts who feel that no travel writer can get a free hotel room night without it clouding his judgment, that nobody can write honestly about a destination if someone from the destination covered her plane ticket to get there.

In my 22 years of experience, this just isn't supported by the reality of what gets printed. I once got so annoyed with someone who took this stance that I sent her 20 of my hotel reviews for a certain city and challenged her to determine which hotels had hosted me and which ones I had simply toured and reviewed without staying. She flunked miserably, getting one of the hosted ones right out of five and guessing that four had put me up that really had not.

This attitude is fading fast due to budget issues though, so fewer and fewer editors now take such a hard line. Overall this is a good thing for writers, but it demands a level of professionalism and honesty some newbies just haven't acquired yet.

Press trips and hosted stays are probably as old as travel writing itself. Just look at the marketing value of "George Washington slept here!" or "As seen in The Odyssey!" The first thing I would do if I opened a new hotel would be to put together a list of travel writers I wanted to invite. It's far cheaper and more effective than getting the word out through advertising. Destinations with huge budgets put a lot of money into bringing writers in on press trips and destinations with tiny budgets still do everything they can to at least get writers in the area involved in getting them some press.

If you've ever wondered why you suddenly see a place like Dubai, Namibia, or Jordan featured in seemingly every publication you pick up, here's why: they spent a lot of money luring in writers and they spent a lot of money advertising in the big magazines to influence them to send their own writers. (Sometimes this is a clear tit-for-tat arrangement, sometimes it's more subtle, but over time you'll see a clear correlation between the advertising and the editorial coverage in most large magazines.)

If you're honest and a good writer, it shouldn't matter whether the magazine paid, the tourism bureau paid, or you paid. Some people aren't honest though, and some are just whores. They'll write anything the hosting company wants them to write. It'll be a boring story, everything will be flattering, and there will be very little conflict or depth. This is what gives rise to the derogatory term "press trip story."

> *I recently had a completely upsetting lunch sitting next to a couple who consider themselves so wildly successful as food/luxury travel writers because of the number of 'free trips' they get to simply write about it in their own blog--which generates no income on its own. If you just want to write positive, glowing reviews of the places you go, be a copywriter for the industry clients. It pays a hell of a lot better.*
>
> ~ Shelly Rivoli of TravelsWithBaby.com

On the other hand, if you're a skilled writer who speaks the truth, you can still get a great story out of a press trip, provided it's not crammed tight with irrelevant stops and there's at least a smidgen of free time to go get some color and some quotes. I've won multiple writing awards from stories that have come out of press trips or individually sponsored trips, more than I've won from situations where I paid my own way, frankly. Many successful writers I have hired over the years as an editor can say the same.

The key to making this work and to retain some integrity is to find a real angle. What would you write about no matter who is paying? What aspect really interests you personally? Where's the personal connection to your background or history—or that of your travel companion or family that is along? What story can you tell that nobody else has told before?

If you can write great articles from your trips that are genuine and you enjoy the hosted travel, there's a way for everyone to win. I can only remember one PR person chiding me for writing something honest; they have mostly only complained about factual errors. For the writers who can strike the right balance, there can be a long string of fabulous trips they may not have been able to ever afford on their own.

> *I was just able to take a week-long trip that was worth about $10,000, totally free because of my blog. My cash income from my blog may be low, but experiences like that trip are so worth it to me.*
> ~ Lillie Marshall of .AroundTheWorldl.com

Press Trips and Online Media

Once upon a time, press trips were a simple affair. Public relations people and CVB (convention and visitors bureau) people knew exactly who to invite. They made a few calls to their A list (magazine editors and major newspaper editors), they then made a few calls to their B list (reliable freelancers and newsletter editors), and the invite list was done. Later as staff positions dried up and some publications got all high and mighty about appearing to be neutral, freelancers got more invites.

Then everything turned upside down when new media took over. As newspapers became irrelevant in the travel world and some blogs started pulling in more readers than your average print magazine, some (but still not all) travel tourism people started to wise up. They invited multi-outlet influencers instead of print editors with a specific circulation and they saw a flood of new visitors to their websites. A year later, they were still getting press out of it. They started inviting personalities with a huge social media reach too, knowing this would send more visitors to their own feeds.

Now that many websites have far more impact on where people go and where they stay than print publications ever did, public relations people are struggling and flailing when putting together their lists. They know that some writers have a much bigger influence than others, but it's harder to measure when you don't have easy benchmarks like circulation numbers and full-page ad values.

There are still benchmarks, of course, but they are different. Now it's about traffic, Alexa rank, search engine positioning, inbound links, Moz rank, "follower" numbers, and engagement. Obviously this is more complicated and takes more effort to research, but in the end the criteria are the same. How much influence does this person have on the right kind of potential travelers? How many people read what this person has to say?

Some people are shoo-ins and they get more press trip invites than they can ever accept. Magazine editors, famous bloggers, and freelancers that are regulars at top-tier magazines or websites have to pick and choose which trips they will accept. Fortunately I'm in that category myself now, but wasn't until new media started becoming a force that couldn't be ignored. Up to about early 2008, I'd frequently see press trip invites with a qualifier that I needed to have an assignment from "a print publication with a circulation over 100,000." Never mind that I could get an assignment from a website that reached four or five times that many people every month and the article would keep generating clicks for years. Or that my own blog reached 50,000 people and I had complete editorial control. I'd get turned down in favor of a writer from a mid-market newspaper that nobody under 60 was reading anymore.

When I surveyed writers in preparing this book, some listed one of their big frustrations as trip invites that are conditional upon acceptance from an outlet that meets the organizer's criteria. "It's often hard finding additional outlets, including print or online sites, with circulation or traffic sufficient to qualify me for inclusion on press trips." Says Debra Dunning Brouillette. One time that challenge worked out especially well though. "I started an online tropical travel column on Examiner.com in 2009. From contacts I made in requesting information for posts, I was invited on a press trip that required a print assignment. I sent e-mail pitches to two newspapers. One was accepted, and I was able to go on the trip. I still freelance for that newspaper."

Some writers struggle to get onto any press trip at all, anywhere. Their freelance assignments are all over the map and each time they have to query anew with a story idea—along with everyone else trying to get an assignment for the same trip. Or they write for some small newspaper or website with very few readers and the people paying for the trip feel the press payoff isn't sufficient. Remember, this is at heart a business transaction. The publicity you will generate must have a value greater than what the host is laying out in expenses. Otherwise, it doesn't add up.

Most travel writers who have been at this for any length of time fall somewhere in between. If they've found a good niche they'll get invited on trips that tie in nicely. If they have a track record at specific publications or blogs that matter, they'll get invited on trips fairly regularly.

Sponsorship and Individual Hosting

For the sake of the story, being hosted on an individual basis is far preferable to a group press trip. In this arrangement the host covers some or all expenses and/or a hotel hosts you because you are writing about them. Your schedule is your own and you have plenty of time to do real research, focusing on just your angle(s).

Besides the whole ethical quandary this potentially raises with the hosting, there's the problem that the hosting company or person may still feel completely justified in monopolizing your time and controlling parts of your schedule. In *Smile While You're Lying*, Chuck Thompson says, "One of the problems with accepting comps at swanky resorts is that you end up paying for them with dinners so boring they leave you wanting to scrape your own face off with a souvenir conch shell."

Most narrative feature writers cringe at the idea of a group press trip, being herded around in a van and having everything served up on a fast-moving itinerary. They much prefer to get part of the trip covered, like airfare and some hotel nights, and then have a loose schedule that allows more exploration and interviewing. In these cases it's not a matter of an invite landing in an e-mail box, but rather the writer proposing an individual trip to the right tourism bureau contact or commercial enterprise.

Some writers have success with a third way: going on a group press trip, but tacking a few extra days on the end for individual research. In many cases your contact will go along with this, especially if all that's required is a different date on the plane ticket and you're on your own for expenses on the extra days.

Be advised that individual hosting requires a solid assignment (you may be asked for an assignment letter from an editor), a blog or site with major traffic, or a great track record that shows you will deliver. No tourism bureau person wants to lay out a thousand dollars or more on a risky bet. They want a sure thing. If you can deliver many sure things—as in four or five articles from that one trip—even better. They'll be happy to hear from you again in the future.

Keep in mind that individual hosted trips may mean more money out of your own pocket. Group ones are not really "free" either unless you're a total moocher. You'll need to bring money for tips, for starters, and the higher up the luxury scale you go the higher those tips need to be for your driver, guide, masseuse, and bellhop. And yes, sometimes you'll need to make your way somewhere on your own or—egads!—find your own transportation from the airport.

How to Get In On This Action

If you do want to go on press trips—and there are a lot of very good reasons to avoid them remember—it is largely out of your hands. Most writers who go on these hosted trips are invited. That's the key word—"invited." Lists of who is going are often filled out before anyone else gets wind that a trip is even happening. The higher the price tag, the higher the standards. So a regional food festival you can drive to may be easy to get in on. A luxury safari tour to Africa? Much, much tougher.

Sometimes it just seems like blind luck and a lot of it does come down to relationships, but overall the writers invited on press trips are invited because they can deliver an audience that is attractive to the person laying out the money. If the writer's work isn't worth more than the cost to host them, they usually won't be on the list.

So the best way to get invited on trips is to make a name for yourself in one of two ways. The first is to own a niche, meaning you can deliver a very targeted readership. If you have the highest-ranking website for dude ranches in the American West, you're pretty likely to get invites to dude ranch press trips (but not much else, unfortunately). If you are known as the person who gets the most articles published about Croatia, you shouldn't have any problem getting on the list for trips to Croatia.

The other way is to get known for delivering, whatever the subject may be. This goes back to that idea of getting other things published in a variety of outlets. I've been invited to Iceland, South Africa/Botswana, Thailand, Colombia, Honduras, Guatemala, Panama, British Columbia, Hungary, and a bunch of places in the US and Mexico—for a start. What did they have in common? Next to nothing. Out of those trips have come articles for dozens of publications with a wide variety of slants. In most cases, I delivered three or four different pieces from each trip. The PR people loved me, I made a bit of money on my side for the investment in time, and for the most part I managed to put out work I was proud of. I had a blast too. So when writers pooh-pooh press trips as never lending themselves to a good story, I can point to my experience and say, "Well, it depends..."

Now I don't have much trouble getting onto trip lists and if I call with a proposal for a custom individual trip, I can usually get something worked out—assuming there's any money there in the budget and the PR person is not some ditzy recent college grad who doesn't know which way is up. Neither is always a given, so understand that sometimes you will not be hosted in the place you want to go, no matter how much you plead and how big the opportunity may be.

When there's no money, there's no money. This is especially true for airfare, which these days must usually be paid for out of the tourism bureau's budget. Most airlines are incredibly stingy now and they know they are so hated by consumers that they don't even bother trying to get positive press anymore. So, if you can pay to fly there yourself (with money or frequent flyer miles) or if the place is in driving distance, you'll find the tourism board people to be much more receptive to your requests.

If you're a general travel blogger with a big verified audience or someone with a crazy huge social media following, the slant becomes almost immaterial. You will get invited or hosted just because the hosting company or destination wants to reach lots of eyeballs. They want big numbers to put on a report and you're an easy way to get those numbers.

So how would those requests work out—how do you approach it? I get this question a lot, so here's a sample letter you can modify to suit your needs. The idea of this is to show, in no uncertain terms, what you can deliver. Crass as it may be, this is a business transaction. They give you something, you give them something, and hopefully everyone is happy.

Typical Hosted Individual Trip Proposal

Dear Key Contact,

I am a freelance travel writer who has contributed to xxx, yyy, and zzz and I am interested in visiting [location] to write a story about [angle] for [publication]. [Information on why this area appeals to you, your connection with it.]

I would be interested in coming [time frame] for x days and would like to explore [explanation of suitable activities].

To put this story together, I am looking for press hosting in terms of [list what is needed such as airfare from your city, hotel nights, admission tickets, and meals]. I expect to place [list expected story length and publication(s)].

I am open to suggestions on making this story great and look forward to your input.

You can see a sampling of other things I have written at [insert portfolio site] and I would be glad to discuss specifics on the phone at your convenience.

I look forward to visiting [location] and sharing my experience with [circulation/monthly visitor number] readers [and if applicable, add social reach.]

Name and phone number

The more details you can reasonably supply the better. If this is just for a single outlet, say so. But if there's potential for more and you'll send 20 social media updates, include that information as well

There are several potential outcomes to this e-mail. The first is that you are ignored. In that case you should follow up by e-mail in a week then by phone after that to see if they are ignoring you, if the answer is no, or if the e-mail never made it through. You can't assume it's any of those without any feedback.

The second outcome is that you are denied. Try to find out why, because it may be the publication, it may be you, or it may be a lack of money in the budget.

The third is a maybe, dependent on you fulfilling some other requirement (such as an assignment letter), changing your dates, spending less time there, or staying at the state park lodge instead of the Ritz Carlton.

The best outcome is a yes, and then you start working out the details. If you get a yes, make sure both of you are clear on what will be provided. After the trip, stay in touch and be sure you come through with your end of the deal. This doesn't mean writing that everything is lovely when it's really not and ignoring every urge to make a negative observation. As long as you're honest and your comments are based in fact, you can't get criticized for negativity. What it does mean is that you deliver on what you promised. Get the story done and get it published.

I take pride in the fact I have *never* gone on a trip or accepted some kind of hosting that didn't result in at least one story placement. To me, taking a hosted trip without delivering any press is just plain slimy and there are very few cases where that writer who didn't keep up his end of the bargain can be considered anything other than a moocher. Even if that magazine you were writing for went under or the newspaper canceled its assignment after the fact, you should not let that story go. There are plenty of other outlets that will publish your story—if the angle is any good. So hunt around and find one, regardless of the pay. Rework the slant if necessary. Otherwise you will lose respect and get blacklisted in a hurry. Just as travel writers talk amongst themselves, so do PR agency people and visitors bureau publicity directors. If you're seen as a taker and not a giver, you're going to have a tough time in the future.

When you do get invited, act like a responsible and empathetic adult. Don't be a demanding prima donna. Show up on time. Take notes. Don't get so drunk on free booze that you make a complete ass of yourself and embarrass your host. Be professional. Word gets around quickly if you're not.

Tax breaks

One of the clear perks of travel writing, if you do it right, is that you get major tax benefits by being able to deduct expenses from your trips. First a disclaimer: I'm no accountant. The tax laws are in constant flux, so consult a professional before acting on any of the deductions advice in this section and don't take my word as gospel.

The general guideline for deducting business expenses are that there needs to be a clear connection between the expenses and an expectation of making an income from the action of incurring those expenses. The expenses cannot be deducted in pursuit of a hobby.

For many, travel writing *is* a hobby. There is no logical way they will make more in income from their travels than they spend on the travels—ever. The IRS will give you the benefit of the doubt for a time, but after that you need to show a profit. For it to be considered a real business, you are expected to have made a profit in three of the last five years.

This means you could lose a fortune for a couple of years, net a few hundred dollars annually the next three years, and you're legit. Keep losing money every year, however, and you are not a professional for tax purposes. Deducting expenses in that kind of situation could invite an audit. The pursuit eventually needs to look like a business and not just something you do for fun.

This is another reason working for a blogging sweatshop that pays you a small percentage of small revenue does not make you a travel writer, at least in terms of your tax classification. Neither does having a zillion social media followers but only making $200 from your blog. Unless you deduct almost nothing, you can't make enough money to exceed your expenses. Spending $1,000 and writing it off because you made $25 for an article can only work over time if you balance that trip with others that earned more money. You need to find other ways to create income related to your travels.

There is a workaround, though, if you think long term. There's no minimum or maximum amount on gains or losses. You can "lose" an unlimited amount in your zero profit years and gain a measly profit in your net positive years. With careful planning and bundling of expenses/income into different calendar years, you can follow the letter of the law and still lose money (bigtime even) for a while.

I did that when I was first starting out, losing a lot for two years and then showing a profit after that. At first the profit was pretty modest, but now that I make a real income from this, I can deduct quite a lot every year. Since I write and edit for so many outlets and have editorial control at some of them, there are very few trips I can't deduct as a business expense.

What you can deduct

Again, get a tax advisor to help with your specifics, but in general you can deduct the following in the US if the expenses were incurred in pursuit of a story you published or tried really hard to publish, assuming your expenses were not covered by a publication hiring you.

- Airline tickets
- Train and bus tickets
- Hotel room charges
- Rental cars and gas
- Mileage for your own car
- Taxi charges
- Admission charges for museums and attractions
- Books and research materials for your story
- Travel magazine subscriptions
- Your Internet service
- Seminars and professional dues
- Half your meal expenses while on the road
- Whatever you pay an assistant or intern
- Hosting and domain name charges
- Business equipment and office supplies
- Tax preparation expenses (because you're self-employed)
- Medical insurance and travel insurance
- Co-working facilities and Wi-Fi charges

The following are a little dicier, but can be deducted if you can prove you needed them to do your job and you work from home

- Phone service (if you do interviews, phone pitches
- Cable service (you need some shows/networks for research and ideas)
- Specific software and apps needed for your job
- Massages (if it's a spa story), booze (if it's a cocktail story), or wine (if it's a winery tour story) are all fair game with the right documentation.

As you can imagine, this all quickly adds up to a sizable sum. Even travel writers making good money have little trouble erasing a significant portion of that income through deductions—a positive or negative depending on how you look at it.

Of course if you only go on press trips or on trips where a big magazine is paying your expenses, you won't be laying out a lot of cash. Still, items like airport transportation, tips to service personnel, and meals while in transit to and from the destination can really add up. Several times I've spent a couple hundred dollars on a "free" press trip because of tips to safari guides or trekking guides.

To make this work, you need to keep meticulous records. Stock up on ink cartridges, jot down all your cash outlays, and save all those scraps of paper—even the handwritten ones in a different language and currency. Or use a phone app that turns receipt photos into organized records. I've never been audited, but if I ever am it's not going to be a pleasant week for the IRS man. He'll get boxes of receipts from multiple countries in a variety of currencies and he'd better be able to read Spanish.

I sleep well at night knowing that if I ever do get that IRS letter, I'll be ready and able to justify every expense I've claimed. Some push it further than this and will probably get away with it, but I figure the guidelines are fair and generous enough on their own without trying to overdo it. Claim what's defensible and if it feels fishy, it probably is.

Remember too that the goal is to make money, not to create deductions. The advantage of being a travel writer is that every trip has the potential to be another batch of write-offs. If you're not really working on anything related, though, it's a vacation, not work. Set yourself up for enough ongoing success financially and your net income will be higher.

I feel like this is one big advantage of being a blogger or running your own site. You have far more control over what gets published and paid, so it's easier to justify the expenses as leading to some sort of income. If you have to go pitch an editor for every single possible trip, you don't have as much ammo to defend those expenses.

There's a bit of a gray area in one area, though: the idea that you *tried* to get paid for writing about a trip, but gosh darn it, the genius of that big feature idea wasn't recognized by any of the editors you queried. If you can show you sent out repeated query letters and truly tried to get a piece published from your two weeks on the coast of Italy, in theory you can write off those expenses. If you were ever audited, that paper trail would be sufficient, but apply some common sense. A new writer who has never earned more than $50 for an article is going to have a hard time proving that a $6,000 trip to Bhutan was really a possible money-making venture. Save that leap for when you're successful.

Earn While You Sleep

Running an online business of your own is different than writing articles for someone else. The worldwide web is open 24/7, even while you sleep. So you can earn money around the clock.

You have to tend your virtual garden regularly, but the site doesn't care if you're around or not. You can literally make money while you sleep, especially if you have a worldwide audience. There's no feeling like going out for happy hour or a hike and coming back to find you've made more in that time than you did earlier in the day while you were pounding away behind the desk. It's nice to open your dashboard in the morning and find you earned money while you were having happy dreams. This is the real payoff for all that time toiling away for cheap or free in the beginning: real freedom later on.

One interesting byproduct of being a writer in the digital age is that those who own their own content on the web aren't constantly in pitching mode to keep food on the table. If a successful blogger goes on vacation for a week, she still gets paid. If a successful webmaster goes on a two-week vacation in an Italian villa and doesn't add anything new to his resource site, the money will keep flowing anyway.

You can't continue this practice forever, of course: even static resource sites need updating now and then. With blogs you need to "feed the beast" on a regular basis to have fresh content or you start losing readers. Still, even with blogs you can "future post" by writing things in advance and having then go up while you are away. The point is, you can go on vacation for a week or two completely off the grid and still have some income generated each day. It's the closest a freelancer gets to a paid vacation.

There have been weeks where I made more money not logging on once than I did being online nonstop in the office. One of the greatest things about publishing on the web is that the earnings are mostly generated by traffic. Readers keep coming to the site whether you are making tweaks or not. Your traffic may dip a little if no new posts are going up, but not by much—at least for a week or two. Sometimes a key media outlet has linked to my blog and traffic has soared while I was hiking or rafting; I was oblivious to the fact my ad revenue had doubled for the week.

Next Steps to Success

Always deliver more than you promise, and deliver it on time.
~ Bob Sehlinger, Publisher, Menasha Ridge Press

I can talk for 50 pages about my personal experience and what has worked for me, but everyone comes to the table with different skills and experience. So in this section I will give my advice that will lead to success, but temper it with lots of wisdom from others.

I also want to let the editors and publishers tell you what to do since they're the ones who—unless you are purely a successful independent blogger—will be the ones paying you for your writing.

In the early part of this book I listed some personal qualities that are important for travel writers. This section is about putting those qualities to work for you, as well as some concrete steps to take in developing yourself as a travel writer.

Develop a Good Portfolio Site

Before you do anything else on this list, spend the time or money to develop an attractive, professional portfolio site. Make an investment in your future, just as you would by taking a class. Ideally register your domain name at the place where you'll purchase hosting so you don't have to move it later.

I didn't do this as soon as I should have, but my dawn-of-the-Internet-age website on the old Geocities platform was decent anyway. The one I've had and tweaked since 2005 is great (www.TimLeffel.com). I paid a talented designer in Argentina $250 to set that up for me the first time, then about half that later for a graphics update, then $90 last time around to make it fancier and mobile-responsive. Every time that money was a great investment. Here are a few more good ones to check out, some fancy, some not, but all effective:

Nicholas Gill – nicholas-gill.com
Mark Johansen - markjohanson.com
Amy Rosen - amyrosen.com
Ellen Barone - ellenbarone.com
Rory MacLean – rorymaclean.com
Gabriel O'Rorke - gabrielororke.com
Peter Moore - petermoore.net
Matt Villano - whalehead.com

Notice that in most cases the person snagged the domain in their own name, though Peter Moore had to grab a .net one instead of .com. Really the suffix doesn't matter much: only a few people will automatically put your last name and .com in a browser instead of doing a search. If you have a really common name, you can stick in a middle initial, use a whole different phrase, or put something like "writer" or "writes" on the end: www.joeblowwrites.com.

Try to get some version of your name though since that makes it easier to rank #1 for your name then and remember that you can put dashes in like Nicholas did and achieve the same result. Most search engines treat a dash like a space between words, so tim-leffel.com is just as effective as timleffel.com, for instance. It may even be better if your name is not clear when both are mashed together (like Carollynn or Tomotis).

Make certain you have an online and a social media presence. You need to have a workable website. Whether you plan to make that your money-maker or to use it as your portfolio and a jumping off point to other things, you must have a website.
                    ~ Susan Lanier-Graham, freelancer and blogger

---

Do this now. Today! Ideally from wherever you're going to purchase hosting, but if the thought of researching that stresses you out, you can register the domain at Hostgator, GoDaddy, Dreamhost, or wherever and move it later. It will usually cost you $8 to $15 a year depending on the host.

After you've bought the domain name, you can find a good designer by asking around, by using Craigslist locally, or by using

Upwork, Envato Studio, 99 Designs, or Fiverr. These are sites where freelancers gather to bid on projects. You post what you want (be specific as possible, preferably with examples of what you like) and designers bid on how much they would charge to complete the project. Or in some cases you pay a set fee for a specific outcome. Money goes into escrow and they get paid when the job is complete.

Then don't just put it up and forget it! I was amazed as I was finding current entries for the examples how many sad, outdated, and abandoned portfolio sites I saw. If you're going to be a pro, then look like a pro! That means ponying up a little cash to get mobile responsive and current looking, plus some time to add new links or material.

As Sheila Scarborough noted in a blog post she did once, most people—including her—neglect this gateway page because it's a lot of trouble to redesign it and it's not much fun to maintain. "It is a visual wasteland and I'm too cheap to spend any money on it. I'm embarrassed to include the URL on my business cards even though it would be easier for my customers to find me there.." She then asks, "Is your personal website an embarrassing entrance to your online house?"

Giving a terrible first impression is a bad move. This is your billboard, your personal business pitch, and what's almost sure to show up on the first page for searches of your name. If the site is good, this is what you want in the No. 1 spot. I can't stress enough how important it is to have this site show up first in Google rather than some old article you wrote or your Facebook page. Editors and employers are impatient.

Real grunt work in building something worth showing off isn't always as fun as sending tweets or updating your Facebook page, but those things won't get you many assignments. You also can't control which of them shows up in search engines and where. So get your act together as soon as you have anything to say about yourself and develop a good portfolio page.

Hire a designer if you really want to look professional. But if you're really hurting for money, hunt around for a good template from a hosting company or a WordPress theme you like. You can usually get a decent template from the place where you are hosting the site. It won't be as great or as customized as something you invest real money in, but if you pick the right one at least it won't be embarrassing. You will need to learn their interface and probably eventually some basic HTML to tweak the graphics later if you don't use WordPress, but you'll need those skills anyway, so get on it.

My advice today would be to put this book down and go get something on Contently.com first if you're a freelancer. Then hire someone to tweak a WordPress theme for your own domain, with your host company.

But there are some other dead-simple solutions like Wix.com or About.me that look slick and give you a place to shine. (See Dana McMahan's portfolio site built with Wix at www.bodybybourbon.com). Squarespace has made it possible to build a website via simple (and attractive) drag-and-drop functions rather than coding or installing a template, something many of us have wished for since the birth of Netscape.

There's no one hosting company I'd recommend whole-heartedly, but remember that for a portfolio site, ease of use is more important than anything else since you won't get a lot of traffic on that site anyway. The best deal out there is usually at iPage.com, where you get hosting, a template of your choice, unlimited e-mail (at your domain), and free 24/7 phone support for a few bucks a month. Hostgator has some attractive template features too with their lowest-priced package.

The other option is to build it with the blogging software WordPress, which has lots of advantages (for one thing it's free apart from the hosting) and the themes keep getting better looking every year. I'd strongly advise hiring someone to set it up, after picking a template that's suited for lots of static pages on one long scrolling one. Just remember that WordPress requires regular updates and maintenance.

After it's set up, use that portfolio site as your showcase. You post links to articles on it, a feed from your blog, your LinkedIn page, your Twitter stream, whatever. Just make sure you're linking to things that are professional, not your personal Facebook page filled with baby photos, your dog, and the flower garden in your back yard. This is a business page meant to show you off as a professional, remember?

Don't put this off until you have a big body of work to list. Get the house built now and then hang your work up on the wall as things are published. If you hate looking at blank spaces, go write some free articles or guest blog posts to get things rolling.

Write Good Query Letters

As I mentioned earlier, there are entire books devoted to the art of the pitch—writing query letters. When you're starting out, it pays to spend a lot of time on this if you intend to write articles for others as it's the only way you'll get work and the only way you can plead your case.

> *The ability to pitch well has been a big key to my success, as it's the pitch that gets the commission in the first place.*
> ~ Lara Dunston, freelance writer and author

In its simplest form, a query letter is a short pitch about the idea, information about why you're the person to write it, and why it's right for that particular publication. In cases where the editor doesn't know you and the idea is the main selling point, the first paragraph or two are a taste of your writing and how you would present the material, so typically you would include the lead paragraph from the actual article you plan to submit and then a more explanatory paragraph. Then a paragraph or two on the rest. Sign off and end it.

Edit it to the bare essentials. Many editors won't even read a long query letter. They can tell in a paragraph or two whether it—and you—are worth considering. And they don't have the time or patience to be your grammar coach or writing teacher. So make it great and make the first two paragraphs have what really matters.

Typical Query Letter

Dear [Real Name],

First paragraph that draws the reader in—an approximation of the actual article lead.

Second paragraph with more explanatory info about the story. What makes it special.

Third paragraph about why that publication, where in the publication, and why you're the person to deliver the story.

Any information about timing, photos, and word count.

I look forward to hearing from you soon,

Signature
Portfolio site link or About page of blog
Phone number

In the days of stamps and letters a query letter was not supposed to be more than one typed page. If anything, editors have even less patience now, so edit as tightly as possible. For the few newspapers still buying freelance material, the actual query letter isn't very important: those editors want to read the whole story.

Many experienced writers have written a four- or five-paragraph query letter for years. Once you become established, the format above is superfluous. Once an editor knows you and trusts you, just a simple summary of the idea is enough. One writer I know was flown to the other side of the world to work on a huge feature assignment for a big glossy travel magazine after submitting this query: "I want to go to Yap and I don't know why."

He could get away with that because of his track record. There are a few writers who work for me at Perceptive Travel who don't have to send much more. I know they're talented and will turn even the most mundane destination into an interesting read by pursuing a unique angle. They understand what we want and deliver it.

Sell yourself, but don't oversell yourself. Let your work stand for itself and be direct, concise, and polite. Don't be a stalker. Sending one follow-up e-mail is fine, even encouraged. (My inbox is overflowing on a daily basis and it's impossible to keep up with the writers I already have established relationships with, let alone respond to cold pitches.) If enough time goes by, maybe send another. Beyond that, you've crossed into the "annoying" category. No one wants to work with annoying. It also decreases your chances of being tapped on the merit of a future pitch.

Also: Pitch one idea at a time! Bombarding editors with 18 different story ideas is a great way to get ignored. We just don't have that much time. Start small and earn trust.

The formula for an effective pitch is simple, really. Here it is: Write a short (1-3 sentence) summary of your idea that addresses these four questions:

Why THIS? Why NOW? Why US? Why YOU?

Let me know if you have a particularly high level of familiarity with a place or topic. In fact, pitch me stories that get at those strengths. There's nothing I hate more than writers that assume an air of authority when writing about a place they spent 24 hours in. Ick.

~ Leslie Trew Magraw of National Geographic Online

I tend to lead with my credentials now in freelance queries instead of the story idea for the same reason. First I want the editor to know I'm a pro. Then we can talk about the idea.

What nearly every editor really desires from someone they don't know is this: a writer who gets what their publication is about and either proposes ideas to match or nails assignments that are handed down. Understand the publication well and then pitch something that fits, but something that hasn't been published there before—or at least in the past few years. From the editor's standpoint, if the writer is a proven entity elsewhere, that makes saying yes even easier.

You have to get used to looking into the future too. With magazines, Christmas is in July and summer travel is in January.

That's how far ahead they're working on stories. At least ten times now I've gotten a rejection that basically said, "We just did a piece on that." What they are calling "just did" turns out to be an issue that won't hit the stands for two more months, so I couldn't foresee that, but the point is I need to pitch it elsewhere. They've "published" it in house and the editor is looking six months out from now.

Many magazines publish an editorial schedule (often in their "advertise with us" section on the website) and the ones that don't still furnish one to some of the database services mentioned in the resources section at the end. You can study these to get a jump on what they want down the road.

> *Successful freelancers are proactive, always on the lookout for work and willing to put a LOT of time into researching publication etc. to create the perfect pitch.*
>
> ~ Sophie Couwenbergh, freelance writer

For books, you don't send a query, but a proposal. This is a far more complicated endeavor, so go get a book specific to this subject before diving in so you can do it right. For a book proposal you have to show writing skills, show credentials, show that you have a platform to get the book marketed, and that you have the attitude of a professional.

> *The most common mistake we see are book proposals and manuscripts laden with misspelled words and grammatical and punctuation errors. also shudder when anyone sends me a book proposal addressed to 'Dear Sir.' Prima-donnas and narcissists are another turn-off. Any author who approaches us demanding special attention, and claiming they deserve to be moved to the head of the line will get rejected.*
>
> ~ Angela Hoy, Publisher at Booklocker

Be Original and Creative

No one at present dares to state the obvious: growth in society may not come from raising the average the Asian way, but from increasing the number of people in the "tails," that small, very small number of risk takers crazy enough to have ideas of their own, those endowed with that very rare ability called imagination, that rare quality courage, and who make things happen.

~ Nassim Nicholas Taleb in *Antifragile*

There have been many far better trumpet players than Miles Davis. David Gilmour would never win a guitar virtuosity contest. Woody Harrelson will probably never win as many Oscars as Daniel Day Lewis. A lot of people thought Jackson Pollack was a joke as a painter. Jack Kerouac didn't get a lot of respect as a writer at first. Each of these people has or had something going on that intrigued people. There was a unique creativity evident enough to make people notice.

Too many freelancers make the mistake of spending hours crafting perfectly polished query letters instead of spending hours coming up with original ideas that will make them stand out. If it's been written already, why do you want to write it again? If it's a story or advice column that we can already find on the web, why pitch it to a magazine? As Sean O'Neill, former editor of *Budget Travel* once said, "Why should you be paid to do what someone else has already provided to a global audience for free?"

In the age of instant Google queries, that means it's harder than ever to be original, but also much easier to make sure your idea is original before you start pitching it or blogging about it. I would argue that O'Neill is being too generous to his editor colleagues— every month I read glossy magazine "listicles" I've read a dozen times before in different forms—but he would probably tell me most of those came out of groupthink staff meetings rather than being pitched by a freelancer.

> *There are travel writers who see destinations and travel writers who see stories. Those who are in the latter camp are much more likely to succeed. Nobody wants another article on Buenos Aires, but they might want an article on the city's obsession with secret hangouts, like speakeasy-style bars and "puertas cerradas" (closed-door restaurants). Writers who are always thinking about what's new, exciting and unique, and who can find an interesting lens from which to focus in on a destination, will jump ahead of the pack.*
>
> ~ Mark Johanson, freelance writer

Even if your publication has a staff of one rather than a conference room of editors, don't retread what others have already done. And consider following the advice of author Jeff Jarvis: 'Do what you do best and link to the rest. Don't regurgitate what someone else has already written when you can link to that info instead. Focus on providing your own fresh original reporting or insights."

If you want to get noticed, either as a pitching freelancer or a blogger creating content that draws readers, originality is key. Sure, in the short term you can draw lots of clicks online with forgettable top-10 lists and steams of posts with "best" or "worst" in the title, but that doesn't build a long-term audience of engaged readers. Editors, publishers, and media people don't call you because you're good at writing linkbait listicles that will get you retweets and Facebook likes. They want to hire writers with something fresh to say.

Earlier in this book I gave examples of stories that came out of a three-week trip to Peru. I went back three more times later and covered other angles. I've been to Ecuador three times, but if someone sent me there again, I could come up with many more ideas for articles that nobody has ever written before. If I couldn't do that, I'd consider myself a failure as a creative nonfiction writer. If you want to be a successful freelancer—or even a good blogger— finding multiple creative angles is key. Ideas are your real currency.

In the magazine world, the writing doesn't happen until you sell the idea. Writing past paragraph number two is pointless if nobody likes the idea to start with. If you're a blogger, who wants to visit your blog to read the umpteenth standard post about visiting Petra or staring at the Grand Canyon? Tell us something fresh.

> *My advice? Pack light and think creatively about your story. People want the arc of a story even in the tiniest piece of writing. Writers who are good at teasing a story out of any material are the ones who will make a name for themselves.*
> ~ Zora O'Neill, author and freelance writer

One of the worst rookie mistakes you can make is sending an editor a note that says something like, "I'm going to Paris in June. Could you use any stories from there?" Many aspiring travel writers feel that telling an editor they are heading off to some certain spot on the other side of the globe will result in an enthusiastic invitation to write about it. But here's some news: editors are not short on people who are willing to head off to this place or that to write about it. Don't assume just going somewhere is a reason to write an article. Or even a blog post. Even remote corners of the globe are visited by more writers than we need. Unless you're going to be the first person landing on Mars, you'd better find a good story angle.

This doesn't mean you can't write about popular tourist spots, but you'd better be able to find a truly unique slant that has never been tried before. Wherever you are going, you need to think like a journalist and dig for something an editor will find refreshing—even if that editor is you. Every place I've been to has something interesting going on that nobody is writing about; it just requires researching before you leave, talking to people once you get there, and walking around. Heck, sometimes you can even ask: "What do you wish travel writers would talk about more for your town/city/resort area?"

Edward Readicker-Henderson went to Hawaii for *Islands* magazine and wrote a feature story about…ukuleles. Darrin DuFord went to New Orleans and wrote about a team that hunts nutria (giant rodents) along the levees. Adam Sachs went to Berlin and wrote about covering three days of expenses for a couple on the same amount the two of them spent for just one meal at a gourmet restaurant on Day One. None of these regurgitated the same tired tourist info about Hawaii, New Orleans, or Berlin.

> *There is so much free travel writing available nowadays. Everyone has a blog. To be different, you have to present a unique angle, perspective, and voice, instead of sharing generic information anyone can write. Draw on your special experience, delve deeper with research, provide juicy details instead of clichés, and try to establish an emotional connection with your readers.*
>
> ~ Yilin Wang, freelance writer

It is also easier to find a fresh angle, however, if you skip the popular tourist spots altogether. I blew off Prague and biked the greenways of Moravia. My family trip stories have been on cities like Huntsville, Anna Maria Island, and Lexington in the US, or Real de Catorce, Cuetzalan, and Ayutthaya abroad. The best India story I ever published was about the hash-smoking sadhus in the mountains up north, nowhere near the main guidebook sites.

The writers I know who get the most print work are the ones who always find something fresh to say, no matter where they're going. The bloggers who get noticed and build a tribe of readers (not just social media followers) are the ones doing something original on a regular basis.

Look Beyond the Obvious

If you do want to write for others—and I suggest even full-time bloggers should do that for a financial hedge and for link-building purposes—then research the whole wide world out there beyond the travel section of a magazine rack. Plenty of print and web publications put out travel articles, but in a way that suits their readership.

I've written for or been quoted in *Money, Kiplinger's Personal Finance,* the *Wall Street Journal, MSNBC.com*, and H&R Block's blog, for instance. These were travel pieces with a financial angle.

You also see travel articles in the likes of *Elle, Shape, and Women's Health*, but with an angle at least somewhat related to fashion, health, or well being. There are a whole slew of independent online sites covering these same issues and they may be even more interested in your pitch if you frame it correctly.

What else is related to travel? Cars, motorcycles, business, shopping, clothing, design, and tech for a start. Food magazines have travel stories in nearly every issue, as do many regional or city magazines. Just as people travel to break up the routine of their life, many non-travel magazines look at these pieces as a nice break from their usual narrow focus on one topic. They just have to relate to the overall slant.

> *If you're a newbie, don't waste your time trying to break into national magazines right off the bat. You'll find yourself frustrated and broke. Instead, explore new avenues within the travel realm (or write for your city publication first to build up a portfolio of your work). The industry is changing so rapidly that those of us who survive these changes do so because we are malleable and haven't stuck to one set path or approach to travel writing. There are so many other opportunities out there beyond writing for the handful of (barely surviving) travel magazines that offer very limited real estate.*
>
> ~ Kristin Luna

Even within travel, there are dozens of custom publications you won't find on any newsstand, but that pay decent (or sometimes great) rates and aren't as competitive. Did you know Four Seasons, Ritz-Carlton, Belmond, Small Luxury Hotels, Fairmont, Waldorf-Astoria, Conrad, Palladium Hotels, and Autograph Collection all put out their own magazine? Or that this is just the start? Did you know airline publications in other countries commission stories in English about your country?

If you're not normally having the kind of experiences that they're publishing, study them anyway for those short and sweet front pieces on trends and narrow local topics where they have properties. Most of the major cruise lines have their own magazine too, which of course they want to fill with stories on ports where they stop. Some car brands have their own magazines, which naturally cover some road trip options.

Build relationships

The key, as is true in any business—especially a highly coveted art form—is to create alliances. Fellow travel writers that I met on press trips proved to be great allies, showing me the ropes, sharing war stories, getting me on to other trips, introducing me to PR companies, and turning me on to media outlets. Relationships. relationships, relationships.

~ Karen Loftus

That's the advice from my friend Karen Loftus, whom I met on a press trip to Iceland many years ago. We reconnected again at an Adventure Travel Mexico conference and we still keep in touch regularly. I've had dinner with two other writers who were on that trip when I visited their city. I've had drinks with another in her city since.

There's a lot of serendipity in being a freelance writer. Tips and assignments can come from odd places you never would have expected. Knowing the right people can make the luck a lot more frequent.

When I've launched new projects and it was time for me to hire writers, most of them ended up being people I knew already. I wasn't an editor when they met me, but I turned out to be one later and I felt best hiring the writers I already knew and trusted. The others I've hired have come from referrals. It's an old axiom of business that people find a way to buy from or hire the people that they like. Not the people who are most in their face, mind you, the people that they *like*. So meet people, make friends, find a way to help those people out and someday they might return the favor. That's what makes the world go round.

New writers and bloggers should keep just three things in mind really. 1) Aggressively hone your skills and continually strive to become a better writer. 2) Build relationships within your community through social media. 3) Start an e-mail newsletter yesterday—e-mail is the single best long-term strategy for building a direct line of communication with your fans and readers.

~ Shannon O'Donnell of AlittleAdrift.com

There are different approaches to this, however, and social media has been both a boom and a bane in this respect. I've got thousands of Twitter followers than I know absolutely nothing about and I know people who have 1,000 "friends" on their personal Facebook accounts, but not many real ones they can depend on for help with something. It doesn't take long to reach a point of diminishing returns with these too-easy tools for networking, especially when you're mixing business and personal contacts.

How you deal with this is up to you. Some people can juggle 100 contacts and have meaningful relationships with all of them. For others the number may be more like 25. For me, one contact I've met face-to-face or spent a half hour with on the phone trumps nearly all the ones I've never actually talked to except through a software tool.

Whether it's through LinkedIn, the Travel Blog Exchange, MediaBistro, trade organizations, or Twitter, having quality contacts (and not just *lots* of contacts) will definitely help your career over time. Go to conferences that make sense if you can. Meet other writers in your city if there's a community there. Spend time on message boards or Facebook groups that cater to travel writers. See the resources section for suggestions on all of these.

> *I credit my success to tenacity, thick skin, and above all making contacts. Your contacts in this business are like gold.*
> ~ Susan Campbell, freelance writer

Edward Readicker-Henderson says he has met most of his contacts face-to-face, and he credits much of his success to that. "At this point, I'd say the vast majority of work comes from editors I know personally, and I'm just lucky that I know some really powerful editors."

When I asked John DiScala, better known as Johnny Jet, what he would do differently if he had it to do all over again, he said, "I would network my tail off. Go to travel conferences make friends with people like you and other well-known personalities and try and write for them for free just to get my name out there."

Don't forget that every contact with an editor is another opportunity to build a long-term relationship. So don't blow it by being unprofessional or telling lies. "Writers forget, or don't know, that I've been a freelancer myself and so I know many of the tricks in the book," says Stuart MacDonald of TravelFish. "If a person can't follow clear instructions—for instance, don't send attachments—what is the chance of them being able to follow more complex editorial instructions? We don't give writers a style guide for the sake of it—they're expected to read and follow it. The good ones deliver what we want, on deadline and generally require very little (if any) editing. Trust is paramount."

If an editor trusts you, that person will give you more assignments, will recommend you to others, and will want to chat with you at cocktail parties. Earn that trust every time and your network will grow.

> *Do as much networking as possible, online and offline, getting to know as many people as you can in the industry and building relationships. People who have the ability to hire prefer to hire people they like (assuming everything else is equal), so be sincere and get to know people.*
> ~ Larry Habegger, Executive Editor, Travelers' Tales Publishing

Persevere, but Be Patient

The Professional endures adversity. He lets the birdshit splash down on his slicker, remembering that it comes clean with a heavy-duty hosing. He himself, his creative center, cannot be buried, even beneath a mountain of guano. His core is bulletproof. Nothing can touch it unless he lets it.
~ Steven Pressfield in *The War of Art*

"Keys to my success? I think perseverance. After being rejected, I stepped back and approached things from another angle. When that didn't work I tried another. Eventually I got my bit of dumb luck and I got 'inside.' I was also lucky that my first book did well enough for my publishers to want to publish another one."

That's from Peter Moore, author of great travel narrative books including *Vroom with a View* and The *Full Montezuma*. He kept at it, still working a day job, after his first book proposal was "promptly rejected by every publisher on the planet." Seven books later he's still making it work.

Chris Epting also has close to 20 books in his biography and makes a comfortable living on royalties, assignments, and speaking engagements. When asked about his success, he says, "The keys have been persistence, tenacity, and follow-through."

To prove that even the most successful writers have moments of doubt, widely published consumer advocate Christopher Elliott said when I interviewed him for the first edition, "I'm not sure if I've broken into travel writing yet! But assuming I have, my key to success is persistence. Never stop!" I think he can safely say he's made it now, with this simple line appearing on his About page: "In more than two decades as a journalist, I've either worked at or appeared in almost every A-list outlet."

Susan Griffith, a freelancer who has penned multiple editions of books on traveling and working abroad, says, "So much success in writing is based on luck added to a huge amount of patience."

I'm nothing if not persistent. Every time someone said no I redoubled my efforts. And I pitched way outside my league, sending ideas to big-time outlets as if I were somebody they should consider hiring. Then one of them did. And sometimes, to my great surprise and delight, they came to me.

~ Dana McMahan, freelance writer

This is echoed by nearly everyone who looks on paper like an "overnight success." Some form of the word persistent came up in the answer of almost every writer I surveyed when I asked what separates successful writers and bloggers from the also-ran.

I'm all for quitting if something is not working, but many get intimidated or frustrated and quit before they've really had time to tell. (Read Seth Godin's short book *The Dip* on how to figure out when to cut bait and when to keep sweating to make something happen.)

Some will give a nod to dumb luck, a kind editor, or being in the right place at the right time, but it's that ability and willingness to keep at it after repeated rejections and setbacks that separate the winners from the losers. Granted you need a modicum of talent, but the most brilliant writers aren't usually the most successful ones.

Those are too hung up on being artists to keep marketing themselves when it gets hard. Like it or not, successful writers are usually successful salespeople—even if they hate the whole thought that this is what they have to be.

My advice would be to write consistently good material for at least a few years before trying to make much money off of it. Prove yourself first. Then, if you're still interested and haven't burned out, you'll know you're in this for the long haul.

~ Amy Whitley of PitStopsforKids.com

David Farley sees it from the writer's side, but also from the teacher's side. "For many years I've taught travel writing (at New York University and Gotham Writers' Workshop) and the students who have been the most successful weren't the most talented in the class; they were the most determined and driven. You can always become a better writer through practice and study, but that determination has to come from somewhere else."

Find your core area of expertise

Wikipedia's demonstrated that they can provide the big answers but all the little answers are not there yet.

~ Fraser Cain, editor of UniverseToday.com

I've said it many times in many ways in this book: Dominate your niche and success will follow. The assignments will be easier to come by, you'll eventually get media attention without trying very hard, and you can credibly start your own site or blog that will draw readers in—instead of having to bust your tail every day to pull people to your site.

Have you ever been on one of those streets of similar restaurants in a tourist town, all jammed together in a block or two, competing head-on? From Peru to Turkey to India I have and for me it's not a pleasant experience. Touts are shouting at me to come into their restaurants, waiters are waving a menu in my face, someone is tugging on my sleeve if I even glance at what's inside the place. If it weren't for the meal deals and the free drinks they often throw in, I'd skip the whole street.

If you start a generalist travel site, that's how aggressive you need to be to make people come eat at your table. As soon as you stop constantly promoting (through friends, through social media plugging, through outright begging for links), traffic drops. When you ramp up the hype, though, you run the risk of turning people off by seeming like a shameless shill. After a while, your pitches are about as welcome as ones from a telemarketer during dinnertime.

What if, however, you're the only pizza restaurant on a street full of seafood shacks? What if you have the only bagel shop in the whole city? You won't please everyone that way, but people will find you on their own and you won't have to drag anyone in against their will.

Figure out what makes you different or better than the thousands of other aspiring writers out there. Discover what aspect of travel gets you the most excited and find a niche that needs filling around that area. Find a fresh place where a hole in the market and your interests can intersect. Find the corner of passion and prosperity: what can you cover better than anyone in a way that will attract others who care about that place or subject?

The first key was choosing a topic I'm passionate about, as it's the only reason I've kept writing regularly for 8 years and counting. Consistency is another key. It's not enough to simply write whenever you want, you need to show up day in and day out to build your online presence, name recognition, and readers' trust.

~ David Lee of GoBackpacking.com and MedellinLiving.com

Owning your niche is especially important if you're a blogger or author. A study from Cession and George Washington University found that 89% of journalists reported using blogs for their online research. Only corporate websites (96%) are used by more journalists when researching online for a story. These reporters are seeking out people who know a lot about a specific subject. One of the first things they'll do is a blog search. If you keep popping up as the expert, you're the one who will get interviewed and quoted.

Travel writing is increasingly a bad field for generalists. There just aren't many generalist publications out there as newspaper travel sections die off and general interest magazines go on life support. For those at the top of the print pyramid it's still mostly fine, of course, so if you're already there then keep covering the world and all its aspects. A small but solid group of travel writers are still making most of their income from print because they're regularly pitching to and getting accepted by the big, established magazines that are still hanging on.

If you're just starting out however, you really, *really* need to find a path of less resistance. That doesn't mean a coffee specialist can't write about beaches or a diving expert can't write about a wine tour, especially after finding some success, but things will move much faster for you if become known and recognized as an authority in one area.

> *The primary keys to my success have been 1) passion for my topic 2) having a very clearly defined niche 3) perseverance. The successful writers and bloggers have a focus, a niche, a professional approach and a never-say-die attitude. They see their writing and blogging as a professional career, not a fair weather hobby.*
>
> ~ Mariellen Ward of BreatheDreamGo.com

Some manage to stretch this niche a bit and cover several areas well, but usually those areas are complimentary. A writer might focus on luxury resorts, destination weddings, honeymoon spots, and the Caribbean, for example. One trip can result in articles for all those subject areas.

> *When I made the jump to freelancing full-time in 1998, I had an idea that I wanted to focus on two of my favorite things—food and travel—and so I steered pitches in that direction, and ultimately niched myself as a food, travel, and lifestyle writer. I rarely cover any topics that don't fall into that holy editorial trinity.*
>
> ~ Charyn Pfeuffer, freelance writer

I and many others have chosen a different way to branch out: by starting new websites or blogs that cater to a specific niche. I never wanted to be a writer that covers travel gear 100% of the time, but when I saw a need for reviews of gear and gadgets that normal people would buy—instead of the super-expensive things featured in *Outside* and *Robb Report*—I started PracticalTravelGear.com. Six years later I sold it for a nice mid-five-figures sum. The blog wasn't all about me, so it was very easy for a buyer to take it over and run it without me.

When I saw that hardly anyone was covering luxury travel in Latin America, even though it was on a major growth trajectory, I launched LuxuryLatinAmerica.com. Since Tim Leffel was already known as the budget travel and cheap destinations guy, I used my first two names as a pen name for the editor. Timothy Scott runs that show. Someday I'll probably sell that one too, but for now it's profitable and gives me lots of travel opportunities in the Americas.

Find a way to be authentic

We're all drowning in words and communication, but most of it can be—and is—easily ignored.

One of the short cuts to authenticity is writing about what you know well. This can be a certain subject or a place—your home or your adopted home. When I asked freelancer Adam Sachs what he would do differently if he had it to do all over again, this is what he said. "I'd move somewhere. Live somewhere outside of Manhattan for a while. Six months, a year, a decade. I don't think there's any formula for ensuring (or even defining) success but this is just something that can't hurt you as an observer of things."

When I asked author Chris Epting if he would do anything differently, he felt he got on the right foot from the start by being original. "Today I think I'd do the same thing I did before when starting out: look for ways to stand out and tell stories that nobody else is telling."

For long articles or blog posts, it's also important to find that elusive thing people talk about but have trouble describing: "voice." When a writer has a voice, the person's prose is unique. Not everyone has this; some people are very successful being chameleons who can adapt to any assignment. If you strive to greatness though, people should be able to recognize your voice in your writing. This is extremely difficult, if not impossible, when writing short pieces for magazines. These get reworked so much by editors that any trace of a voice is gone. With features, blog posts, and books, however, your voice should develop and shine.

> *I don't think success can be ensured by any means. But what I did wrong early on was not try harder. I didn't think bigger magazines would pay any attention to me. Turns out they would. I'd push more to make that jump sooner, spending less time on guidebooks. I would waste less time writing what I thought people wanted, and instead, just spent the time writing my kind of stories. That was a major change for me. When I stopped trying to adapt and just said, "Screw it, this is what I do," my income tripled. Would have been nice to have figured that out sooner.*
>
> ~ Edward Readicker-Henderson, freelance writer

For the most part, voice comes through development and practice, the same way it does for a musician or singer. Over time, that authenticity will shine through.

Authenticity can also be achieved by following good creative nonfiction writing practice. Engage the senses, use lots of examples instead of generalizations, show don't tell, use dialogue from real people (not just cab drivers and bartenders), avoid descriptions we've already heard a hundred times. Describe one incident or scene well instead of trying to cover everything you did on your trip. Remember, most documentaries you see have left out hundreds of hours of footage. Edit just as ruthlessly in your writing.

Be Professional

If there's one piece of advice that's most important, this is it. For most editors I know, professionalism is a non-negotiable requirement.

Editors don't have the time or patience to deal with writers who don't have their act together. Very few are willing to hold your hand, correct your spelling, soothe your ego, listen to your personal problems that got in the way of completing the assignment on time, or indulge your organizational idiosyncrasies. There are too many other writers out there who are ready and willing to do it right. As Victor Ozols said when I asked him what advice he would give to budding writers, "Make your deadlines. Be one of those people who always meets their deadlines."

This may be a hobby for you, something you do for fun even, but for the people who would pay you, this is a business. Forget that and you're dead before you've started. Most editors will say outright that they'd rather have a competent writer who is dependable than a brilliant writer who is unreliable. Doing what you've promised shouldn't be hard, but it's amazing how many writers blow it in this area.

As Stuart McDonald of TravelFish says, "Obviously writing skill is important, but also an ability to meet deadlines and to not be a time waster. When you're running your own business and relying on freelancers, you don't (or shouldn't) have the spare time to indulge people who don't have the above qualities."

Editors may differ in lots of ways: what kind of queries they like, what kind of writing they prefer, and how formally they define their agreements with writers. If there's one thing that almost all agree on, however, it's that sloppy writers who aren't professional aren't going to get any slack. It's amazing how far you can go by delivering flawless copy submitted on time, every time.

"Flawless" doesn't mean your brilliant prose won't be edited, but it means that you did everything right. You ran a spell check and then had another set of eyes check the text manually. You carefully read the guidelines or style sheet and followed those instructions to the letter. The story is formatted correctly. You double-checked the deadline and got the piece in on time or early. You submitted any additional materials, such as sidebar info or photos, in the manner and format specified by the editor.

New Writers' Mistakes:

1) Some do not read the articles on the website.

2) Some do not read the writers' guidelines.

3) Some expect to be paid for any piece they submit, period, while we only accept submissions on spec—except for those who are proven contributors.

4) Some refuse to allow their pieces to be constructively critiqued in order to fit our editorial or the unique requirements for success on the web.

5) Some are closed to learning how to write articles that are of interest to others, and assume that their own experience will be of interest to all. (I believe those who read all successful forms of media learn to incorporate that intuitively in their writing.)

Good Writers' Trairts:

1) They have read the best articles on the website and may even want to improve them or offer another perspective.

2) They have read the writers' guidelines.

3) They see gaps in our coverage and offer ideas in detail on how they might approach them.

4) They are open to being edited.

5) They evolve as writers and as travel writers article by article, year by year. They then open up a world of options. The very best continue to experiment and learn.

~ Gregory Hubbs, Editor and Publisher, TransitionsAbroad.com

As I was writing this book I got an e-mail from a freelancer asking me for the second time what the deadline was for her article. I replied back with the answer and then reminded her the deadline was in the contract she already had in hand. "Yes, but I filed it away," she replied. "It was easier to just zap you and ask."

Very wrong answer!

That writer got another big X mark on my mental professionalism checklist when that happened and I haven't hired her since. The laziness displayed in that e-mail reply has stuck with me ever since—especially since this was on top of six e-mails sent earlier about the content of the contracted piece. Some of those questions repeated what we had already discussed in earlier e-mails. (Your e-mail program has a search function. Use it!)

An editor is not your psychiatrist, your life coach, your writing instructor, your spell checker, your grammar doctor, your personal Googler, or your travel planner. Some rare ones may befriend you and nurture you if they feel like it, but each one is a *customer* buying something from you in a business-to-business transaction. A customer with very real time constraints and a career-hardened lack of patience for ineptitude.

As Paris-based Karen Fawcett says, "The key to my 'success' was being willing to be there, chase fire engines, generate my own ideas for articles and ALWAYS file on time."

Many editors are more approachable than you would think if you deserve their attention and are a qualified match for their publication. They'll kick around an idea on the phone or discuss what would work best on your upcoming trip across the ocean. All of them are busy, however, so if there's not a clear payoff to your call or e-mails, they don't want to be wasting time. It's always useful to forget about yourself and remember the question that guides the actions of most good sales reps and diplomats: "What's in it for the *other* person?"

What does the person on the other end of the conversation have to gain? Come to them prepared and ready to answer this question, get to the point, and then deliver on your promises if you get an assignment. If you get a no, don't argue. Bow out graciously, thank them for their time, and live to fight another day. Getting the last word may make you feel better, but it's not going to help your long-term prospects.

I have some personal pet peeves as an editor that I know are shared by many others when it comes to professionalism, so here's the inside scoop on how to do things right.

1. Keep your promises and meet your deadlines. You only get one free pass, if that. As former Lonely Planet book editor Brice Gosnell told me, "One writer's aunt has died four times now I think. It was a running joke in the office until

we didn't use that writer anymore. One time, okay, but when the same person is late multiple times, they're out."

2. Edit your material well before sending it. Unless we're chatting over a beer somewhere about a potential story idea, I generally don't have time to be your sounding board and angle shaper. Sure, I'll make your article better sometimes through editing, but it should be 95% there before I even get it.

3. Follow the guidelines and the contract. If the style guidelines say, "Third person past tense," don't send an editor an article that's in the first person and present tense. If the agreement you signed says, "2,000 words max" then don't send some 3,500-word novella and give me the chore of chopping it in half. If the guidelines say "American English," don't send a piece with British spellings and cockney slang terms.

4. Don't ever send a query that completely defies the guidelines, thinking your idea is so great that the editor will say, "Oh, forget those silly guidelines." The odds of this succeeding are right up there with the most unpopular boy in high school taking the hottest cheerleader to prom or the local rabbi asking to go to the cathedral with you for midnight Mass. If the requirements say something like "Book authors only," "writers with top-tier magazine experience only," or "bloggers who can commit to 10 posts per week," then only query if that requirement applies to you.

Not following directions is a common mistake with both old and new freelancers. We list a generic-sounding e-mail address on our acquisitions page for people to use when contacting us.

cont/d ...

Freelancers think that using connections to get my e-mail address and contact me personally might give them a better chance, but it actually decreases their visibility because I get so much other e-mail. Follow the directions on my site, take my experience requirements seriously, and write a fantastic cover letter that shows a knowledge of our books and how your experience relates to them,

> *and I will notice your résumé—and use it if I have a project that seems like a good fit, even if it's a couple years later.*
> ~ Grace Fujimoto, Acquisitions Director at Avalon Travel Publishing

Develop a Good Work Ethic

As I noted at the beginning of this book, being "on assignment" is often no picnic. It's not uncommon to work all day every day for a week or two straight. Longer if you're a guidebook writer.

Here's a Perceptive Travel story excerpt from Rachel Dickinson, who was blogging every day from Ireland for another publication before getting stuck there because of a giant cloud of ash from Iceland.

Everyone had a story. The drunk in the bar. The doorman. The maid from Lithuania. The taxi driver from West Belfast. And I spent my days in a kind of reporter-mode and it was goddamn exhausting. And at night I'd go into my room and try to craft a little story to post. And I'd drink from the bottle of Merlot purchased from the liquor store and eat bread and cheese for dinner bought at the grocery store and I'd begin to feel sorry for myself in this beautiful country of greenness and melodic voices. Then I'd crawl between the 800 thread-count sheets on my perfect bed hoping I'd sleep. I knew I couldn't whine about it lest I get slapped.

And each day was the same. Eat breakfast. Look for the story. Plot the trip. Take a white-knuckle drive. Go to another fabulous hotel. Then eat from the grocery store because I couldn't bear to eat out because they don't really get the table-for-one thing in Ireland. No one eats alone. So I started really looking forward to going home.

Working hard is part of the game for anyone expecting to make real money at this. All the lazy freelance writers you will meet are people who depend on a spouse, a parent, or retirement savings to pay the bills. I'm not saying it's impossible to be a slacker and earn good money as a travel writer, but I have yet to come across someone who is that mythical exception. Read Michael Shapiro's excellent book, *A Sense of Place*, to get a good feel for the writers' life. Even the authors you feel should be able to kick back and take it easy now—Simon Winchester, Bill Bryson, Jan Morris, Rick Steves—still put in full days and then some in front of their computer or doing research on site.

If you work for others, they will expect you to give it your all. If you work for yourself, your readers will expect you to give it your all. Either way, don't choose travel writing because it looks easy. The pros only *make* it look easy on the page.

Part of having a good work ethic means giving full focus to what's needed instead of doing what's fun. Most travel bloggers spend an inordinate amount of time on social media because it's fun. That and snapping iPhone shots on a press trip are easy. Most could do better by putting time into more difficult things like freelance articles, guest posts, book projects, media outreach, interviews, real research, and producing writing with real depth.

To do real work, you have to focus on that work and give it your all. There's a scientific reason why shutting off distractions results in better work. There's clear evidence that multi-tasking just makes you bad at multiple things simultaneously.

> *The often-used phrase "pay attention" is apt: you dispose of a limited budget of attention that you can allocate to activities, and if you try to go beyond your budget, you will fail. It is the mark of effortful activities that they interfere with each other, which is why it is difficult or impossible to conduct several at once.*
>
> ~ Daniel Kayneman in *Thinking, Fast and Slow*

Develop a Thick Skin

Doug Lansky seems like the picture of success, with lots of great books under his belt for Rough Guides and Lonely Planet, a column in the *Guardian* newspaper, regular stories in the biggest magazines, and a long list of industry keynote presentations on his record. It didn't come easy though. "When starting, you'll probably need to 'collect' about 40 rejection letters before you see much progress," he says. "I worked my ass off to get started—12 hours per day for about five months, then I kept working hard after that."

But it's important to put all this in perspective. "It was helpful to visit the Rock and Roll Hall of Fame in Cleveland and see all the rejection letters that The Beatles and Rolling Stones received," he adds.

Timothy Ferriss notes the following in his updated version of his runaway bestseller on lifestyle design: "*The 4-hour Workweek* was turned down by 26 of 27 publishers."

As David Farley says, "There's a ton of rejection in this business; know that even the successful writers get rejected frequently."

Like most travel writers, I've been rejected by more magazine editors and book publishers than I care to count. It still happens to me on a regular basis now even. I don't keep track; I just bounce off and move on. It's hard not to take it personally, but that gets easier over time as you realize a lot can keep an idea or article from generating a yes with one particular editor. For me, articles that have been dismissed outright by one editor have often been picked up elsewhere and then won some kind of "best travel writing" award. Maybe the editor didn't get it, but more likely the timing or fit just wasn't right.

> *Anyone who can't handle rejection or constructive criticism will never make it in the writing or blogging world. There are many editors wanting to help you become a better writer. Sometimes 'no' simply means 'not now.'*
>
> ~ Beth Blair, freelance writer and author

Nobody is perfect, including the managing editor in an office on the 36th floor in Manhattan or the webzine editor working in his pajamas. As much as they hate to admit it, those who do the hiring often make their decisions in a heartbeat, based on emotion as much as the merits of the pitch. If they're in a bad mood or it's the end of the day and happy hour is calling, they may not give your query the attention you think it deserves. What makes it to the "maybe" pile one day may get deleted after a few seconds another day.

Or maybe you made a typo and got immediately dismissed. Or you spelled the editor's name wrong. Or you clearly didn't read the guidelines so your query went straight into the virtual trash bin.

Odds are, for a variety of reasons, you will get rejected more often than you get accepted. At first, the ratio may be 100 rejections (or no responses) to one. A year or two later, the ratio should be much better. If not, you're doing something wrong. If you get to a ratio that's better than 10-to-1, you're doing well and if half your pitches get a yes you're a huge success.

Those who aren't rejected probably are becoming lazy and not trying to break into new outlets or get published in a different type of media. It takes a thick skin to be a freelancer, so learn to take rejection (or being ignored) as a routine matter. Learn from it when you can, forge on and keep trying when there's no response to go on. Tweak the idea and try it elsewhere. Pitch that editor with something different. Dive into magazine editorial schedules and find the perfect angle you can pursue locally. Subscribe to a service that will help you figure out what editors are really craving, such as MediaBistro AvantGuild. Save each rejected idea to revisit later. Use it when you are running your own blog or when you get a regular column where you have creative control. Just because one gatekeeper said no doesn't mean it's not a great idea. Toss it out there and see.

Expose Yourself

When you're starting out, your first goal is to get clippings—virtual or physical—and build a portfolio so you've got something to show editors. Even if you're applying for a blogger's spot on a group blog that pays $5 per post, the editor wants to see what you've written already. *Something* at least.

How far should you go to get exposure and build up a portfolio? Should you write for free?

Nothing inspires a more impassioned debate among writers than this subject. If you want to get people fired up on a message board or Facebook group for writers, raise this question and get ready for a flood of responses.

I'll turn down stupid work for free in a heartbeat, but I'm firmly on the side that says, "Write for free when it makes sense for you."

Many writers will point to some free (or close to it) articles they did that gave them something good to build on. There are many other writers who will tell you that you should *never* write for free.

Your skill is valuable and it's an insult to do it for nothing and you bring down the value of the profession and you wouldn't ask your plumber to work for free and yada yada yada. I've heard all the arguments and they're mostly bogus. A plumber is a tradesman and there are barriers to entry for that profession. Anyone can be a writer and at times it seems that half the population is trying to be.

It's not all that hard to string grammatically correct sentences together. Much of the writing out there is "good enough" for what's required. Look at Wikipedia, which is completely written by volunteers. One recent study estimated that 10 *million* hours of human labor have gone into Wikipedia alone. (About 100 of those went into one vigilante editor's vendetta to take down the Tim Leffel Wikipedia page, which eventually succeeded. Grrrr.) One of the most popular travel sites in the world is TripAdvisor, which is almost completely written with "user-generated content" that didn't earn anyone a cent from their prose.

You can't fight this trend. Whining won't help. This is your competition now if all you can do is express opinions or regurgitate facts about a destination. To earn money from your writing, you need to inspire, inform, or elevate better than the masses can do for themselves.

Remember, nobody owes you a living because you printed business cards saying you're a writer or you paid for a weekend workshop. To earn money doing this, you truly have to earn it, generally by covering something far better than anyone else.

If you're going to compare professions, compare travel writers to aspiring musicians, actors, songwriters, fashion designers, painters, or sculptors. These people all work for free sometimes until they've really made it. For some they never go beyond that— the passion remains a hobby. Fun jobs with low barriers to entry pay less. That's life. If you don't like it, go to law school so you can earn the big bucks making life more complicated for everyone.

In a story on the Black Eyed Peas that ran in the *Wall Street Journal*, Will.I.Am credited much of the group's success to getting its music out there in any way possible. "Not long ago, the band was lending its music for relatively paltry fees for exposure—a common strategy for emerging acts." This got them onto TV sets via advertising and people started humming their songs. They eventually got a better music deal, real concert sponsorships, and then superstardom. "It wasn't about the check," says former manager Seth Friedman.

Exposure opens doors. It gets you in front of an audience; it gets you noticed. It gets links to your portfolio site or blog. Exposure gives you clippings to show editors and it gives you valuable practice. Those who say "exposure doesn't pay" aren't getting exposed in the right place. Or they are bad at marketing and don't know what to do with what they've gotten. Taking gigs that pay little or nothing sure beats sending out query after query that goes nowhere.

> *I've learned that this career (like many) comes with a snowball effect. You have to start small, and one thing leads to another. If I were starting all over again, I probably would have reached out to more local publications to build my portfolio before jumping into the game. I've been fortunate to get a lot of great writing jobs, but maybe they would have come sooner if I had a larger portfolio of smaller outlets at the beginning.*
>
> ~ Ramsey Qubein, freelance writer

For me, exposure has led to mighty things: book deals, article assignments, media coverage, trip invites, and business success. There has been *very* little correlation between article pay scales in the short term and actual long-term monetary benefits. Apart from bragging rights, the biggest magazine assignments haven't done nearly as much for my eventual earnings as a few carefully placed cheap or free articles in the right place have done. It's how you parlay that exposure into something tangible that matters. For example, I used to do a free column that got syndicated by MSNBC. Those stories led to 14 national media interviews and sold a fair number of books from the exposure. The links from them helped my own sites' search engine ranking. The arrangement eventually ran its course, but it was certainly worth the minimal time I put into it repurposing content I already had available. A guest post I did on one super-popular blog sent thousands of new readers to *my* blog and led to tangible revenue from book sales.

Starting your own blog is a sure-fire "work for free" proposition in the beginning. My blog didn't make a cent the first two years I ran it except for selling some books. Eventually it got to a point of covering the mortgage payment each month and has gotten me assignments that didn't require a query. The work started out free, but ended up being a pathway to solid income. In the digital world, it's "no pain, no gain."

Free won't pay the bills, of course, so working for little or nothing needs to be a means to an end. Know what you want to get out of it before signing up. The key is doing it when there's a clear payoff. If the site will send major traffic, bring in new blog readers, or raise your site's Google profile with new links, that's worth a lot more in the long run than what some struggling magazine or newspaper will pay you.

For me, though, if that eventual payoff isn't worth roughly what I could be making on an hourly basis doing something else, I've got to pass. And if somebody like *Forbes*, AOL, or an airline magazine asks me to write for free, I'll get as indignant as any writer. Downright insulted, actually. If a huge publication with lots of editors on the payroll can't afford to pay the freelancers creating its content, I don't view it as a reputable business. If a major corporation can't pay as much as a one-person blog publisher, they shouldn't call themselves a publishing company. That's just exploitation—and bad management.

Forbes even had the gall to ask me to contribute a column with no pay, but then said in the same request that I couldn't accept any hosting or press trips. Since when did slave labor come with conditions? Think about how desperate you are for exposure before you fall for an "opportunity" like this just because it comes with a name brand attached. That gleaming name brand may be losing its luster fast in the new media world.

Only you can determine what is worth doing for no pay or low pay. Naturally your standards are going to be lower when you have no experience than they will be later, the same as with a musician or actor. Once you start getting paid work on a regular basis, you can scale back on jobs you've taken just for "exposure," but don't treat that as a dirty word. Nobody gets anywhere in the creative fields without ample exposure, be it an obscure indie film, a community theater part, a free concert in the park, or a travel article that puts a showpiece on that blank slate of writing clips. Just don't let a person doing the hiring wave that word around as a way to avoid paying for good work.

Become a Great Writer in Any Media

Write. Write. Write. Then write some more. And if you feel you've had enough, it'd probably be a better idea to do something sensible like becoming a dentist or raising rabbits.

~ Rory MacLean, writer, author, and novelist

If there's one bit of advice that's relatively agreed-upon among the best narrative writers I know—the ones who win prizes and get into book anthologies regularly—it's that being a great "writer" should be the foremost goal, not just being a narrow-casted "travel writer."

> *Try to be a good writer and a good traveler, but not so much a travel writer. Too many people are infatuated with the title of travel writer, but the best travel books and features are usually written by plain old writers.*
>
> ~ Nicholas Gill, freelance writer

There are a few different paths to becoming a great writer, but utilizing all of them can't hurt either.

You can take any kind of creative writing course offered at your local college or participate in workshops held in most cities. Or enroll in a travel writing workshop or course taught by someone who knows the ropes. The best is probably the Book Passage conference held in the San Francisco Bay area each year, but there are others taught by great writers and editors, including some that are featured in the book you are holding now. (For my own course offerings on the income side of things, see RealMoneyWriters.com.)

The best ones allow ample time and occasion to rub shoulders with successful writers and editors and to get your work critiqued. If this is not part of the agenda, the cost should be significantly less.

A less expensive method that many writers feel is equally important is to read a lot. Read a lot of magazines (not just travel mags), read a lot of newspapers or news sites with good international sections (not just the travel section) and read a lot of great books (a mix of travel, novels, and non-fiction). People who do *not* read a lot usually make that obvious in their writing. They use a lot of clichés, they don't use enough dialogue, they don't engage the senses, and they have trouble constructing a sustained narrative. Too often, they come off as a hack just in it for the perks. Writers are readers and readers are writers. Build some time into every week to read and as with healthy meals, make sure you're getting a balanced diet.

Almost every experienced writer will tell you to write often as well. Preferably every day, but at least on a very regular basis. This doesn't all have to be writing for publication though. I'd estimate that more than half of us working travel writers got our initial practice keeping a handwritten journal on the road. There's a whole great book on this subject by Lavinia Spalding called *Writing Away*. Get it before your next long journey.

> *A lot of people dream of being a travel writer but they don't actually sit down to write. You have to write and read a LOT and have a passion for both. Writing is a craft. It's not something you're born with.*
>
> ~ Laurie Gough, travel writer and author

If you can get a gig writing for a blog or have the perseverance to run your own, that's great practice. It should be combined with other pursuits since blog posts are only one style, but that's a great place to try out ideas, practice different kinds of writing, and find the kind of focused angles that editors are always looking for. This is often as valuable as a collection of clippings too because the person who would hire you can see how you write on your own, not what your articles look like after intervention by an editor.

(Most F.O.B. articles in magazines sound like they were all written by the same person, usually because the editor has had a strong hand in the style and voice, no matter who submitted the initial draft.)

Otherwise, get experience any way you can, even if this means writing for free or cheap sometimes or working for low wages on a guidebook for a few months.

Make sure you are getting feedback on that writing though so you know what you're doing well and what needs work. Playing the violin eight hours a day isn't going to make you a better violinist if you have a dozen bad habits and you're tone deaf. I've seen pieces from writers who have written a regular small-town newspaper column for years on end and what they're putting out is still pure drivel. They've not gotten any better at the craft along the way, probably because nobody has called them out on it and the writer has never asked for advice or aimed higher. Keep an eye on your writing and how it is progressing. If you're not seeing an improvement over time and you're not getting better assignments, suck it up and get some help.

> *Only get into travel writing if you really love to travel and write. If you think it's a good pretext for getting to travel, think again: you can travel just as much by saving up money from another, better-paying job, and just taking off to go vagabonding. So only pursue travel writing because you love to write as well.*
> ~ Rolf Potts, freelance writer and author of *Vagabonding*

What does it mean to be a "great writer" and who decides that, anyway? You could argue that it's all in the eye of the beholder and like pornography or good art, most editors will say "I know it when I see it." Most books on writing well will at least provide a road map though and give you examples of what makes for compelling writing. Plus if you read a lot, eventually you get a sense of why that feature writer for *National Geographic* got the job or why Bill Bryson got a book contract and you didn't. Sure, some of it's luck and some of it's who you know, but great writers who are persistent usually break through eventually.

For certain styles of publication the basic rules are relatively well defined. For example:

Newspapers want tight sentences, as few adjectives as possible, aggressive avoidance of clichés, AP style (in the US), and lots of service information. In my experience, editors at newspapers are the busiest, the hardest to impress, and the least patient with writers who do not follow directions. The longer the feature the more latitude you get, but wasted words are not appreciated here. You may be required to submit photos with your story, either included in the rate or for a separate fee.

Magazines want different things depending on the section. For short articles, they want short sentences that pop and can say a lot without so many words. In my experience, most editors have never met a pun or metaphor they didn't like in these F.O.B. sections. For features, a more narrative, literary style is appropriate, with powerful prose that touches on all the senses and tells a story. Crafting and careful editing are extremely important before you hit that "send" button. Most of all, the editors want something unique and written specifically for them unless it's a custom publication for the likes of AAA, Geico, or RCI, where conventional roundup destination stories are still the norm. For smaller publications, you may be required to submit photos with your story, either included in the rate or for a separate fee. Larger ones will usually hire a professional photographer or use stock photos.

Websites and Blogs want copy that will appeal to search engines. The prose takes a back seat to keyword phrases. So a clever headline and a meandering lede/lead that would work great in a magazine will be a dud for something on the web. The headline and first paragraph need to clearly define what the story or blog post is about. That may appear to be dumbing it down, but reality is that people read differently online, so it's not just for the Googlebots that these elements are simplified. Like it or not, your writing for the web needs to grab a reader within a couple seconds or they're moving on. A good photo or two helps and readers expect links they can follow for more information. Rules can be broken, but in general you need to write in shorter sentences in shorter paragraphs, with more subheads and other elements to break up the text. This doesn't mean being careless or sloppy, however. Succinct writing still needs to be good writing.

> *Learn to write first before you worry about how to pitch or social media or WordPress or whatever. That might sound very old-school but I still can't get over how many bloggers can't write.*
> ~ Lara Dunston, freelance writer and author

Trade Publications vary greatly depending on the audience, but in general they are most interested in conveying the facts. Do your homework and write like a reporter. Editors appreciate good writing, but only if it doesn't get in the way of what needs to be conveyed to meeting planners, travel agents, or tour companies. For most trade magazines, revenue comes from regular advertisers and high subscription fees, so positive stories and slants greatly outweigh any negatives about the given industry. You will seldom need to submit photos for these stories as stock photos are commonly used.

Guidebooks are clearly meant to guide, so the prime objective is to convey as much useful service information as possible within the pages that are available. What not to include is as important as what to leave in, so writers do not have the luxury of wasted words and meandering sentences. Occasionally you can stretch and show your skills in the sidebars or special sections, but for the most part good guidebook writing means efficient writing. Depending on the publisher, you will often be required to perform other functions, such as sketching out maps or submitting photos of the popular sites. Some require you to shoot photos along the way.

One last bit of advice on writing well: open your horizons across all media. Watch great films with powerful scripts instead of senseless action flicks. Watch great dramas on TV where every word matters instead of ditsy people arguing in interchangeable reality shows. Listen to songs with great lyrics. If Bruce Springsteen, Harlan Howard, or Tom Waits can tell a character's whole story in four minutes, maybe you don't need as many words as you think to make an impact. Take lessons from other media and it will make you a better writer.

Travel in a Frugal Manner

Travel writers cover lots of nice vacation spots frequented by people with plenty of money, but in reality most of these writers are getting by on the budget of a backpacker.

There are plenty of travel writers out there right now staying in five-star hotels and getting from place to place on a tour bus or with a car and driver. For some publications that works just fine, so many of the big magazines foot the bill for the experience, but for most writers that's a terrible way to travel on a regular basis. Luxury travel is, by nature, sheltering. I love a thick bathrobe and cavernous hot tub as much as the next guy, but not much of a story is going to come out of that unless I'm writing a hotel review.

Putting aside the fact that most travel writers earn well under six figures, luxury travel and good writing don't go together very well. To write good stories you need to take unscripted excursions, talk to new people, eat in restaurants with no tourists, and see real local color. You need to leave the TV off and say "no thanks" when a doorman counters your subway question by offering the "special car" service.

The writers who do reputable work that stands the test of time tend to stay in smaller hotels built for mingling. They take public transportation. They eat where the locals eat, preferably in the local market now and then.

The other reason to travel in a frugal manner is that you then have some slim hope of earning a profit from what you are writing. Just one night in a luxury hotel costs more than you would get paid for the average travel article, so unless all expenses are covered by the publication or you're hosted on a press trip—both rare when you're starting out—you want to keep your expenses low.

This is why a great number of excellent writers are current or former backpackers, especially bloggers with a big audience. They already know how to wring the maximum experiences out of the minimum expenses. The hack writers who never met a press trip they didn't like, however, are completely lost without a guide and prearranged transportation to take them around. I can usually spot those kinds of writers' stories after reading the first two paragraphs. They're predictable, boring, and don't tell me anything I couldn't have found out myself through a quick Google search.

Sure, those blue bloods doing feature stories for the *New York Times* and *Departures* magazine can afford to stay at the best suites at the best hotels because they don't really need the money. But what comes out on the page is more often than not best perused when you're ready for a nap. As David Mamet said in his book *True and False*, "Where in the wide history of the world do we find art created by the excessively wealthy, powerful, or educated?"

If your entire history of travel is a stream of luxury resorts, air-conditioned deluxe taxis, and cruises, the best thing you could do for your future writing career is to go spend weeks in a cheap country with $1,000, a journal, and a backpack. Your writing will be more interesting and you'll probably have an easier time finding a wealth of angles. (Or get an internship at a luxury magazine and hope it turns into a real job!)

Of course, there is one way to spend time in a foreign country without eating up all your savings: get a real job. One thing Rolf Potts, David Farley, and many other writers have in common with me is that we have all spent more than a year teaching English abroad. Besides this being a great cultural experience, it allows you to have a home base in another country while earning a decent living. Others write while they're on a volunteering mission or are working for the Peace Corps.

As former Moon guidebook author Joshua Berman says about travel writing, "Do it and have fun but don't expect it to pay for anything for a while. Find other forms of cheap travel to finance it—like volunteering or studying abroad, or working seasonally in another country."

Now that we're in a digital nomad era where it's so easy to work abroad as a telecommuter or entrepreneur, there are fewer excuses not to follow this path at some point. See my book *A Better Life for Half the Price* for more, at CheapLivingAbroad.com.

But Invest Freely When Needed

A year and a half before I moved out of Nashville, a neighbor of mine put his house up for sale. When I moved away he still hadn't sold it. He's a contractor, so it was expertly renovated, impeccably maintained, and he had moved to another house on the same street, so it stayed clean and uncluttered.

We were in the midst of a housing slump and this particular house was priced a bit higher than the neighborhood norms because it had a pool, but the asking price was not out of whack with comparable sales. So why didn't it sell quickly?

Nobody knows for sure, but it can't help that the only indication it was for sale was a cheap "For Sale" sign bought at Home Depot, with the owner's phone number scrawled on it with a Sharpie. This guy understands construction and staging, but he obviously doesn't understand marketing.

Leaving aside the benefits that a Realtor could provide, what kind of impression does this lousy sign send to potential buyers? How much more attractive would this house be with a professional wooden sign, a good website with lots of photos, and an attractive flyer available to potential buyers driving by?

To me it seems ludicrous to sell a $400,000 house with a crappy looking $10 sign. It's also ludicrous to market yourself as a professional writer if you're not willing to invest any of your own money in development and marketing. In my experience, this is the main factor separating the six-figure writers from the ones who struggle to cobble together enough for rent and food. The former invest in growth and knowledge, the latter try to spend as little as possible on their career.

If you struggle to justify buying a $15 book filled with good advice or $55 for an annual AvantGuild membership through MediaBistro, or $10 a month for an e-mail newsletter service, then you lack a basic understanding of the term "return on investment."

If you're not willing to spend any of your own money to attend conferences, to travel in pursuit of a great angle—even if it means losing money on the article sometimes—then you're going to need a tremendous amount of luck to make it. You'll constantly be at a disadvantage compared to those who are willing to invest for knowledge and an edge.

Few of us writers can pin our success on one turning point in particular, but usually there is at least a certain period of time when things started getting easier. For me there were several inflection points, all following investments I made in my career that had no guarantee of paying off. I spent six months working on a book, with no guarantee I'd earn anything from it, and even paid for the cover design and POD setup fees on my own. I paid a hosting company for a domain name and website at the same time, and then spent another month building the book's resource site. I started a blog without ever dreaming it would become a profit center. I started writing articles that tied into my book with little regard for what kind of payment was attached.

After all that, I got more assignments and the media started calling me for interviews. Then I paid to attend some conferences and networking events. Pitching got easier. Making money got easier.

I later paid a talented designer to build a custom portfolio site to my specifications. Editors started taking me more seriously. I had control of what showed up No. 1 in Google for my name and it looked impressive.

Later as I branched out into running websites, I paid designers to do it right and I paid freelancers to provide content. I never asked any writer to work for free. I hired assistants to do a lot of the HTML coding and social media grunt work so I could focus on high-value tasks instead. Time after time, I invested real money to create real value.

Most people are, fortunately for me, too timid or too cheap to make all these risky, long-term investments in their future. So it was easy for me to leap ahead of them all and stand out. With a range of different revenue streams, it has been easier for me to weather the storm if something went wrong in one particular area because a recession hit or a country I was covering fell out of favor.

I'm not the only one who has discovered this "success through investment" philosophy. Most of the webmasters I've profiled in this book have gone down the same path. None of them sat back and waited for the work to come. None of them depended on sweat equity and what they could get for free online to build a business. The old saying, "You've got to spend money to make money," has been abused by some start-ups as a reason to blow through millions of dollars, but at an appropriate level it's true for almost any entrepreneur, freelancer, or solopreneur.

Want to set yourself apart from the pack? Spend constructive money on yourself and your career. Attend conferences now and then. Pay for access to good information. Pay designers to make you look like a pro. Look professional and gain professional knowledge to turn this writing thing into more than a hobby. My experience is only anecdotal, but from what I've seen this willingness to invest in the future is what sets the six-figure travel writers and editors apart from those who struggle to get their earnings past the pocket money level.

Act Like a Business Owner

Approach this with an entrepreneurial spirit, and do all that you need to do to make this business successful. Put in the long hours, be prepared to wear lots of hats and learn new skills, and remember to take time to balance the work with what you love (hopefully travel, and travel writing!).
~ Jessie Voights of WanderingEducators.com

If you run a blog, treat that blog as a real business or it will never become one.

If you're a freelance writer, run what you do like a service business, trading your precious time and output for money.

According to the Freelancers Union, about 40 percent of their members had trouble getting paid in in the past year and three of four had experienced trouble collecting earned income at some point in their career.

Not that self-publishers don't have risk as well, but I'd rather get stiffed for ads that ran in the sidebar for a couple weeks than for an article I slaved over and incurred expenses to research.

As I've said before, being a freelance writer is not an endeavor for the meek. Even if you're a part-timer, treat this like a business. Get promises in writing. Ask for payment terms before taking an assignment. Be persistent about getting paid when the terms have been met.

Figure out how much your time is worth on an hourly or weekly basis and push to make your writing efforts produce that amount. Unless this really is no more than a hobby for you, don't treat it like a hobby. Treat it like a business: You, Inc. It's hard to earn like a pro if you don't have the outlook of a pro.

Learn New Skills

Travel Writer 2.0 is not just a writer. To succeed in the future, you will need to be more like a Swiss Army knife than a switchblade that can do one thing only. Continual education and practice in new areas are essential.

> *Embrace the hustle. Not the negative aspects of that term, but to be a freelancer, you have to be everything: writer, photographer, pitcher, self-marketer, social media specialist. Your brand is you. There are no days off.*
>
> ~ Jill Robinson, freelance writer

Unless you're regularly appearing in one of the top-tier magazines, it's very hard now to be a writer without also being a photographer. A blog without photos is pretty boring and most web editors expect you to illustrate your own stories. Otherwise they have to go buy photos from a stock agency or hunt down Creative Commons ones on Flickr. So if you're not already a good or great photographer, take a course to learn the basics of framing, lighting, cropping, and creating drama.

There are also books and inexpensive courses out there on basic HTML coding, video editing, and blogging. There are also plenty of free online tutorials if you take the time to hunt around. Invest time, money, or both in making yourself more valuable by being able to do more than string sentences together. But don't let the technical considerations be an excuse for not starting now.

> *Just start. Way too many people obsess about the layout of their site, and create no content. Just write! The rest can evolve as you grow and get readers.*
>
> ~ Lillie Marshall

Keep Focusing on What Earns an Income

The key to success as a writer is focusing on what's is bringing in money now and what's likely to bring in money later. There are 100 things that can pull you away from what I hope you're trying to do: write. Some are complimentary (like producing photos and videos), but some are just fun distractions that make you feel like you're getting something done even when you're not.

If you've gotten this far, you know I have some strong opinions on what matters and what doesn't, but the only person who can say what works in your case is you. Keep experimenting with new tools and new means of communication; when one works, give it your all until it doesn't. But if you want to be a travel writer or blogger, be sure you're writing and blogging often and saying something worth reading.

> *A lot of bloggers are distracted by design, or SEO, or the latest tools and forget to just keep delivering useful content over and over.*
> ~ Darren Rowse of ProBlogger.net

Enjoy

Travel writing is supposed to be fun. Not as fun as being on vacation, but more fun than being a lettuce picker in the Arizona sun. That's why you want to do it, right?

If you look purely at the financial rewards, this is a lousy job. Most travel writers could double their income by taking a corporate job writing RFP responses or software user manuals. We do what we do because we get up in the morning excited about our day. We love the giddy feeling of walking onto an airplane and knowing we'll walk off in a strange new land. We like to wake up in a new bed and wander through local markets. And although the thrill fades a bit over time, it's exciting to see your name in print—even pixilated print.

So if you're not having fun, return to that "passion and expertise" section. Do not pass Go; do not collect $200. Because you won't collect many dollars if you're not passionate about the subjects or the places you're covering.

Get that part right, follow the advice in this book, then have fun. If you become a success—whatever that means for you—this can be one of the most satisfying and enviable jobs on the planet.

See you on the road!

Last Calls to Action

There are a lot of tasks and steps in this book you just finished that will help you on the road to success. Here are two more that will take your writing career up another notch.

1) The Travel Writing 2.0 Success Newsletter

Once a month I dish out advice, provide info on cool tools I've discovered, and pass on tidbits from recent interviews. Sign up at TravelWriting2.com/newsletter and you'll get some kind of bonus as well.

2) The Real Money Travel Writers Course

If this pursuit will always be a hobby for you and you're okay with that, have fun. If you want to ramp up your earnings though and make real money as a travel writer or blogger, I've got a self-guided course or a mastermind group with personal coaching that provides action steps and accountability. See the details here:

RealMoneyWriters.com

Travel Writing 2.0 Resources

As I said in the beginning, this book is meant to be a jumping-off point. Here's where to jump off to when you're ready to develop your skills, find markets for your articles, or start earning money as a blogger or travel website owner.

You can find a more comprehensive set of resources for freelance writers in other places, including at the Media Bistro website: mediabistro.com/resources/.

Sometimes you want something a little *less* comprehensive though, so here's a pared-down list of books and sites that are useful. They may be out of date before the ink is dry though, so keep digging! For a current version of this list that is updated and has links to click, go to the resources tab of www.TravelWriting2.com. (I'm running detailed interviews there as well.)

Some of these are free, some require a fee.

References and Databases

The following resources and databases commonly list editors to pitch to, their e-mail address, and a phone number for the main desk. A bit of sleuthing will often accomplish the same thing for free (a magazine masthead will have somebody's e-mail address under the business/advertising part you can extrapolate). When time is money, a database will get you rolling in a hurry.

Your local library (for magazines and reference books)

A good newsstand (at Chapters or Barnes & Noble you can write down key masthead info and study the issues without buying every one.)

TravMedia.com – sends out editor alerts and collects press releases in one place.

Scott American Corporation's travel media directory for sale - scottamerican.com

FeaturesExec has a database of editors in Europe
Bookmarket.com has downloadable agents and publishers lists
Publishers Marketplace has databases and a query service at PublishersMarketplace.com
FreelanceSuccess.com has a database of magazine editors to query

There are also some very expensive ones of questionable validity available from Cision, Vocus, Gorkana, Bulldog Reporter, and others, but you probably need a PR agency connection or job to justify the cost.

Job postings and leads

FreelanceWriting.com has links out to multiple job boards, so that's the best place to start.
WritersWeekly.com site and newsletter
JournalismJobs.com
Freelanceconnect.com
Press4Travel.com (European)
BloggerJobs.biz
TheWriteLife.com/jobs
Jobs.Problogger.net
TravMedia.com

Upwork.com (you pay a portion of revenues)
Sologig.com (you pay a portion of revenues)

MediaBistro.com Avant Guild service (job postings and some content are free)
FreelanceSuccess.com (database of editors, workshops, and courses)
RealWritingJobs.com (mostly low-paid content mill work)
FlexJobs.com

Writing Websites, and Newsletters

Some of these are specific to travel writing, some are for freelancers in general. Many post a steady stream of openings for bloggers and are therefore a better source for online opportunities for beginners than some of the above.

Travel-writers-exchange.com

WriteToTravel.blogspot.com

FabFreelanceWriting.com/blog/

WritersInCharge.com

FreelanceWritingGigs.com mediabistro

MediaJobsDaily -.com/mediajobsdaily/

Bookmarket.com – from book marketing expert John Kremer

GoinsWriter.com – The blog of Jeff Goins, an expert on writing and marketing books.

Contently.net Freelancer section and blog

MenWithPens.ca/blog

TheRenegadeWriter.com

FundsForWriters.com

Communities

Travelblogexchange.com – otherwise known as TBEX

SATW.org – Society of American Travel Writers

NATJA.org – North American Travel Journalists Association

IFWTWA.org – International Food, Wine, & Travel Writers Association

TravelMedia.ca – Travel Media Association of Canada

BGTW.org – British Guild of Travel Writers

TravelWriters.co.uk – Travel Writers UK

TravelBloggersAssociation.com – Professional Travel Bloggers Association (PTBA)

Outdoor Writers and Photography Guild - owg.org.uk

Australian Society of Travel Writers - astw.org.au

Writers & Photographers Unlimited - wpu.org.uk

Various Facebook groups – search by interest

Fizzle.co – Membership group with unlimited courses and active message board for online content business owners

MediaKitty.com – a place where PR/marketing people connect with writers for announcements, press trips, and help with assignments.

HelpAReporter.com – THE place where journalists seeking sources post their needs. If you're an expert on something and want media attention, subscribe for free.

Travel Writing and Creative Non-fiction Courses

There are a million of these, it seems, but the following survive on results and good word of mouth rather than extreme hype and hard-sell direct mail pitches. Assume they all have a substantial fee.

Self-PublishingSchool.com – Chandler's Bolt's free intro course and paid in-depth one on publishing your first book and marketing it.

Travel Writing Workshops from Rory MacLean and Dea Birkett - travelworkshops.co.uk

Matador U - matadoru.com/

Paris Creative Writing workshop - Pariswritingworkshop.com

MediaBistro writing courses and webinars - Mediabistro.com/courses/

Writer's Digest courses and webinars – WritersDigest.com

Bookmarket.com has seminars and e-books related to writing, book proposals, and book marketing

Amanda Castleman's courses - Writers.com/castleman.html

If you live in New York City, check into the Gotham Writer's Workshop. If you are in San Francisco, check into courses run by Larry Habegger.

Tribe Writers (TribeWriters.com) and Intentional Blogging (goinswriter.com/intentionalblogging) by Jeff Goins.

Start a Blog That Matters - by Corbett Barr at Fizzle.co

Fizzle - offers courses on specific and tangible steps for the online entrepreneur. They cover things like growing your e-mail list, starting a podcast, increasing traffic, creating better content, creating videos and more. (fizzle.co)

Make A Living Writing – various courses on Article writing and pitching to editors. (makealivingwriting.com)

Who Pays Writers? – Anonymous updates with just word count and pay rates submitted by users (whopays.scratchmag.net/)

Last, you can see options to learn more from **me** on several levels at RealMoneyWriters.com

Professional Networking Conferences

American Society of Journalists and Authors - asja.org/
North American Travel Journalists Association – natja.org
Society of American Travel Writers – satw.org
TBEX – Now3 conferences: North America, Europe, and Asia
Professional Travel Bloggers Association
Book Passage Conference – bookpassage.com
International Food, Wine, & Travel Writers - ifwtwa.com
British Guild of Travel Writers - bgtw.org
Travel Media Association of Canada - travelmedia.ca
Outdoor Writers and Photography Guild - owg.org.uk
Australian Society of Travel Writers - astw.org.au
Writers & Photographers Unlimited - wpu.org.uk
Travel Classics Conference – TravelClassics.com

Good Starting Points for Your Library of Writing Books

Travel Writing by Don George
Break Into Travel Writing by Beth Blair
Writing Away by Lavinia Spalding
A Sense of Place by Michael Shapiro
Smile When You're Lying by Chuck Thompson
Writer's Digest Guide to Query Letters by Wendy Burt-Thomas
Telling True Stories by Mark Kramer and Wendy Call
The Elements of Style by William Strunk Jr.
Grammar Girl's Quick & Dirty Tips for Better Writing by Mignon Fogarty

31 Day to Build a Better Blog by Darren Rowse (also available as a 31-day podcast for free)
*The Well-fed Write*r by Peter Bowerman
The Soul of Place by Linda Lappin
Bird by Bird by Ann Lamott
On Writing by Stephen King
You Are a Writer (So Start Acting Like One) by Jeff Goins
The War of Art by Steven Pressfield.
On Writing Well by William Zinsser

E-books and Reports

If there's a writing blog or podcast you follow, that's a good place to start to dig in deeper. You can find other good e-books at WritersWeekly.com and WritersDigest.com.

These are from people I trust:

31 Days to Build a Better Blog by Darren Rowse
A Practical Guide to Going Digital by Christine Gilbert. Also see her Blog Brilliantly course (AlmostFearless.com)
*Write a Winning Book Proposa*l by Michael Hyatt. Fiction and non-fiction editions

Otherwise, the number of reports and e-books you can buy has exploded the past few years and anything I put here will be out of date within months. Make use of the great search engine and recommendation engine at Amazon. Fire up the Kindle and start getting schooled.

Book Publishers and Agents

If you want to publish a book through the traditional route, find an agent or publisher through one of the following:

PublishersMarketplace.com
LiteraryMarketplace.com
PublishersandAgents.net
AgentQuery.com

Many of the vanity press, print on demand, and e-book publishers are flaky and just out to make money off your setup fees, but here are a few with transparent terms and reasonable costs. I've only used the first two, however, so do your homework and read all the fine print.

Booklocker.com
CreateSpace.com (Amazon)
GuideGecko.com
Smashwords.com
Fastpencil.com
Lulu.com
Scribd.com

Other Writing Websites to Learn From

Make a Living Writing (makealivingwriting.com)
FreelanceWriting (freelancewriting.com)
AllIndieWriters (allindiewriters.com
Travel Writing 2.0 (travelwriting2.com)
Problogger.net

Where to Find Assistants and Contractors

Except for Craigslist, assume these all have some kind of fee, either up front or built into the rates. I've used most of these and have had the best luck for ongoing virtual assistants by using Craigslist in places like Mexico City, Guadalajara, San Jose (Costa Rica), and Panama City. I use Fiverr and Upwork every month for WordPress fixes, design work, Kindle conversions, proofing, and promotion activities.

Craigslist.com – Post ads at home or in foreign cities
Perssist.com – Virtual assistants platform for hire by hours
Outsourcely.com – browse and hire remote workers
VirtualStaffFinder.com – Finds candidates in the Philippines
OnlineJobs.ph – Provides access to Filipinos looking for positions
Fiverr.com – Hire people for specific tasks

Upwork.com – Hire people for specific tasks or ongoing arrangements

Sologig.com – Similar to Upwork but not as well-known

Envato Studios – Similar to Upwork but not as well-known

Taskrabbit – Hire locals for tasks in certain U.S. cities

Matching Sites for Sponsored Posts/Assignments

These are coming and going quickly, so just consider this a starting point and I can't guarantee they'll all be around two or three years from now.

Contently.com

Izea.com

TapInfluence.com

Blogness.net

Cooperatize.com

BloggerBridge.com

Featured Travel Writers

A whole bunch of writers contributed their opinions and stories to this book and trusted me with data on their income and earnings mix. I'm incredibly grateful.

In the first edition I listed all their bios, but the list was a lot longer this time and would have added too many pages. So to read more about anyone quoted in the book, they're all in one place here:

TravelWriting2.com/bios

Acknowledgements

First up, thanks to all the writers and editors who were generous with their time and advice. One guy jabbering for 200+ pages on one subject can get old, so thanks to all of you for making this a more interesting and helpful book to read. Marija Vemic did the front cover illustration and then Arbëresh Dalipi did the final design.

Thanks to those who gave me constructive criticism on the initial draft and helped with proofing. Special thanks to Terri Marshall from that list, who does most of the posting on the TravelWriting2.com blog.

Angela and Richard at Booklocker have provided more support through four editions of *The World's Cheapest Destinations* than I've gotten from any traditional publisher, so thanks to them for providing a good book publishing platform that actually makes business sense for all parties.

As usual, my family put up with me working more hours as this book was being written, but I'll make up for it with some good vacations after it's out.

Lots of editors hired me over the years when that was the only way to make any money as a writer, so thanks to all of them who printed my work—especially those who hired me multiple times! Thanks also to the web editors who have mostly taken their place the past few years.

I wouldn't be able to make it as a travel writer and publisher without all the book buyers, blog subscribers, and readers of my websites who have supported my publications and my advertisers. You've kept me from being a starving artist and have indirectly contributed pocket money to a whole lot of freelancers. Thank you for coming along on the rides.

Index

CPSIA information can be obtained
at www.ICGtesting.com
Printed in the USA
BVHW040844180721
612146BV00008B/602